Pornography Law

XXX MUST NOT BE TOLERATED

Pornography Law

XXX MUST NOT BE TOLERATED

Brajesh Rajak

Universal
Law Publishing Co. Pvt. Ltd.
NEW DELHI - INDIA

2011 Edition

ISBN : 978-81-7534-999-5

Published by
UNIVERSAL LAW PUBLISHING CO. PVT. LTD.
C-FF-1A, Dilkhush Industrial Estate,
(Near Azadpur Metro Station) G.T. Karnal Road,
Delhi-110 033
Tel : 011-27438103, 27215334, 42381334
Fax : 011-27458529
E-mail *(For sales inquiries)* : sales@unilawbooks.com
E-mail *(For editorial inquiries)* : edit@unilawbooks.com
Website : www.unilawbooks.com

Recommended citation: *Pornography Law: XXX Must not be Tolerated,* Brajesh Rajak (New Delhi: Universal Law Publishing Co. Pvt. Ltd., 2011)

Computer Typeset at Aesthetic & *Printed* at Vishal Binding House, Noida.

FOREWORD

It delights me to write the foreword to this book. It adds to my delight because Mr. Brajesh Rajak happens to be one of the promising students of the National Law School of India University, Bangalore of which I happen to be the Vice-chancellor at the moment. That which has a tendency to deprave and corrupt has always been despised by any civilised society. That which titillates and that which is vulgar would be debasing. Connubial bliss is full of love and affection whereas obscenity and pornography are repulsive. The quality of freedom lies in moderation, otherwise it will degenerate into licentiousness. A Khajuraho sculpture is an aesthetic delight whereas a porn movie is disgusting. The perennial debate as to what borders on obscenity and what amounts to pornography has raised many interesting intricacies seemingly defying resolution .

The author has made a bold attempt to suggest way outs basing his studies on the spectrum of comparative frame. The Oriental and the Occidental diversities and the intractable cultural diversities make a universal and unifying approach not that easy. The young writer deserves appreciation of all those, who strive to prevent the homosapiens from going down to the bottomless perdition, for his genuine and painstaking effort to promote judicious restraint.

Prof. R. Venkata Rao
Vice-chancellor
National Law School of India Univeristy
Bangalore.

PREFACE

"I think it quite likely that there is no such thing as good pornography. If it's good, then it's not pornography."

—Vincent Canby

An increasing number of shocking incidents around the world concerning pornography have made the subjects and the State alike ponder over pornography and the resultant disastrous disturbances. Pornography has been a subject matter of constant and continuous debate between intellectuals from various schools of thoughts including Marxism, Liberalism and Feminism. The tentacles of pornography-related problems continue to increase their spread by each passing day, inviting more concern and more consciousness among all those who are directly and indirectly affected by it. The haunting predicament of Pornography has emerged, especially after shocking incidents such as the DPS MMS and the Anara Gupta scandals, as a serious concern among parents, school authorities and lawmakers, to name a few.

Needless to say, regulation of pornography has to be the first step towards its termination. The fact that there is no category of law, at least in India, known as pornography is not less than an irony. In many countries, pornography is enveloped within the laws dealing with obscenity and understood only to mean a subset of obscenity. Pornography may be said to suffer from the problem of a definite definition. However, such an inconsequential issue should not be reason enough behind a consequential lack of interest in regulating the same. Thus, more than mulling over any particular definition of pornography, the concern should thus shift towards regulation of pornography.

The development of laws dealing with pornography in India can be traced from its common law antecedent to the most recent decisions in India. The Indian Judiciary has also followed the development in laws relating to obscenity in United States. Pornography is also supported by advocates of pornography by identifying it as a part of speech and protecting it under the garb of right to free speech and expression. Nevertheless, the Indian judiciary has been reluctant to admit that the pornography enjoys protection of freedom of speech and expression.

The term 'XXX' has become an identifier of pornography after the organization issuing rating for the movie started using 'X' rating for movies that contained explicit, non simulated sex. Initially, 'X' ratings were used to indicate that the movie is not suitable for minors but does not have pornographic content. However, gradually pornographers also started placing 'X' rating to identify the adult content in them. The number of Xs on the cover of a movie signified the intensity of adult content present in the movie. In course of time, video sharing websites started using 'XXX' to signify that the videos present on their websites are pornographic in nature. These facts added to making 'XXX' as an identifier of pornographic content.

This book has been written to probe into the moral, physical and mental harms of pornography. An attempt has been made to study the laws of obscenity that are prevalent in United States and United Kingdom which has guided the lawmaking authorities in India to make legislations to deal with obscenity. The alleged protection of freedom of speech has also been tried to be scrutinized in a different chapter in this book. There is a separate chapter which provides solution to the prickly problem of pornography, identifies problems in enforcement of laws that is followed by solutions for the same and makes recommendations to repair the lacunas present in present laws in India that deal with pornographic content.

I am indebted to Prof. (Dr.) R. Venkata Rao, Vice Chancellor, N.L.S.I.U., for his constant support and encouragement and for being kind enough to write a foreword for this book. I am also grateful to Universal Law Publishing Company Private Limited for publishing this book. I would also like to thank my friends Sonal Jena and Kunal Ambasta, and especially Bodhisatta Biswas for his valuable contributions in the form of suggestions while writing this book. I express my gratitude to Kanishk Thakur, Ishita Bhaduri and Prateek Anil Shreevastava (NLIU) for assisting me in the research work.

November 2010 **Brajesh Rajak**

CONTENTS

CHAPTER 3
ADJUDICATING PORNOGRAPHY IN UNITED STATES

CHAPTER 4
ADJUDICATING PORNOGRAPHY IN UNITED KINGDOM

CHAPTER 5
ADJUDICATION OF PORNOGRAPHY IN INDIA

CHAPTER 8
CONTRACTUAL ASPECT OF PORNOGRAPHY CONTRACTS

UNITED STATES ACTS AND ORDINANCES

INDIAN STATUTES

TABLE OF CASES

J

K

L

M

N

CHAPTER 1
PORNOGRAPHY AN OVERVIEW

Pornography is much debated subject among scholars all over the world. There are differences in opinions among scholars about harms (including both physical and moral) of pornography. They have also refused to accept the existence of any casual link between pornography and alleged harm caused by it. This Chapter attempts to deal with the viability of their arguments by providing an overview of the cause and effect of pornography.

What is Pornography?

Pornography is seldom attempted to be defined by lawmakers. It was attempted to be defined by Mackinnon-Dworkin while drafting an Ordinance for Minneapolis.[1] Their definition of pornography is based on subordination of women. However, pornography is also about subordination of children (both female and male) and adult male sex workers. It includes portrayal of people engaged in or descriptions of ultimate sexual acts including vaginal or anal intercourse, fellatio, cunnilingus, anilingus and masturbation,[2] representation of women as a whore by nature,[3] depiction of women enjoying forceful penetration, ejaculation and manipulation of genitals is clearly visible[4] and publication of sexually explicit materials which have the tendency to deprave and corrupt the mind of people.[5] Exploitation, subordination, dehumanization of workers engaged

---

1. In the 1983 Ordinance for Minneapolis drafted by Andrea Dworkin and Catherine Mackinnon Pornography is defined as graphic sexually explicit subordination of women, whether in pictures or in words, that includes women being presented dehumanized as sexual objects, things or commodities or they being presented as sexual objects who enjoy pain or humiliation or being presented as sexual objects who experience sexual pleasure in being raped or being presented as sexual objects tied up or cut up or mutilated or bruised or physically hurt or being presented in postures of sexual submission, servility or display, or women's body parts including but not limited to vaginas, breasts and buttocks- are exhibited, such that women are reduced to those parts or women are presented as whores by nature or women being presented being penetrated by objects or animals or women being presented in scenarios off degradation, injury, torture, shown as filthy or inferior, bleeding, bruised or hurt in a context that makes these conditions sexual.
2. Bruce A. Taylor, "Hard-Core Pornography: A Proposal for a Per Se Rule", 21 University of Michigan Journal of Law Reform 255, 272 (1987-88).
3. Randall D.B. Tigue, "Civil Rights and Censorship Incompatible Bedfellows", 11 William Mitchell Law Review, 81, 85 (1985).
4. Deana Pollard, "Regulating Violent Pornography", 43 Vanderbilt Law Review 125, 155 (1990). In the Deana Pollard model of definition of pornography she describes violent pornography to include depiction of physically violent act between and among those engaged in sexual activity. Physically violent Acts include assault, battery, murder, rape, torture and coercion by physical force.
5. *R.* v. *Hicklin,* (1868) LR 3 QB 360.

in pornography and sexual explicitness of the product, are some of the identifying factors of pornography. There is no particular category named as pornography in law. It is also considered to be more aggravated form of obscenity. Pornography is usually regulated by obscenity laws.

There is no unanimous agreement upon definition of pornography among scholars. Courts have also refrained themselves from attempting to resolve the debate of definition of pornography. However, it can be better understood by differentiating it from obscenity and erotica.

Obscenity and Pornography

Obscenity includes all materials that are filthy, indecent and offensive to modesty and decency.[1] For example a portrait in which a man is following women to rape her may be considered obscene, but it is not pornography. Pornography is a subset of obscenity. Pornography requires sex as an essential ingredient of the matter in question. Obscenity does not include the religious epics, artistic masterpiece and contemporary erotica and so pornography also does not include any of them.[2] Obscenity is defined in many legal regimes and explained by Courts in a very elaborate fashion. There is a lot of jurisprudence available upon the definition of obscenity. Pornography is inalienable part of obscenity that focuses upon dehumanizing its actors by presenting them as mere objects engaged in gratifying sexual desires of customers of pornography. Pornography is a limited term but obscenity is wide enough to include acts like bar dancing that are capable of offending the morality and decency of society.

Erotica and Pornography

Pornography is different from erotica. Erotica is understood to mean portrayal of pleasure of sexuality within a positive emotional relationship.[3] Erotica is about admiring sexual activities. If couple is depicted in the form of portrait, writing or video, where they are voluntarily engaged in sexual activity, where there is no question of exploitation, where there is no degradation of sex and dehumanization of the workers engaged behind production of such material, it is erotica. Erotica is accepted by many societies across the word. In western culture, the explicit treatment of sex continued in the form of medieval bawdy ballads and poems of Chaucer, Dunbar and others or in part of art and poetry of renaissance Florence or in the form of French farces of fourteenth and fifteenth centuries, or in the form of Elizabethan ballads and poetry.[4] In India, it is found in Kamsutra and also visible in the paintings of Ajanta and Allora and Khajuraho Temple. However, pornography dehumanizes and degrades sex. It turns people indulged in sex as commodities capable of being bought and sold. In a nutshell pornography objectifies humans. Actually erotica is literature or art intended to arouse sexual

1. Oxford English dictionary.
2. Nadine Strossen, Defending Pornography: Free Speech, Sex, and the Fight For Women's Rights 55-56, 258-59 (1995).
3. David Linton, "Why is Pornography Offensive" in Harry Lesser, Ethics, Technology and Medicine p. 123, 1988.
4. Attorney General's Commission on Pornography, Final Report 234 (1986) available at porn-report.com.

desire but pornography is about pictures, writing or other material that are sexually explicit and patently offensive to community. The supporters of pornography usually refer to erotica while referring to pornography. Hence the problem lies in definition of pornography as understood by them. If the supporters of pornography try to understand the difference between erotica and pornography then, they would also be agreeable on the point that pornography must not be tolerated.

Pornography as a Moral Offence

Pornography is seen as self regarding activity by supporters of pornography. It is argued that pornography is a matter of privacy of an individual that is protected by the constitution. An argument is often advanced in favour of pornography that it is self regarding activity of a consumer which can not be regulated by society using law even if it harms the consumer. The most which society can do is to persuade, instruct, advice or avoid that consumer. This argument is based on Mills harm principle that suggests that State should illegalize only those offences in which offender causes harm to others and not to self.[1] However, this principle ignores the fact that there are certain offences based on foundation of morality of the society. Certain activities are offence because they are immoral. This morality is not a matter for private judgment. A society is made up of community of ideas that are not only political but also include ideas about the way its members should behave and govern their lives.[2] A common morality is the price paid for social cohesion.[3] The William's committee in United Kingdom that was set up to review the laws concerning obscenity, indecency and violence in display, entertainment and publications also appears to have accepted that society can legitimately enforce criminal law to preserve its common morality.[4]

Society's Right to Prohibit Certain Activities

Another argument was also put forth by Lord Devlin which was termed by the eminent scholar of jurisprudence, H.L.A Hart as Social Disintegration Thesis. According to this thesis, society has the right to penalize deviation as it does to prohibit treason; it is called as right to prevent its own social disintegration.[5] Anything which can disintegrate the society and violate peace by causing disharmony in society can be prohibited using law by society. Section 144 of Indian Penal Code is an example of a tool used by society to preserve peace in society. This section prohibits assembly of five or more persons; holding of public meetings and carrying of firearms. Ronald Dworkin, the famous jurist, describes this disintegration thesis as society has the right to prohibit those activities which would bring significant changes in social institution upon which society's positive

1. J.S. Mill's First Harm Principle in Nils Holtug, "The Harm Principle" 5(4) Ethical Theory and Moral Practice, pp. 357, 359, 2002.
2. Devlin, The Enforcement of Morals, p. 9, 1968.
3. Susan M. Easten, The Problem of Pornography, p. 27, 1994.
4. T.R.S. Allan, "Right to Pornography" 3(3) Oxford Journal of Legal Studies 376, 377 (Winter 1983).
5. Rolf E. Sartorius "The Enforcement of Morality" 81(5) The Yale Law Journal, 893 (April 1972).

morality places very high value.[1] Hence, an activity that has the potential to affect a social institution which is considered to be very important by society and the effect caused to such institution can violate peace in the society then such activity can be prohibited by law. For example, marriage is considered to be a social institution upon which the positive morality of society places a high value. Same sex marriage is an activity which has the potential of bringing up significant change in the social institution because it can change the whole concept of marriage as it is commonly understood in the society. Marriage is usually understood to be a bond between a male and female. Hence, marriage between individuals of same sex can be prohibited by society using law as a tool.

Positive Morality

Coming to the next vital question: what exactly is this positive morality of society? Now the question what this positive morality of society is? One thing is sure that positive morality is not a constant phenomenon because it cannot be said that positive morality of ancient society of India is same as the positive morality of present India. Hence, to ask what the ancient sages would have thought about playboy magazine is similar to asking what they would have thought about computers. Also, positive morality, common morality or shared morality of society can not be a unanimous opinion of all the people in a society because it is very difficult to have such a unanimous view in a society. If certain people in society have a principled position on a particular point and such a principled position is consistent with the other principles attributed to it, then such principled conviction of society could be called as positive morality, shared morality or common morality of society. Here, unanimity among reasonable man is required, not among all the men of society. The society has the right to enforce only those principled moral convictions, not all the moral convictions. For example, if certain people in Society think that Dance Bars are immoral then until and unless it is established that those people are reasonable men of society and their argument is based on principled moral conviction (protection of Indian culture) consistent with other principles which can be attributed to it, such a view can not be enforced with the help of law. Determination of reasonable people is not a tough job as we just have to be sure that they are not criminals, goons or other antisocial elements of society.

In India, the presence of section 377 in Indian Penal Code clearly shows that Indian society has also utilized the tool of law to preserve its common morality. Section 377 that penalizes sexual activities between couples of same sex is a self regarding activity that does not harm others in society but is an offence because the common morality of society treats this kind of sexual activity as immoral and society has made use of law to preserve its common morality. According to concept of legal paternalism also, an act can be prohibited to prevent harm to the actor itself by state.[2] The justification behind such prohibition is the person harming himself will be better off if such an activity is prohibited. Hence, even if pornography is

1. Dworkin, "Lord Devlin and Enforcement of Morals" 75 Yale Law Journal 986 (1966).
2. J. Fienberg, "Offense to Others", p. 187, 1987.

considered to be a self regarding activity, it can be prohibited by state to prevent harms to sex workers, producers, distributors, purchasers of pornography.

Is Pornography a Self Regarding Activity?

Pornography cannot be considered to be a self regarding activity because it brings sex into public sphere. It commercializes sex. It depicts subordination and exploitation of women and children. Women and children are those segments of Indian Society that need care and protection. Hence there is no question as to why such depiction of subordination and exploitation of women and children in public sphere must not be tolerated. It is doubtful that pornography makes any contribution in the healthy development of society but corrupts the minds of people by its low quality material which also diverts them from more worthy self-enhancing occupation.

Radcliff Richards, an eminent philosopher[1] argues that if sex is accepted in private sphere then there is no reason to condemn it when it comes within public sphere and commercialized by market forces. However, the publication of private activities by market forces is a very important fact because commercialization of sex means profit.[1] The profit in pornography industry attracts organized crime that exploits workers in pornography industry. To ensure more profit, the criminals engaged in organized crime ignore the fact that whether the consent of workers is obtained voluntarily or forcefully. Increase in demand warrants more supply. Increase in supply of sex workers encourages trafficking in women and children. In India, where workers of pornography industry are rendered incapable of free choice due to absolute poverty, unemployment and illiteracy, there is a strong presumption that most of the workers in the pornography industry are exploited till the extent that degrades and dehumanizes their existence as a human.

Establishing a Causal Link between Pornography and Organized Crime

In the organized crime of pornography a consumer demands a portrait of a couple indulged in sexual activity. The offender contacts his agents to arrange workers who are willing to do such act. There is a great probability that consent of these workers would be affected by the factors mentioned in above paragraph or it could be obtained through use of force that may take form of rape also. This is a causal link between pornography and sexual offences. This causal link cannot be said to be affected by remoteness of cause in the Indian context where there is a strong presumption of involuntary consent.

However, such a causal link can be argued by supporters of pornography to be absent in case of pornographic depiction of hypothetical humans which is based on the imagination of a pornographer. For example, in case of animated pornography or imagination of a book author there is no question of involvement of sex workers who would be exploited in the process of obtaining pornographic material. Nevertheless, there are reports which suggest that even these kinds of pornography cause individual, social, moral and ethical harm and causally related to sexual offences.[2] The animated depiction of pornography encourages

1. Susan M. Easton, The Problem of Pornography, p. 27, 1994.
2. Attorney General's Commission on Pornography, Final Report 234 (1986) available at porn-report.com.

and legitimizes pornography. They contribute in the process of desensitization. For example, when the animated pictures are circulated in the market, people may become desensitized from them after certain time period. Then they would demand more sexually explicit content that would include human workers in pornography industry.

Desensitization

The process of desensitization is visible in the form of upcoming websites on the internet everyday. Earlier there were websites providing animated imaginary photographs of nude women indulged in sexual activities. Then new websites depicting couples in sexual intercourse came up. When people became desensitized from these websites, MMS, video clips and pictures showing sexual intercourse of celebrities began circulating through those websites. After desensitization from such form of pornography, websites depicting graphic sexual fantasies involving rape, torture, bestiality, excrement, vomit, cannibalism, and necrophilia began prevailing in the market.[1] After this, the next stage was the publication of websites showing boiled naked women and people eating them.[2] Now the question is how many people in this world would consider these depictions as mere fantasies? People claim to distinguish between fantasy and reality but they fail to acknowledge that the actions in pornography are happening to real people who are experiencing real pain, degradation or humiliation.[3] There is no guarantee that these depictions will not be imitated by sexual offenders. The crux of this argument is that such type of imaginative and animated pornography is actually the first step of consumers towards other form of pornography that exploits workers. Hence all forms of pornography must be regularized by law.

In case of porn websites like pinkworld.com, worldsex.com and youporn.com where porn is available in abundance and for free, also the same arguments given above applies without any restrictions. Porn is always in demand and seeing such type of porn increases appetite of consumers; that is why the next step of these consumers turns towards paid supply of porn.[4] This stage of pornography takes the form of organized crime and the consumer becomes a part of this organized crime.

The Problem of Imitation

The imaginary depiction of unusual sexual activities could be imitated by people. That would increase sexual offences. For example sex scenes portraying women enjoying sexual exploitation depicted in a movie or a portrait may be imitated by individual on partners and strangers. In India, where there are

---

1. http://www.sickestsites.com/last visited on 19/02/2009.
2. http://daha.best.vwh.net/boiled/main.shtml
3. Pamela Paul, Pornified: How Pornography is Transforming Our lives, Our Relationships and Our Families, p. 44, 2005.
4. Elizabeth Harmer Dionne, "Pornography, Morality and Harm, Why Miller should Survive Lawrence" 15 George Mason Law Review 611, 622 (Spring 2008).

incidents of people dying while imitating Shaktiman[1] and Krish,[2] a possibility of such imitation can not be denied in its entirety. A series of cases in United States and United Kingdom affirm that sexual offenders have imitated pornographic materials while committing sexual offences. In *R.* v. *Halloway*[3] Lawton L.J. has said that it is not uncommon for the judges to deal with sexual offenders who have undoubtedly been incited to engage in criminal conduct by pornographic material. He further opined that pornography has a corrupting influence. Hence, a causal link between pornography and sexual offences can not be denied in its entirety.

Reports in Support of Harm Produced by Pornography

Williams Committee Report

William's report produced by William's committee which was set up in 1977, reviewed the laws related to obscenity and concluded that adults can be allowed to view pornography unless it could be shown that harm has resulted from pornography.[4] The harm in question was not moral harm but a certain kind of physical harm that should have been resulted and must share a causal link with pornography. It also said that restriction can be imposed where the material in question appears to involve exploitation of a person who at the time was under 16 or where actual physical harm is inflicted on that person or a sexual activity is appeared to be offensive to reasonable people, then restriction can be imposed.[5] Hence, this committee advocated restriction on child pornography. However, on the issue of pornography other than child pornography, the committee recommended to restrict only such pornographic materials where harm is inflicted on the workers involved in production of pornography or if such activity is considered to be offensive to reasonable people. Here, the committee's recommendations were not at all related with the positive morality of society. It recommended that the materials in question must have offensive elements involved in them to be prohibited.

Centers for Disease Control and Prevention Report

Based on in-depth interviews and public testimonies of pornography employees, the Centers for Disease Control and Prevention[6] in the United States conducted a Childhood Adverse Experience Study and found that 90% workers in pornography industry are survivors of child abuse. There are other findings as well, for example, one in four girls were sexually abused before the age of 18 and

---

1. Bhaskar Ghose, "The Television Story" 25 (25) *Frontline* (December 6-19, 2006) available at http://www.thehindu.com/fline/fl2525/stories/20081219252507800.htm
2. "Krissh Stunts, Not for Immature" The Hindustan Times, July 2, 2006 (Mumbai Edition). A boy jumped down from the balcony imitating stunts in the 'Krissh' Movie.
3. (1982) 4 Cr App R (S) 128.
4. Attorney General's Commission on Pornography, Final Report 234 (1986) available at porn-report.com
5. Susan M. Easton, The Problem of Pornography, p. 143, 1994.
6. http://www.cdc.gov/nccdphp/ace/index.htm

one in six boys was sexually abused before the age of 18. An estimated 39 million survivors of childhood sexual abuse exist in America today.[1]

Other Reports

Another Study that was conducted by a Medical Healthcare Foundation in the United States on workers in pornography industry showed that 66 to 99% performers were suffering from a disease known as *Herpes* which is a non-curable disease.[2] Chlamydia and Gonorrhea among workers in pornography industry was found 10 times greater than others.[3] Another shocking report concluded that 70% of sexually transmitted diseases occurred in female pornography workers.[4] The environment of pornographic workplace very often results in suicide or suicidal ideation,[5] post traumatic stress disorder,[6] sexual trauma,[6] sexual addiction[7] and substance abuse.[8] These studies try to establish a link between pornography and physical harms that can be reasonably associated with it. They are evidence of the fact that pornography does not cause only moral harm of mental harm but it also causes physical harm.

In the United States, several women also reported that pornography was the root cause behind their divorce.[9] These women found their husbands watching porn and imitating the sexual acts shown in pornographic materials on them. Pamela Paul's book '*Pornified*' gives an overview of how men, women and children are affected by the ubiquity and mainstreaming of porn.[10] These studies reflect the social harm of pornography affecting lives, reputation and wellbeing of a member of society.

The Attorney General Commission on Pornography's report in United States also unanimously concluded that pornographic violence harms women and recommended that the Government should take appropriate measures to minimize such harms.[11] Michael Flood who conducted a study in a dozen countries and

---

1. Abel, G. Becker, J., Mittelman, M., Cunningham-Rathner, J., Rouleau, J. & Murphy, W. "Self reported sex crimes on non-incarcerated paraphiliacs" 2(1) Journal of Interpersonal Violence, 3 (1987).
2. Adult Industry Medical Healthcare Foundation – www.aim-med.org
3. Peter R. Kerndt, MD, MPH Director, Sexually Transmitted Disease Programme Los Angeles County Department of Public Health. "Worker Health and Safety in the Adult Film Industry." May 21, 2008.

   http://bixbyprogram.ph.ucla.edu/lectureslides/Kerndt_5-21-08.ppt
4. Kerndt, "Worker Health and Safety in the Adult Film Industry." http://www shelleylubben.com/sites/default/files/LA_Public_Health_9-17-09.pdf.
5. http://www.shelleylubben.com/suicide-deaths-us-porn-industry-1970.
6. http://www.prostitutionresearch.com/prostitution_research/000021.html
7. http://www.sexualabusesurvivors.com/SexualIssues.htm
8. Attorney General's Commission on Pornography, Final Report 234 (1986) available at porn-report.com
9. Pamela Paul, Pornified: How Pornography is Transforming Our lives, Our Relationships and Our Families, p. 166, 2005.
10. http://www.pamelapaul.com/pornified.html
11. Attorney General's Commission on Pornography, Final Report 234 (1986) available at porn-report.com. at 322-351 (1986).

carried out a report at the Australian Research Center of Sex, Health and Society, said that there is compelling evidence from around the world that pornography has negative effects on individuals and communities; it shapes sexual knowledge; it is a very poor sex educator because it shows sex in an unrealistic way and fails to address intimacy, love, connection and romance.[1] There are researches which reveal that on-line pornography plays an accessory role in negative social issues such as child abuse, violence against women, rape, inequality, relationship and family breakdown, youth crime, promiscuity and sexually transmitted diseases.[2] These reports are an effort of various Governmental and Non-Governmental organizations to establish a causal link between pornography and the depravity caused by it in the society. Even if it is accepted that these reports are not a conclusive proof of link between pornography and instigation of sexual offenses, but it cannot be denied that pornography does have something in it that is offensive and harmful to society and it must be prohibited if society wants it to be prohibited using the tool of law.

Indian Context

However, these reports are not conclusive when seen in the Indian Context. Here the situation is very different from England and U.S.A. In India, there are very few sex workers who join pornography industry voluntarily for livelihood. Many of them are coerced physically or economically. Hence, a thorough research by Government Organization is needed to find out a causal link between pornography and sexual crime. There are various organizations which are raising voice against pornography by helping the sex-workers to move out from their profession and also by preventing transmission of Sexually Transmitted Diseases but they have not tried to engage in research activities to find out any causal link between pornography and sexual offences. The absence of any such study in India and the inapplicability of The Meese Commission Report in Indian Context can not support pornography in India but it only furthers the point that the research work that was conducted by researchers in foreign context, if conducted in Indian context would bring out a clear and strong causal link between pornography and harm associated with it. After studying the framework of porn industry in India in this book, one will have absolutely no doubt about it.

Link between Pornography and Sexual Behaviour

Pornography must be regulated on the ground that it acts as an incitement to sexual hatred and violence against women in the same way that racist and fascist literature acts as an incitement to racial hatred prohibited under the law.[3] This is very true because the sexual exploitation of women working in the pornography industry works as incitement to sexual offenders. Pornography symbolizes that such kind of behaviour is acceptable and practical in society. Hence all the

---

1. www.timesofindia.indiatimes.com/life/relationships/parenting/Boys-who-watch-porn-indulge-in-casusal-sex/articleshow/5494353.cms
2. www.netsafety.nic.in/internet.htm
3. Anna Marry Smith, "What is Pornography: An Analysis of the Policy Statement of Campaign against Pornography and Censorship", 43 Feminist Law Review 71, 75 (Spring 1993).

material containing pornography must be regularized by law because it can incite sexual hatred. Itzin C. who has written a book titled 'Pornography: women, violence and civil liberties' also proposes that incitement of sexual hatred to be ground for regulation of pornography which is threatening, abusive and insulting or degrading or damaging to women.[1]

An argument may be advanced that pornography arouses offensive sexual behaviour in men often raised in abusive homes, men who are hostile towards women, self centered, having poor social skills. Even if this argument is accepted then also you cannot limit their reading without controlling everyone's.[2] These men are also part of society and anything which affects their interest can not be denied regularization by law.

Moral Harm of Pornography

The word 'harm' cannot be understood to mean only physical or financial harm. Moral harm is more important than physical and financial harm because it relates to the dignity and decency of human being. Even if there is no possible way for scientific measurement of such harm the acts causing moral harm must be condemned because the conscience of the society demands so.[3]

The argument which is used to support pornography is usually based on the physical harm aspect of pornography. All reports whether in the United States of America or in the United Kingdom analyze only whether pornography causes any physical harm and whether there is any causation between the physical harm and the pornographic material. However, one forgets to ask whether moral harm is not harm. Is there any moral harm associated with pornography? Does the state have power to illegalize an activity that causes such moral harm to members of society?

Moral harm is a meaningful concept. It is a harm that affects the attitude of a person towards other members of society. Pornography causes moral harm when it appeals to the prurient interest of a person.[4] If it is accepted that reading books which have social, literary, artistic and political merits help a child in his moral development then the books which have obscene content and contain low quality material having the tendency to deprave and corrupt the mind of people could well be said to harm a child's moral development.[5] Then should the legislature not prescribe such filthy material which harms children's moral development?

The Courts in the United States have gone on to the extent of saying "the sum of experience, including that of the past two decades, affords an ample basis for legislatures to conclude that a sensitive, key relationship of human existence, central to family life, community welfare, and the development of human personality, can be debased and distorted by crass commercial exploitation

1. Itzin C., London Daily News (20 April, 1987).
2. Andrew Coppelman, "Does obscenity cause moral harm?" 105(5) Columbia Law Review 1635, 1671 (June 2005).
3. Attorney General's Commission on Pornography, Final Report 234 (1986) available at porn-report.com, at 303.
4. *Roth* v. *United States,* 354 US 476 (1957).
5. *Paris Adult Theatre* v. *Slaton,* 413 US 49 (1973).

of sex."[1] Pornography is nothing but the commercial exploitation of sex which has ample power to distort the basic structure of the community.

Joel Fienberg, an American philosopher has argued that morally corrupting a person does not cause any harm to him unless he has any antecedent interest in being good. However a reply to his argument has been given by Harry Clor, an American Thinker who says that if Fienberg is right, then the effort of children educators to promote children's moral development would be said to be raw exercise of power.[2] The fact that the State has an interest in promoting the moral development of members of the society is a strong point to support the argument that anything which is contrary to the moral development of people and therefore averse for the well-being of society must be regulated. According to the concept of legal moralism also, an act can be legitimately prohibited, if it is inherently immoral.[3] If it can be established that pornography is legally immoral then even if it does not harm and does not offend to anyone in society, it can legitimately be prohibited.

Once it is established that moral harm is actually a kind of harm which has some meaning attributed to it, it cannot be denied that morally bad literature contributes to affirm morally bad social values and norms. They confirm that such morally bad social values and norms are normal, usual and acceptable in society. Pornography literature seeks to confirm that people are objects *i.e.,* it seeks to objectify human beings. It therefore treats people as tool to gratify lust, as lacking autonomy, as interchangeable with other objects, as lacking in agency and as something whose feeling and interest need not be taken into account.[4] It confirms that people are capable of being sold and bought in the market. Sex is a commodity, which can be commercially exploited. When commercial exploitation of sex is accepted in society then all the characteristics attributable to commercial exploitation also become acceptable. The first characteristic of commercial exploitation which is maximization of profit and minimization of loss also becomes acceptable. To maximize profit by commercial exploitation, illegal trafficking, child abuse and sexual offences are encouraged. Hence, a clear causal link can be seen between literature having the tendency to affirm morally bad social values and its effect on society.

According to Posner, "literature continues to be an important component of high school and college education because it affects in stretching student's imagination, multiplying his cultural perspective, broadening his intellectual and emotional horizons and offering him a range of vicarious experience."[5] It can be said that pornography literature is a form of literature that shortens a student's imagination and leads him in a wrong direction; it also narrows his intellectual and emotional horizons by depraving and corrupting his mind.

---

1. *Paris Adult Theatre* v. *Slaton,* 413 US 49 (1973).
2. Andrew Coppelman, "Does obscenity cause moral harm?" 105(5) Columbia Law Review 1635, 1671 (June 2005), at 1642.
3. J. Fienberg, Offense to Others, p. 24, 1987.
4. Martha C. Nussbaum, Objectification, in Sex and Social Justice, p. 213, 1999.
5. Richard A. Posner, Sex and Reason, p. 335, 1992.

Is there a Need of Deterministic Causation?

The question is whether there is any causal relationship between photographs of sexually explicit violence and sexual offences? An argument may be forwarded that a deterministic causation cannot be established between photographs or videos of sexually explicit violence and sexual offences. Deterministic causation means that a particular factor is essential for a particular consequence to follow.[1] Without the presence of that factor, the consequence would have never taken place. The presence of that factor would always lead to happening of that consequence. Such causation cannot be attributed to pornography because it is not necessary that without pornography, sexual violence would never take place. To agree on the necessity of deterministic causation would mean to reject that cigarette smoking results in lung cancer because it is not necessary that every person who smokes cigarette would suffer from lung cancer or *vice versa*.[2] However, it is true that Cigarette may cause lung cancer and there is a causal link between cigarette smoking and lung cancer. Hence even if without pornography also sexual violence is possible, pornography does not always result in sexual violence, it can be argued that there may still be a causal link between pornography and sexual violence.

It is not always necessary that the cause is a necessary condition for the effect. A cause can also result in the effect if coupled with other causes. Hence even if sexual violence may occur without any relation with pornography, it cannot be denied that pornography plays a vital role in occurrence of sexual violence. There is no need to establish a deterministic causation between sexual causation and pornography. For instance a curfew is imposed not because there is something wrong if people would go out at night but because there is possibility that under some circumstances a crime may occur in that area. There is no need to establish a deterministic causation between the curfew and the harm caused by it (offence). There are many offences where there is no need to establish deterministic causation, mere possibility of harm being inflicted is enough.[3] On the same lines, it can be argued that there are sufficient grounds to regularize pornography because it may lead to commission of sexual offenses, it may cause unnatural sexual practice.

Pornography and Private Morality

In *Lawrence* v. *Texas*,[4] the Supreme Court in United States declared that mere morality is not a sufficient basis for criminal legislations that restrict private consensual and sexual conduct until and unless there is harm to a third party. The harm done to parties in the suit is also immaterial. It is possible to view Lawrence case as deregulating private morality and also as a set of norms that have no apparent impact on anyone but the subjects of the particular action or are not

1. Peter Van Invagan, An Essay on Free Will, p. 170, 2002.
2. Frederick Schauer, "Causation Theory and the Causes of Sexual Violence" 12(4) American Bar Foundation Research Journal 743 (Autumn 1987).
3. One of them is under Arms Act, 1959, where mere possession of certain weapon is an offense.
4. 539 US 558 (2003).

appropriately the subject of governmental regulation.[1] It means that the Lawrence case deals only with private conduct and not a conduct which is published, circulated and consumed by consumers and prohibits interference by law in private sphere. Since pornography is a conduct which is published, circulated and consumed outside the private sphere; Lawrence case does not have any implications on pornography. However, it has been very well argued by Elizabeth Harmer Dionne, the Harvard Law Olin Fellow, that it is difficult to demarcate a line between private morality and public concern.[2] Activities done in the private sphere may have sufficient potential to impact public sphere as well. Voluntary selling one's own body parts or entering sexual or physical servitude could appear to be private matters but many societies may think that such a conduct should be prohibited.[2]

Pornography as an Exception to Rule of Law

Pornography is an exception to rule of law. Rule of law is a concept of jurisprudence that declares that everybody is equal under the law. Pornography causes harm to society through social conditioning that fosters discrimination.[3] The production of pornography industry goes far beyond mere exploitation of gender and racial stereotypes, brazenly celebrating vicious and fundamentally immoral acts of misogyny, misanthropy and racism.[4] Pornography creates stereotypes representation of women and becomes the basis behind unequal treatment of women in society. Rule of law is based upon equal treatment of individuals. Hence pornography clearly goes against the principle of rule of law and a State that supports pornography clearly violates the principle of rule of law.

In the words of a sex worker, pornography normalizes and legitimizes sexual abuse which they experience as sex worker and it also works as introduction to prostitution, it is also used as groom and to train them.[5] Pornography is able to strengthen the perception that women are objects of lust and they enjoy getting raped. It also reinforces the dominant view of patriarchal society that when a women says no it means yes. Hence, it can be said that it degrades the perception of an ordinary woman of society by identifying her as adulterous, seductress and as object of lust capable of being bought and sold.

Samples of Degradation

The best example of degradation and corruption of girls including 8 years olds is visible in the United Kingdom in the form of Shag Bands. Shag Bands are colored bracelets supposed to be signifying sexual acts. Shag Bands are worn by some school girls and the snatching of a yellow, pink, orange or purple, red, white, green or blue and black band by a boy means that the girl has to give him hug,

1. Robert P. George, "Forum on Public Morality: The Concept of Public Morality", 45 AM J. JURIS. 17, 24 (2000).
2. Elizabeth Harmer Dionne, "Pornography, Morality and Harm, Why Miller should Survive Lawrence" 15 George Mason Law Review 611, 622 (Spring 2008), at 615.
3. Andrea Wolfe, "The Pornography Debate" Lawyers Collective January, 1989.
4. Attorney General's Commission on Pornography, Final Report 234 (1986) available at porn-report.com.
5. Statement of Ms. P., The Minneapolis Hearings pages 14-120.

love bite, kiss, lap dance, flash, oral sex and full sex respectively.[1] Children are being commercially exploited by companies which sell such bands. Pornographic websites are spreading awareness about the availability and utilization of such bands. Many comments of children who are way less than 18 can be seen on those websites about how they used them today.[2] Children are asked to participate in such sexually explicit and vulgar activities even at too early an age to demonstrate their coolness.

Pornography and Racism

Pornography promotes racism. Black women suffer more extreme violence and domination and black men are portrayed as more violent and libidinous. A survey of porn videos available on youporn.com would clearly bring to ones' notice that maximum videos of gang rape depict black men committing rape on a blonde girl. It seems to establish a racist view that black men are morons of an uncivilized society.

---

1. http://www.buzzjack.com/forums/index.php?showtopic=100809
2. http://women.timesonline.co.uk/tol/life_and_style/women/families/article6910040.ece.

CHAPTER 2

PORN INDUSTRY IN INDIA

It is necessary to understand the porn industry in India inside out before recommending any kind of regularization on pornography. Pornography is being circulated in the form of magazines, books, videos, MMS and photographs in India. The abundance of material in different forms has created huge problem in the regulation of pornography. Child pornography is restricted to the private sphere and rarely available on the internet. This form of pornography is circulated in the form of Multimedia Messaging Service (MMS) by the help of mobile phones. DPS MMS is an example of such kind of child pornography where the pornographic video of a girl child was prepared by certain people and distributed through MMS. These kinds of MMS are also used to blackmail the children to engage into perpetual sexual activities with the maker of such videos. The makers of porn videos also force these children to join prostitution. This series of events is just a part of the organized crime known as illegal trafficking.

The porn industry in India has not developed as a big industry like film industry or steel industry due to the laws in force in India and taboos attached to pornography. However, it is commercially lucrative in certain regions like Kerala where it is known as Mal-Porn features porn videos of girls from Kerala and could easily be found on video sharing websites or other internet websites. Pornographers are criminals who are actually involved as pimps in prostitution and also engaged in illegal trafficking, but they rarely make porn. They purchase porn from the makers of porn videos who are usually somebody related to the victim. The maker of such videos may be the brother, friend, schoolmate, husband or landlord of the victim. Such videos are usually made by hidden cameras which may be hidden in the changing rooms of hostels, hotels, shops or bathrooms. In many cases, images or videos are created without the consent of the persons involved and unscrupulously circulated for commercial gain. Such activities are not only a blatant invasion of privacy but they also attack an individual's dignity.[1] While discussing pornography in India, the contribution of savitabhabhi.com can not be afforded to be ignored. The material available on this website depicted a woman who is somebody's wife and somebody's sister-in-law as being lustful, adulterous and someone who fantasizes sexual activities with multiple persons. The content which is being distributed by websites like savitabhabhi.com and magazines like Debonair, Fantasy, Chastity, Royal Magazine, Dafa-302 not only degrade sex but also dehumanize women in Indian society by depicting them as lustful objects. Such form of pornographic content degrades people, mostly women,

1. www.tech.in/should-adult-porn-websites-be-banned-in-india.html

and depicts them as existing solely for the purpose of others (usually men), in a manner that most people would consider humiliating.

The porn industry in India is now transforming from little cottage industry to a big profit making venture. Even the Chief Justice of India has expressed his desire to ban pornographic websites immediately.[1] The reason behind development of such huge concern is the display of advertisement of pornographic websites without the permission of the viewer. Such uncontrolled display of porn advertisement banners usually come out while browsing the internet at home or business meetings and are sufficient to offend the people browsing internet.[2]

The porn sites available on the internet are being used by child molesters as electronic superhighways to look for victims, they are pedophiles' playgrounds due the special feature of anonymity where they can hide their identity using newsgroups, chat rooms, and exchange information through e-mail and interact with children. Child molesters use these sites to lure children with games and establish online relationships with them. These websites are also being used by criminals to change identities, forge passports and smuggle children.[3] Animal pornography is rare in India, but it is equally offensive as any other form of pornography. Animal porn is like child porn, it is also a disturbed human behavior that we must not tolerate because it causes suffering for animals and we have to protect them.[4] It is an irony that countries like Netherlands are supporting such type of pornography.[5] Pornography is like moral cancer that is eating at the moral fabric of our society.[6] The areas where pornography is made and distributed also spoil the environment of surrounding areas.

Pornographic movies are popularly known as blue films in India. The production of these films is mostly done outside India and they are largely imported. There are very few blue films available in the Indian Market, which are made in India involving Indian citizens in the production work. The problem lies in the rating system of the United States where movies containing explicit sex scenes are given PG ratings and importers of such films distribute these films to children without any problems because Indian Law only prohibits distribution of R and X rating films to minors. Films containing extremely sexual and pornographic material are also permitted for distribution and viewing in United States under X (NC-17) category though minors are not allowed to view these films in any situation.[7] These films are illegally imported in India by the Piracy mafia which imports pirated C.Ds. of these films through Dubai and Nepal. These films

1. www.tech.in/should-adult-porn-websites-be-banned-in-india.html
2. Adultfriendfinder.com is one of those sites whose advertisement banner could easily be seen while surfing internet even when the person browsing the internet is using safe search features.
3. www.netsafety.nic.in/internet/htm
4. www.rnw.nl/english/article/move-ban-animal-porn
5. www.rnw.nl/english/article/move-ban-animal-porn. Netherlands is the biggest distributor of animal pornography.
6. www.afa.net/detail.aspx?id=2147484806.
7. http://www.mpaa.org/2007-Theatrical-Market-Statistics.pdf

are also downloaded via internet websites including youtube.com.[1] In India also the Censor Board of Film Certification issues Adult certificate to certain films that contain sex scenes but these films do not have pornographic content in them. These pornographic movies are often aired by Cable T.V. operators at night time or often viewed at home using CD players and V.C.R.

The pornographic Industry in India is an underground industry largely operated by underworld. The blue films are imported in Mumbai which is the center for underworld activities. Dawood Ibrahim, the Don of the underworld is the father of piracy in India.[2] Through the underworld, pirated pornographic content reaches Mumbai from where it is distributed throughout India.

Connection between Organized Crime and Porn Industry

Pornography is emerging as an organized crime in the form of human trafficking in India. The workers involved in the pornographic industry are obtained through human trafficking. Human Trafficking is an organized crime of illicit trade where abused persons especially children and women are treated as commodities to be traded and re-traded without the slightest concern for human rights.[3] This trade supplies the raw material for prostitution and pornography because 80% of the people being traded are women and children and among them premium is more for young females.[3] The victims of human trafficking are forced into prostitution and dance bars. Dance bars provide perfect environment for nourishment of pornography and other activities associated with it. However, now an order of the Maharashtra Government to shut down dance bar has curbed this problem to a large extent.

Pornographic videos include sexually explicit material involving sadomasochistic activities where whips, iron rods and chains are used on women performing the sexual acts. The sexual activities start with a man making sexual advancement to a woman that is, if rebuffed results in forced intercourse and if accepted then the women can be seen begging for more.[4] Exploitation films that are subcategories of slasher films show sexual activities in a bad light including scenes of extreme violence being inflicted on performers. Exploitation films are low budget horror films specialized in suggestive or explicit sex, sensational violence, drug use, nudity, freaks, gore, the bizarre, destruction, rebellion and mayhem.[5] After viewing these films nobody would be agreeable on the point that such form of pornography must be tolerated in the society. The supporters of pornography either do not have knowledge about such form of pornography or they tend to ignore it. Thus, this book aims to provide sufficient knowledge about the pornography industry and the possible harms (both physical and moral) attached

1. www.bluefilms.com
2. http://news.outlookindia.com/item.aspx?658255.
3. Welcome Speech by Director, CBI, Seminar on Organized Crime and Human Trafficking available at http://cbi.nic.in/speech/dcbi_orgcrime_20090511.php
4. A survey of porn video on youporn.com and videos under various categories in pinkworld.com and worldsex.com can be looked into for further reference.
5. http://www.allmovie.com/essays/exploitation-movies-bikers-babes-and-slashers-5.

to it, so that the intellectuals of modern society can form an unbiased opinion as to whether pornography must be tolerated or not.

Such forms of pornography no doubt encourage aggressive behaviour towards women. These materials increase the acceptance of myths that women enjoy being coerced into sexual activity, and they enjoy being physically hurt in sexual context and that as a result a man who forces himself on a women sexually is in fact merely acceding to the real wishes of the women, regardless of the extent she seems to be resisting.[1] Even if, all those people whose behaviour is aggressive to women will not commit sexual offenses, but there is no guarantee that pornography would not be a causal link of sexual offences for some of them.

What should be Prosecuted?

On the issue of what should be prosecuted, the Meese commission in United States has recommended that nudity involves lewd exhibition of genitals, materials that are sexually violent, materials that are non-violent but degrading, and materials that are although highly sexually explicit and offensive to many contain neither violence not degradation.[2]

Advertisement of Sex Chat on Phone

Many Indian Newspapers contain advertisements of phone numbers for making new friends. These friendship services offer sex chat in the guise of friendship and also arrange customers to meet girls by charging hefty amount of money and thereby offending the moral fiber of society.[3] The sex workers engaged in such industry are for their emotional labour which is related to generating lustful thoughts and unchaste ideas in the mind of caller, thereby depraving and corrupting his mind. MTNL the premier telecom service provider in Mumbai has blocked 21 such services for violating the undertaking to keep out obscene material.[3] These sex chat operators had undertaking with the telecom service provider company for keeping out obscene material from their services. However, providing sex chatting facility to customers and arranging a meeting for immoral purposes clearly demonstrates that the sex chat operators have violated the undertaking because of which the telecom operator decided to disconnect their chat lines. The Court in *Pratibha Naitthani* v. *Union of India*,[4] case also passed an order restraining newspaper and periodicals from publishing any advertisement that amount to advertisement to prostitution having sexual overtone or any representation that violated section 3 of Indecent Representation of Women (Prohibition) Act, 1986. This directive of the Court covers advertisements of obscene chatting with girls on mobile phones.

---

1. Attorney General's Commission on Pornography, Final Report 234 (1986) available at porn-report.com. at 327.
2. Attorney General's Commission on Pornography, Final Report 234 (1986) available at porn-report.com., at 377.
3. http://timesofindia.indiatimes.com/india/No-dirty-talk-please-were-Indians/articleshow/42343477.cms
4. AIR 2006 Bom 259: (2006) 2 Bom LR 1180.

Adult Book Store

The adult book stores are the source of corrupting the minds of readers by selling pornographic books. They are more than paradise for sex addicts and perverts. The books in these stores contain hardcore pornographic books including books on child pornography, prostitution, she-males, someone else's spouse, sex with teenagers, animals, multiple partners and depicting sexual violence including rape and torture. There are no official adult book stores in India unlike foreign countries such as Netherlands where adult book stores are legal. However, in spite of illegalization of selling obscene books in India, pornographic books are being sold and bought frequently. These books are available at book stalls at railway stations, bus stands and markets and secretly sold like pornographic DVDs are sold at DVD stores. Prohibited Magazines like Playboy can also be found in India in such bookstores.

Multimedia Messaging Service (MMS)

Morphed pictures and videos of Famous Celebrities are downloaded in mobiles and sent to others *via* Multimedia Messaging Service. There have been incidents of famous actresses morphed pornographic video being circulated through MMS. There are MMS being circulated of other famous bollywood actresses whose photographs and videos have been morphed. These MMSs have become huge source of income for the MMS service providers because the transmission rates for MMS are very high. After every incident of introduction of a new MMS in the market the frequency of transmission of MMS increases and organizations earn supernormal profit. These MMS contain pornographic clips of couples which may be manager and secretary of any famous corporate firm and their bathroom, bedroom scenes, honeymooning couples, couples in the park, or morphed videos next to India Gate or the Taj Mahal.[1]

The fact that viewing pornographic videos in private is not illegal in India, works as catalyst to the production of pornographic MMS. Anyone can make such videos with the help of a mobile with video camera facility and transmit such video to others until reported. Only when it is reported to the police, does it become a case of public exhibition of obscene material and prosecuted under the law.

Hungry Generation/Hungryalists

The word Hungry Generation refers to poets of 1960 and early 1970's in India associated with a literary Movement in Bengali Language.[2] These poets have published works that would have even melted Vatsyayana's pen.[3] This generation attempted to break the norms of mainstream literary genres. The work of followers of this generation also impacted other literatures of other languages in India. With times the writings about sexual activities in Indian literature became more and more erotic and later on turned into pornographic writings depicting women as an object of lust.

---

1. www.atimes.com/atimes/Southasia/GG28DF01.html
2. http://www.library.northwestern.edu/spec/pdf/hungrygeneration.pdf
3. http://www.time.com/time/magazine/article/0,9171,830799,00.html

CHAPTER 3

ADJUDICATING PORNOGRAPHY IN UNITED STATES

To understand the methods of adjudication of pornography in United States, let us first understand the history of regulation of obscenity. Nobody noticed the need of regulation of pornography until 1663 in England, when Sir Charles Sedley was convicted for getting drunk, removing his clothes and uttering profane remarks and pouring urine over the crowd below the tavern balcony.[1] This was the first case where mere indecent behaviour was regulated by the law in England. This case is considered to be the pioneer of regulation of sexually explicit material in the world. However, Charles Sedley was punished for the offence of committing breach of peace.

Even after this case, there was no direct law to punish pornography. This situation of law was reiterated in the case of *Queen* v. *Read*[2] where Lord Justice Powell said that the book named 'fifteen plagues of maidenhead' is surely about printing bawdy stuff but can not be considered to be an offence of libel because libel must be against a person or persons or against the Government. He also said that it is surely a stuff not to be mentioned publicly but there is no law to punish it and judiciary cannot make law. The conduct of punishing such books may amount to corruption of good manners but that is not sufficient to punish it. However, after this case the reaction of judiciary towards pornographic material changed from compulsion to active dislike.

Edmund Curll who published *Venus in the Cloister or the nun in her smock* was convicted in 1727, however the reason behind this conviction was that the book also contained anti-catholic remarks that was sufficient to amount to breach of peace.[3] John Wilkes was also convicted for publishing *Essay on Women* but his prosecution was largely based on his activities that amounted to political dissent.[4] Hence even at this time there was no case where the conviction was obtained on the ground of mere obscenity.

It was Vagrancy Act of 1824 which provided penalties for publication of indecent pictures.[5] Section 3 of the Act also punished every common prostitute

1. *King* v. *Sadley,* 83 Eng. Rep. 1146 (1663).
2. 92 Eng. Rep. 777 (1708).
3. *Dominus Rex* v. *Curll,* 93 Eng. Rep. 849 (1727).
4. *The King* v. *John Wilkes,* 95 Eng. Rep. 737 (1764).
5. Full act available at http://www.statutelaw.gov.uk/content.aspx?activeTextDocId=1029462.

wandering in public street and public highways or in any place of public resort and behaving in riotous or indecent manner.

In United States the position was almost the same as United Kingdom. There was no reported conviction on the ground of mere obscenity as there were no legislations before 19th Century. The state of Vermont passed a statute in 1821 to ban circulation of obscene material, that was followed by State of Connecticut and other states. By the middle of 19th Century the production and distribution of obscene material was a crime throughout most of the United States.[1] Anthony Comstock crusaded for larger restriction on pornography until his death in 1915 when he announced with great pride "I have convicted persons enough to fill a passenger train of 61 coaches, sixty coaches containing 60 passengers each and 61st almost full. I have destroyed 160 tons of obscene literature."[2]

A great development in the field of obscenity law was seen in 1930 when Theodore Dreiser's book *An American Tragedy* was found obscene by Supreme Judicial Court of Massachusetts.[3] The Court also pronounced that the seller of the book has no right to presume that the children to whom the book might be accessible would not read the obscene passage or even if they read, they will continue to read on until the evil effects of obscene passages were weakened or dissipated with the tragic denouement of tale.[3] This judgment revealed the attitude of American Judiciary towards circulation of pornography to children that became the foundation behind laws regulating circulation of pornography to children.

Adjudication of Pornography

This chapter deals with the questions such as how would we determine which substance has the tendency to deprave or corrupt the mind of people? Should a statute determine the exact nature of material which can corrupt the mind of people or should it be left to the judges or jury or someone else? Should the judges apply community standards in the determination?

In United States, statutes have helped the judges by providing qualification for the prohibited materials since 1873. The Comstock Act which was enacted in 1873 gave a qualification of such materials. That provision of Comstock Act, is now present in 18 USC 9 (1978) in the form of section 1461. This section provides that every obscene, lewd, lascivious, indecent, filthy or vile article, matter, thing, device or substance is declared to be non-mailable matter and shall not be conveyed in the mails or delivered from any post office or by any letter carrier. This definition is actually based on publication of pornographic material. Mere possession of pornography is not an offence under this definition. It eases out the task of judiciary as now the judiciary has to only see whether the material in question is obscene, lewd, lascivious, indecent, filthy or vile. However, there is still so much discretion left to the judges to decide whether the material in question actually falls into one of the categories mentioned in the section.

---

1. Donna I. Denis, "Obscenity Law and Conditions of Freedom in 19th Century United States", 27(2) Law and Social Enquiry 369 (Spring 2002).
2. Attorney General's Commission on Pornography, Final Report 234 (1986) available at porn-report.com., at 244.
3. *Commonwealth* v. *Friede*, 171 NE 472 (1930).

***Roth* v. *United States*[1]**

In England, in the case of *R.* v. *Hicklin,*[2] Justice Cockburn laid down a test to determine which material may fall in the prohibited category. He said "I think the test of obscenity is this, whether the tendency of the matter charged as obscene is to deprave and corrupt those whose minds are open to such immoral influences, and into whose hands a publication of this sort may fall."

However, this test was objected in the United States in the *Roth* v. *U.S.*[1] on 3 grounds:—

1. It permitted books to be judged obscene on the basis of isolated pages read out of context;
2. It allowed the obscenity of a work to be determined by its likely effects on unusually susceptible persons;
3. It posited fixed standard of propriety regardless of time, place and circumstances.

Then Lord Brennan corrected the test and said that "a book can be judged obscene only if the dominant theme of the material taken as a whole is so judged; only if it is the likely effects of the material on 'the average person' that is taken into account and only if contemporary community standards are applied to the work." Hence after the *Roth* v. *U.S.*[1] case the attention was shifted from unusually susceptible persons to average person. Here it was also made mandatory to take into account the contemporary community standards.

According to the test laid down in this case, each of three elements must independently be satisfied before a book can be held obscene:—(a) the dominant theme of the material taken as a whole appeals to a prurient interest in sex; (b) the material is patently offensive because it affronts contemporary community standards relating to the description or representation of sexual matters; and (c) the material is utterly without redeeming social value. However, this test did not allow the judiciary to decide whether the material in question has the tendency to deprave and corrupt the mind of people.[3]

This test has very specific features like the requirement of calculating the effect of material after considering it as a whole. This test does not allow a book to be judged obscene merely because it contains a chapter, a page or a paragraph that is obscene or contains material which is lewd, filthy or disgusting and appeals to prurient interest of person. According to this test, if an isolated page of the book contains obscene material, then it can be overlooked if the dominant theme of the book demonstrates a purpose which is related to artistic expression important for the society or the book demonstrates any social value. The test of patently offensiveness requires that the work in question must have the capability to offend the members of society. The effect of the work in question must not be so trivial to be normally overlooked by society. The work in question must be judged obscene only after applying community's moral standards. However, this case did not

1. (1957) 35 US 476.
2. (1868) LR 3 QB 360.
3. *Memoirs* v. *Massachusetts,* 383 US 413 (1966).

explain in detail what this moral standard of community means. Are the standards to be applied local or national? Can a book be judged obscene on the basis of moral standard of a bureaucrat? These were certain questions that were left unanswered by this case.

In *United States* v. *Kennerly*,[1] which was decided in 1913, Justice Hand used the test of 'average conscience' to determine which material falls into the prohibited category. This test was somewhat like 'test of reasonable man' and was equally random. This test required deciding what average conscience is but this test also followed that the effect of work must be judged on an average person, not an unusually susceptible person which means that it is the sensibility of average person that has to be looked into. *Roth's* case (1957) followed the same principle. So, After *Roth*'s case Courts were only concerned with two phrases 'average person' and 'community standards.

Test of Patent Offensiveness

The test of 'Patent offensiveness' was explained in the case of *Manual Enterprises* v. *Day*,[2] where magazine containing photographs of nude males were in question. In this Case Justice Harlan stated that the material in question is not so offensive as to affront current community standards of decency. The test of patent offensiveness was adopted in Model Penal Code in 1962 under section 251.4 which says that a material falls into prohibited category only if, considered as a whole its predominant appeal is to prurient interest, that is a shameful and morbid interest, in nudity, sex or excretion and if in addition it goes substantially beyond customary limits of candor in describing or representing such matters. The last clause of this section actually deals with patent offensiveness.

Test of Utter Lack of Redeeming Social Value

In the case of *John Cleland's Memoirs of Women of Pleasure* v. *Attorney General of Massachusetts*,[3] test of utter lack of redeeming social value was explained. In this case, the Attorney General of Massachusetts brought a civil equity action for adjudication of obscenity of Cleland's Memoirs of Women of Pleasure. The trial court held that the book must is devoid of first and fourteenth amendment protection and stated that any patently offensive book which appeals to prurient interest must not be having utter lack of redeeming social value. The book must not be 'unqualifiedly worthless.' The book in question in this case was found to be having social, literary and historical importance by the Court deciding the matter. According to the Court if a book which has social values is sold in a way that demonstrates that this book has only an object of appealing prurient interest and devoid of any social value, then also the book can not be held to be obscene. This means that the manner in which a book is sold is irrelevant. For example, if *Kamsutra* is sold on worldsex.com by advertising it as an aid to determine the sexual positions of porn actors then also the book can not be banned under this test if it can be proved that *Kamsutra* has social values.

1. 209 F 2d 119 (1913).
2. 370 US 478 (1962).
3. 383 US 413 (1966).

Test of Miller v. *California*

In 1973, in the case of *Miller* v. *California*,[1] a proper test for identification of prohibited materials was laid down by majority. The test provides that the judges should look whether the average person, applying contemporary community standards would find that the work, taken as a whole appealing to prurient interest, or whether the work depicts or describes in a patently offensive way sexual conduct specifically defined by the applicable state law and whether the work taken as a whole, lacks serious literary, artistic, scientific or political value.[1]

This test consolidates the tests laid down in *Roth* and *Manual* Cases. The first phrase of the test confirms Roth Test and the second phrase confirms Manual's Test. Miller case also cites examples to determine as to what are the materials prohibited under the clause of patent offensiveness. It prohibits patently offensive representation or description of ultimate sexual acts, normal or perverted, actual or simulated and also patently offensive representation of masturbation, excretory functions and lewd exhibition of genitals.[2] The *Memoirs* Test was also considered in *Miller*'s test but in a wide way. Here, in place of lack of redeeming social value, the work must depict literary, artistic, scientific and political value. However, even now a lot of discretion is left to the judiciary to determine whether the work lacks such kind of value or not. Currently this test is applied by the judiciary in United States. At present 'mere nudity' is given protection by American Judiciary in the case of *Jenkins* v. *Georgia*,[3] where the issue was whether the film 'Carnal Knowledge' is a material deemed to be prohibited according to the test laid down in *Miller*'s case. The Court on this issue stated that the film shows occasional nudity but nudity alone does not render material obscene under Millers' standards. This was upheld time and again by American Courts.

Lawrence v. *Texas*

In the case of *Lawrence* v. *Texas*[4] that was decided by United States Supreme Court in 2003, the Court declared unconstitutional a statute that prohibited private consensual sexual conduct between homosexuals. It also held that the statute infringed on a substantive due process right. Hence, it declared that right to sexual privacy is a constitutional right enshrined under United States's Constitution. However, Court did not go on the issue that whether there was a fundamental right to engage in sexual activity but it did consider the issue that whether consenting adults were free to engage in a sexual act. On this issue the Court gave an affirmative answer confirming that the due process clause protects such an act. The Court rightly struck down the statute that infringed upon most private human conduct in the most private place, home because the persons in question were consenting adults and there was no question of degradation of sex and dehumanization of person involved in such business. The publication of such conduct would also not have been affected by anti-pornography. However, if there

1. 413 US 15 (1973).
2. Attorney General's Commission on Pornography, Final Report 234 (1986) available at porn-report.com at 25.
3. 418 US 153 (1974).
4. *Lawrence* v. *Texas*, 539 US 558 (2003).

would have been subordination of one person over other with the use of violence on other person then this conduct would surely have been affected by anti-pornography laws. If we see it from another view which is based on public morality then such conduct may be prohibited if it is against public morality and Government has the right to prohibit such conduct if they are against public morality unless and until such conducts are not protected by due process clause.

Sex Toys

There are other forms of pornography which have come up with the development in the field of science and technology. Sex toys including dildos, vibrators and other forms of devices are some of them. People use them for different reasons. Some consider it a useful tool to avoid sexually contracting disease.[1]

State of Alabama's Anti Obscenity Enforcement Act prohibits any person from knowingly distributing, possessing with intent to distribute or offering or agreeing to distribute any obscene material or any device designed or marketed as useful primarily for stimulation of human genital organs for anything of pecuniary value.[2] Texas Penal Code also prohibits sale of obscene devices including dildo, an artificial vagina designed or marketed as useful for the purpose of stimulation of human genital organs.[3] The Anti-obscenity law of Texas does not prohibit only sale of obscene devices but also the promotion of these devices too as it makes an offense if any person possesses with intent to wholesale promotion of any obscene material or obscene devices. If any person possesses six or more obscene devices, he is presumed to posses them with the intent to promote them.[4]

Mississippi Code of 1972 also prohibits a corporation, partnership firm, company, association, business, establishment, organization or other legal entities from distributing obscene sexual devises.[5] Georgia, Texas, Mississippi, Tennessee, Nebraska, Virginia and Utah are the states which have similar bans imposed on sex toys; however, the Anti obscenity law of Alabama provides exemptions for the devices if they have *bona fide* medical, scientific, educational, legislative, judicial or law enforcement purposes.[6] This means that public good defense of obscenity is also available for sex toys in Alabama Code.

The laws banning sales of sex toys are usually challenged on the basis of due process clause that is enshrined in fourteenth amendment to the U.S. constitution. This clause states that "Nor shall any state deprive any person of their life, liberty and property without due process of law."[7] Since the early 1950's this clause was treated by courts to include basic substantive rights and the due process under the clause was known as substantive due process that prohibits an individual from

1. *Reliable Consultants, Inc.* v. *Earle*, 517 F 3d 738 (742) (2008).
2. Section 13A Alabama Anti-obscenity Enforcement Act, 1998.
3. Section 43.21 of Texas Penal Code.
4. Section 43.23 of Texas Penal Code.
5. Section 97-29-109 of Mississippi Code of 1972.
6. http://www.gopetition.com/gopetition-in-the-media/194/alabama-ban-on-selling-sex-toys-goes-into-effect.html
7. U.S. Constitution, 14th Amendment, section 1.

infringing an individual's fundamental liberty, interest, irrespective of the process opted by the Government unless the infringement serves compelling state interest.[1] Hence, it is clear that until the Government can prove that there is a compelling state's interest in banning those materials, the Government cannot ban those materials. In *Lawrence* v. *Texas,* the Court held that public morality does not amount to compelling state interest. It is up to the Courts to decide what amounts to compelling state interest.

In the case of *William* v. *Morgan,*[2] 11th circuit Court evaluated the constitutionality of Alabama's anti-obscenity law. An adult novel dealer, Sherry Williams and American Civil Liberties Union challenged the law on the constitutional grounds including due process clause.[3] The plaintiffs also argued that right to engage in private sexual conduct as accepted a part of substantive right in *Lawrence* v. *Texas,* also includes right to sell sex toys. But the Court distinguished *Lawrence* v. *Texas,* from the present case on the point that in the previous case the Court dealt with a right that was related to private activities of the person involved in the act whereas in the present case the Court has to deal with an activity that is purely public and commercial in nature. Hence, the preposition that public morality does not amount to compelling state interest as upheld in *Lawrence* v. *Texas,* was only applicable to the sexual conduct in private sphere. If such conduct is published in public then the Government has the right to punish such conduct on the ground of public morality.

In the present case, the activities of selling toys in market is purely a public and commercial in nature, so the Courts were right in upholding the statute on the ground of state's interest in preservation of public morality. Hence, it is an established position after william's case in Alabama is that pornography can be prohibited on the ground of public morality. However, this case was not considered by Supreme Court of United States, so there is no national law governing such situation by now. In the lieu of conflicting decisions[4] from other states, the position of law in Alabama can not amount to the law of United States.

Community Standards

Normally Courts apply community standard to find out whether the material is prohibited under the law or not. In United States, *Roth* v. *United States* case mandated community standards to be applied in cases to judge the obscenity of material and in India also the test of community standard has been adopted by Courts from time to time. In United States, the concept of community standard was clarified in case of *People* v. *Finkelstein,*[5] where a book store owner was arrested for

1. Jamie Iguchi, 'Satisfying Lawrence: The fifth Circuit Strikes Ban on Sex Toys' 43 United States Davis Law Review 655, 661 (December 2009).
2. 478 F 3d 1316 (11 Cir. 2007).
3. http://www.usatoday.com/news/washington/2005-02-22-toys_x.htm
4. *Reliable Consultants Inc.* v. *Earle,* 517 F 3d 738. In this case, the 5th Circuit Court held that the Texas Statute prohibiting sale of sex toys is unconstitutional.
5. "Obscenity. Comparison Evidence is Inadmissible for Purpose of Establishing Community Standards under 'Hard-Core Pornography' *Test People* v. *Finkelstein (N.Y. 1962)",* 76 (7) Harvard Law Review 1498 (May, 1963).

selling two obscene books, the counsel of defendant offered in evidence certain other publications in the book stores of New York to indicate the current standards of community and literature. However, the Court refused to accept such evidences on the ground that such evidences are not capable of defining current standards of community's morals. The Court also said that this is not the way the standards of community are made. The presence of other publications in the book stores does not indicate that they are happily bought and sold by the members of community and are accepted by the community. It only shows that such type of publication is available in the market. There is no guarantee that such books would not be considered equally obscene by an average person applying community moral standards.[1]

Since the Supreme Court has intimated that a national rather than a local standard of community tolerance is to be applied in obscenity cases, cases in other jurisdictions should be fully relevant.[2] Thus while in cases of particularly offensive material it may be permissible to find obscenity from the content of the material itself, the defendant should be granted the opportunity to introduce evidence to prove the contrary.[2]

A series of cases in United States point out those standards applicable in cases of judging the prohibited materials are national standards and not the local standards. A material has to be judged keeping in view the history, development and awareness of morality of the nation. Local standards of morality are never constant and bound to change. Hence, taking into account national standards would help the jury in determination of obscenity rather than taking into account of local standards in United States.

Photographic Porn

The objective nature of photography confers on credibility that is absent from other forms of picture making. This form of pornography requires performers of sexual activity and a photographer. There has been no study in India to study the conditions under which these performers appear before the camera and the ill-effects of it in their lives. This form of pornography is visible in social networking websites where people upload photos of nude girl engaged in sexual activities by creating fake profiles. These pornographic images are also visible on websites and calendars illegally published and distributed. These activities have taken the form of organized crime which is clear from the steady increase in number of women receiving offers of nude posing for websites and calendars. Report have suggested that the relationship between pornographers and performers are such that there is very little or no respect for the rights and physical welfare of the latter.[3]

There is a trend of uploading obscene pictures of women on social networking websites by creating fake profiles. The offenders download photos of people from

---

1. "Obscenity. Comparison Evidence is Inadmissible for Purpose of Establishing Community Standards under 'Hard-Core Pornography' Test *People* v. *Finkelstein (N.Y. 1962)*", 76 (7) Harvard Law Review 1498 (May, 1963).
2. *Kahm* v. *United States*, 300 F 2d 78 (1962).
3. Fraser Committee Report, 265.

their profiles and mix these photos with the help of photo-mixing software. It seems to depict the person whose photo is downloaded from his profile indulged in sexual activity in an objectionable position. After creating fake profiles of the victim, the offenders start asking for money from the victims for their dirty deeds. This has taken the form of organized crime and becomes the first step towards other crimes that include preparation of pornographic videos and MMS and human trafficking.

In United States, the Supreme Court in *Paris Adult Theater* v. *Slaton* case[1] said that suppression of obscenity can be justified on the ground that 'public exhibition of obscene material or commerce in such material has a tendency to injure the community as a whole to engender the public safety'. Hence, publicly exhibiting an obscene material including, pictures, images, movies or videos in any form is not protected by law and can be prosecuted if found to appeal the prurient interest of person in whose knowledge the material has been brought.

There is a new ground applied by Supreme Court of United States while considering the ill effects of photographic pornography. The Supreme Court of United States has also justified banning photographic pornography on the ground of personal harm caused to performers of pornography by the publication of pornographic images. In the case of *New York* v. *Ferber*,[2] Court stated that the publication of pornographic material depicting children in the midst of sexual activities (masturbation) does not harm them only because of the sexual abuse involved but also because the published material is a permanent record of participation of children in such activities and harm to them is exacerbated by their circulation. It also stated that the involvement of children in pornographic activities is harmful to psychological, emotional and mental health of child. Child pornography is also not subject to Miller Test. In another case the application of this analysis was extended to the nude cartoon of a famous boxer because of its ill-effects on the boxer.[3]

Child pornography is considered to be different from adult pornography due to intricacies involved in it that are discussed later in this book. In child pornography, children are harmed not only in production process but also after publication of such pornography on internet, or via any other media. It attaches a taint on the future of children depicting them in bad light and characterizes them as offenders of society's common morality. Usually the photos that are uploaded on social networking sites belong to children who are below 18 years of age. Publication of their nude photos either with their consent or fraudulently affects the prospects of their development and it also affects their mental health.

There have been instances when a teenager has committed suicide due to the emotional pressure created around him after publication of her nude photos.[4] The practice of 'Sexting' that is prevalent across the world in certain schools results

1. 413 US 49 (1973).
2. 458 US 747 (1982).
3. *Ali* v. *Playgirl Inc.*, 447 F Supp 723 (1978).
4. http://thecurvature.com/2009/12/2/13-year-old-girl-commits-suicide-after-classmates-spread-nude-photos/

in continuous taunting and harassment of the victims by their classmates and friends. This taunting and harassment leads the victim to take steps like suicide.

Courts in United States have held actionable nude photographs of women whose consent for publication has been obtained fraudulently and also another photograph that was stolen from the home of pornographer.[1] Even after overturning of Indianapolis Ordinance, the law of the land in United States is that the State may prohibit fraud, trickery or the use of force to perform people in pornographic films.[2] These decisions depict the concern of Courts about the ill-effects of publication of pornographic images on the victims of pornography. The Courts seem to have accepted that the effects of publication of pornographic images on the victim are not very different between adults and children. Even adults suffer from the same trauma and humiliation that is suffered by child victims.

The performers perform in the industry not because they have loose morals or they need sex, but because they need money to survive. They are usually struck by the financial conditions and need money to run their livelihood. Hence, the voluntary consent of those pornographers who work in the industry as depicted in the pornographic images is not a conclusive proof as to whether their consent has been obtained fraudulently or voluntarily.

Many a time we wonder why these beautiful looking ladies opt for a career such as pornography. They work in pornography industry not because they are of loose morals but because most of them are sexually abused or otherwise badly damaged as children that renders their body and sexuality worthless to them by abuser. These women are compelled to gratify the desires of men by penetration by two or more males at the same time, gang banged, slapped, choked, spanked, whipped, tied up, tortured, urinated and defecated and drugged to kill their pain or numb their sensibilities.[3]

However, the decisions restrict the application of laws to the photographs that are published fraudulently without the consent of the victim. The decisions tend to ignore the ill-effects of publication of pornographic images that can be suffered by the family and relatives of the victims and the people closely associated with the victims. Even in those cases where the consent of the victim is obtained voluntarily, the humiliation suffered by the relatives, friends and family is similar to the situation when the consent of the victim is obtained fraudulently. Hence, publication of pornographic images must be banned in all situations irrespective of whether the consent of the victim has been obtained fraudulently or not.

Pornography induces fear in women but mostly in those women who have been raped or otherwise sexually abused because it validates and celebrates the criminal behaviour of which they have been victims.[4] There are other reasons also

1. *Braun* v. *Flynt,* 726 F 2d 245 (1984) and *Wood* v. *Hustler Magazine Inc.,* 736 F 2d 1084 (1984).
2. *American Booksellers Association* v. *Hudnut,* 771 F 2d 323 (1985).
3. www.obscenitycrimes.org.socialcost.php
4. "Pornography, Equality, and a Discrimination-Free Workplace: A Comparative Perspective Source:" 106(5) Harvard Law Review 1075, 1078 (March, 1993).

behind dehumanization of women working in those pornographic videos. One of them is such videos are permanent record of the sexual activities done by them before camera. Their sexual abuse becomes someone's pleasure.[1]

In North-Eastern states of India, the women who have been raped or sexually abused by the rebels are harassed by the pornographic videos that are prepared by the rebels while raping them.[2] These pornographic videos become the means of sexual pleasure for the viewers of pornography but this permanent record of their sexual abuse diminishes the future of those victims. These victims are raped time and again by the rebels because of the documentation of their abuse that renders them incapable of getting married or attain any reputable position in society.

In the opinion of Canadian Supreme Court also such degrading and dehumanizing material place women in position of subordination and humiliation as it corrodes women's self esteem and integrity even if they have consented to such acts because sometimes the very appearance of consent makes the depicted acts even more degrading and dehumanizing.[3]

In case of *American Book Sellers Association Inc.* v. *Hudnut,*[4] judge Easterbrook accepted the fact that depiction of subordination perpetuates subordination. The ill-effects produced by pornography are not limited to health of the performers but it extends to affecting employment, social respect and education. It adds to insult and injury to women that they suffer at home by their husbands. Outside their homes, they have to suffer from sexual assaults and rape.

Textual Pornography

Textual pornography is no less harmful than photographic or any other form of pornography. The history of textual pornography is very old. This form of pornography is not only restricted to books, magazines or news papers but it is visible in the form of adult sex stories in many websites on internet that provide pornographic content. These websites contain stories about incestuous sexual intercourse, accidental sexual intercourse and unnatural sexual intercourse and a link to these stories can be found on almost every porn-site.

In the case of *Dunlop* v. *United States,*[5] the publication titled 'The Dispatch' contained obscene, lewd, lascivious and indecent matters in print form on the 11th page of the publication under the heading of 'personal' and 'bath.' It also contained certain advertisements that were obscene. The Court found the defendant, the publisher guilty and sentenced him to hard labour for two years and also imposed $2000 as fine and costs. The Court also held that the question whether the publication in question is obscene, lascivious, lewd or indecent must

1. "Pornography, Equality, and a Discrimination-Free Workplace: A Comparative Perspective Source:" 106(5) Harvard Law Review 1075, 1078 (March, 1993).
2. Subir Bhaumik, 'India Rebels' 'Making Porn Films' available at http://news.bbc.co.uk/2/hi/south_asia/4190570.stm
3. *R.* v. *Butler,* (1992) 1 SCR (452) 489.
4. 475 US 1001 (1986).
5. 165 US 486 (1897).

be calculated on the basis of the capacity of such material to deprave an ordinary reader, his morals and lead him to impure purposes. If such material is capable of lowering the standard which we regard essential to civilization or capable of exciting those feeling which play most of the mischief in this world, then such material is prohibited.

In the case of *John Cleland's Memoirs of a Woman of Pleasure* v. *Attorney General Massachusetts*,[1] where the Memoirs of a woman of pleasure, commonly known as 'fanny hill' were prosecuted and adjudged as obscene. This case followed the Roth's test that the material in question must appeal to the prurient interest of readers. The landmark case in the field of textual pornography is *Kaplan* v. *California*,[2] where a proprietor of an adult book store was convicted for selling a plain-covered book without any illustrations containing repetitively descriptive material of sexually explicit nature.[3] The Court held in clear terms that even if the book does not contain any pictorial content and only contains textual material, it is not protected by the constitutional right to free speech guaranteed by the Constitution. The Government has the right to control distribution of such material to even consenting adults to avoid deleterious consequences. In this case the Court applied Miller's test of contemporary community standard and also accepted that contemporary community standard of the state can also be an apt criteria for determination of the obscenity of the object in question.

Child Pornography

Child Pornography Prevention Act, 1996 defines child pornography to include any visual depiction including any film, photograph, video, picture or computer generated image or picture whether made, produced electronically, mechanically or by other means that is or appears to be of a minor engaged in sexual conduct or if such visual depiction has been created, adapted or modified to appear that an identifiable minor is engaged in such an act or if such depiction is promoted, advertised, presented, described and distributed in a manner that conveys the impression that a minor is engaged in a sexually explicit act.[4]

However the Supreme Court of United States struck down the provisions of this Act in *Ashcroft* v. *Free Speech Coalition*,[5] because the provisions of this Act violated the freedom to engage in a substantial amount of lawful speech. Free speech coalition alleged that the phrase 'is or appears to be of a minor engaging in sexually explicit conduct' was overbroad. The Court opined that the provision of this Act also include virtual child pornography and images produced by more traditional means. It held that the provisions of this Act are overbroad because they prohibit materials that are neither obscene nor produced by exploiting real children and they do not take into consideration the serious, literary, artistic, political or scientific value of the material in question. The Court agreed that the

1. 383 US 413 (1966).
2. 413 US 115 (1973).
3. http://supreme.justia.com/us/413/115/
4. Section 121 of Child Pornography Prevention Act, 1996.
5. 535 US 234 (2002).

Child pornography harms the children because it creates victims in its production but it also said that virtual child pornography is an alternative to preserve serious literary, artistic, political and scientific value of child pornography and should be protected under the free speech doctrine.

It is submitted that the Court was not right in allowing virtual child pornography because such form of pornography normalizes and legitimizes child pornography and equally contributes to the harms caused to the victims of child pornography. It also desensitizes the offenders and induces them to commit an overt act that may include child sexual abuses.

However, this problem has been resolved by the enactment of section 1466A of 18 U.S.C. on Janurary 5, 2009[1] that deals with obscene visual representation of sexual abuse of children. This provision specifically criminalizes the possession and distribution of virtual and comic images of apparent children if they are engaged in sexually explicit conduct and such images lack any literary, artistic, political or scientific value. Section 1466A(a) says that any person who depicts an image that is, or appears to be, of a minor engaging in graphic bestiality, sadistic or masochistic abuse, or sexual intercourse, including genital-genital, oral-genital, or oral-anal, whether between persons or the same or opposite sex would be subjected to the penalties mentioned in section 2252A(b)(1).

Hence, this provision very well covers virtual child pornography because it uses the word 'appears to be.' 'Appears to be' denotes an image created by a painter on computer or canvas which depicts a minor engaged in sexual activity. It also covers images that are prepared by conventional means including hand-painting, drawing etc. in these form of paintings there is no involvement of children and no real child is harmed during the production of pornographic images. The introduction of this provision seeks to affirm that Government in the United States realized that there are harms of virtual child pornography even if it does not harm real children in production process that was ignored by United States Supreme Court while invalidating a provision that dealt with virtual child pornography.

All the laws that deal with child pornography are designed to achieve two main objectives:—

(a) To protect children who are involved in the production process of child pornography;

(b) To prohibit such material to be obtained by wanna-be, in waiting, or impulse driven child sex predators, who the courts, the law enforcement agencies, victims and even the criminals themselves claim, are excited to act out their loathsome fantasies by pornographic images of children.[2]

Laws that deal with virtual child pornography are designed to achieve the second aim of such laws. These laws tend to prohibit the circulation of images that

---

1. www.law.cornell.edu/uscode/howcurrent.php?tn=18&fragid=T18500585&extid =usc_sec_18_00001466—A000&sourcedate=2009-11-06&proctime=sun Nov 8 12:35:36 2009.

2. http://findarticles.com/p/articles/mi_m1571/is_19_18/ai_87024964/

appeals the prurient interest of sex-offenders. Virtual Child pornography has the effect of encouraging child sex abusers and this fact was completely ignored by the Court.

The virtual porn is available in every form of media including, CDs, DVDx, television, Cartoons, Animated Pornography and internet. The problem with virtual child pornography is that it looks like cent per cent real pornography. Today, with the development in computer animation technology, it is possible to create animated characters that resembles with human bodies. The creators are free to make them act in any way and these characters play with their genital organs as desired by the creators. Hentai videos are best examples of such form of virtual porn. These videos depict children engaged in very explicit sexual activities. Hentai videos are available in the form of hentai porn, manga, anime, 3D, and adult cartoons.[1]

Another form of pornography which is very popular among net surfers is poser pornography. In this form, pornography is made with the use of 3D computer graphics and made to represent people engaged in various sexual acts. The bodies of famous celebrities are also designed by 3D animation in a nude 3D image and made to act on the directions of the programme maker or any person authenticated by the programme to give such directions.[2]

There are other forms of virtual child pornography that include adult video gaming. These games have very explicit sexual contents and mainly intended by adult audience. However, there are no means to restrict their circulations to the adult audience only.

In 2003, The Protect Act of 2003 was also enacted in United States with the intent to prevent child abuse and it prohibited computer generated pornography when such visual depiction is a computer image or computer generated image that is or appears virtually indistinguishable from that of a minor engaging in sexually explicit conduct.[3] The provisions of this Act require that the images must be obscene under the test laid down by Miller's test. This provision also tends to cover almost all form of virtual porn that is mentioned above.

In the case of *United States of America* v. *Dwight Edwin Whorley*,[4] Dwight Whorley was convicted of knowingly receiving as a previously convicted person, on a computer 20 obscene Japanese anime cartoons (Hentai) depicting minors engaging in sexually explicit conduct, in violation of 18 U.S.C. Section 1462 and section 1466A(a)(1). The Court rejected the claims of Whorley that section 1462 is unconstitutional because text alone can not be obscene and section 1466A(a)(1) is also unconstitutional because cartoons do not depict actual minors.

The reason given by Court for rejecting claims of Whorley was the definition of obscenity as described in *Miller* v. *California*.[5] In that case, Court defined

1. www.pornhentai.com
2. www.poserporn.com
3. Section 502 of Prosecutorial Remedies and Other tools to end the Exploitation of Children Today Act of 2003 or the 'Protect Act'.
4. Full judgment available at <www.Pacer.ca4.uscourts.gov/opinion.pdf/064288R1.P.pdf
5. 413 US 15 (1973).

obscenity in the context of works which taken as a whole appeal to prurient interest in sex and are devalued of serious literary, artistic, political or scientific value. Even in *Kaplan* v. *California,* case that is described above, the Court very specifically stated that 'works' include both pictures and text. Hence the claim that textual representation of child pornography is protected under free speech is not right. For Whorley's next contention that the virtual cartoon do not depict real minors hence should not be prohibited by law, he relied on *New York* v. *Ferber,* where the Court upheld a state statute that prohibited depiction of actual children in sexual conduct and also on the *Ashcroft* v. *Free Speech Coalition,* where provisions of Prevention of Child Pornography Act were struck down that dealt with virtual child pornography.

The Court opined that the provision in the Protect Act criminalize drawing, cartoon, sculpture or painting that depicts a minor engaging in sexual activity and is obscene and under those provisions there is no requirement that the minor depicted must exist. The language of section 1466A(a)1 and 1466A(c) is sufficiently broad to prohibit receipts of obscene cartoons that do not depict actual minors. These provisions are not unconstitutional because the language of these provisions prohibits visual depictions of minors only when they are obscene unlike the provisions of Prevention of Child Pornography Act and obscenity in any form is not protected by first amendment. Hence, virtual cartoons, images if obscene, are not prohibited under the law and their production and distribution is not protected by the constitution.

Pornography Victim Compensation Act, 1991 that was introduced in the United States Congress allows victim of the crime of pornography to sue distributors of obscene materials and claim compensation.[1] Under this bill the victims of pornography would have been able to sue the producer, publisher, distributors, exhibitors and sellers.[1] However, the bill could not have been passed due to apposition from various sectors of society and now the rights of victims of pornography are governed by Crime Victims Rights Act.

---

1. Henry J. Reske, "Feminists Back Anti-Porn Bill", 78 American Bar Association Journal 32 (June, 1992).

CHAPTER 4

ADJUDICATING PORNOGRAPHY IN UNITED KINGDOM

In United Kingdom, Obscene Publications Acts govern the field and determines the materials that fall within prohibited category. There have been several Acts of the Parliament of the same name including Obscene Publication Act, 1857, Obscene Publication Act, 1959 and Obscene Publication Act, 1964. However, now only Obscene Publication Act, 1959 and 1964 are still in force as amended by latest legislations.[1]

The first Obscene Publication Act was enacted in 1857 when pornography was described as a trade more deadly than prussic acid, arsenic or strychnine. The criteria for obscene material was given in *R.* v. *Hicklin*'s case where obscenity was described as an object having tendency to deprave and corrupt those minds open to such immoral influences irrespective of any literary or social merit.[2] Study of homosexuality,[2] educational pamphlets of sex and contraception[3] were treated as objects having the tendency to deprave and corrupt the minds of people. The reason behind this was that the Act ignored to take into account the social or literary merits of the object in question so even if the object was beneficial for the public interest at large but having the tendency to deprave and corrupt the mind of people then the object will be prohibited by the law. Hence a reform was needed in the law to avoid regulation of objects having literary or social value.

To reform the existing law, Obscene Publication Act, 1959 was introduced which protected regulation of materials which are justified as being for the public good on the grounds that it is in the interest of science, literature, art or learning, or of other objects of general concern.[4] Section 2 of the Act that deals with penalties for publishing an obscene article for gain or not or 'possessing an obscene article for gain (whether for himself or not)'[5] provides that no person shall be prosecuted under this section if he can prove that he has not examined the material for which he is charged under this section or he had a reasonable cause to suspect that the material in question is not the one for which a penalty may be attracted under this section.[6] Hence, this Act provides two statutory defenses to the offender, one is

1. Obscene Publications Act, 1857 is repealed by section 3(8) of Obscene Publications Act, 1959.
2. Susan M. Easton, Page 123.
3. Charles Bradlaugh, *The Queen* v. *Charles Bradlaugh and Annie Besant,* 3, 1877.
4. Section 4(1) of Obscene Publication Act, 1959.
5. Inserted by Obscene Publications Act, 1964.
6. Section 2(5) of Obscene Publication Act, 1959.

public good defense and the other is defense of innocent dissemination. Section 1 of Obscene Publication Act, 1959 lays down the test to determine the prohibited, material under this Act. According to this section an article shall be deemed to be obscene if its effect or (where the article comprises two or more distinct items) the effect of any one of its items is, if taken as a whole, such as to tend to deprave and corrupt persons who are likely, having regard to all relevant circumstances, to read, see or hear the matter contained or embodied in it.[1] This section follows the test laid down in *Hicklin*'s case as far as it refers to the materials which have the tendency to deprave and corrupt the minds of people in whose hands the material of this sort may fall.

This Act goes on to the extent of defining the word 'article' in the section. Article means to include any description of article containing or embodying matter to be read or looked at or both, any sound record, any film or other record of a picture or pictures.[2] Thus this Act includes electronic articles also in clear terms. Under this Act mere possession of article is not an offence but publication of article is necessary. Publication includes distribution, circulation, selling, letting on hire, giving, lending, offering for sale or in the case of an article containing or embodying matter to be looked at or a record, showing, playing or projecting it.[3]

R. v. *Penguin Books*[4] was the first case that was tried under this Act. This case was concerned with the publication of Lady Chatterley's Lover, a novel by D.H. Lawrence. This book contained many filthy expletives and sex scenes. This book was prosecuted for depraving and corrupting the mind of person in who are likely, having regard to all circumstances, read, see or hear the matter contained in the book. The publishers resorted to public good defense that was introduced in the 1959 Act under section 4(1). The book was adjudged one of literary merits on the basis of expert testimony.

The provision of public good defense was examined by Queens Bench in the *Reg.* v. *Calder and Bayers* case.[5] In this case Queen Bench realized that a paradox has been created by enacting public good defense because the legislature hardly have contemplated that a book that can deprave and corrupt readers can be justified on the ground of public good. To solve the paradox Court resorted to concept of standard of proof. The Court of Appeal laid down that the jury must find beyond reasonable doubt that the effect of the book is such as to deprave and corrupt significant portions of people who are likely to read it. After finding so, they must consider the number of readers that are likely to be depraved or corrupted and strength or tendency of such work to deprave or corrupt a person. Then they must weight these factors against the books' literary or other merits to decide on a balance of probability as to whether the book is entitled to enjoy public good defense or not.

1. Section 1 of Obscene Publication Act, 1959.
2. Section 1(2) of Obscene Publication Act, 1959.
3. Section 1(3) of Obscene Publication Act, 1959.
4. 1961 Cr LR 176.
5. (1969) 1 QB 151.

The provisions of this Act are criticized on the ground of being too vague.[1] The Act allowed too much discretion to the jury. It was also criticized on the ground of being too weak to control pornography. The main objection behind this Act is how to determine what object can deprave or corrupt the mind of people. Who are those people, the Act refers to? It is not at all clear from the wording of the act whether the criterion to be used is the ordinary person or the person most likely to read it, or the most vulnerable reader.[1]

It was expected that these problems would be solved by the 1964 Amendment Act but that Act did not make any changes in the definition of obscenity in the Act leaving it as vague as it was before. However, this Act made possessing an obscene article for gain,[2] and keeping negatives for the purpose of production of obscene Articles[3] offenses within the purview of this Act.

In case of *D.P.P.* v. *Whyte*,[4] it was said that an article can be considered to be obscene only in relation to its likely readers. It is the primary job of jury to decide who these people are and whose minds may be depraved or corrupted by the material in question. In *Knuller Ltd.* v. *D.P.P.*[5] the Court clarified that the people referred in the Act are not unusually susceptible persons but ordinary people and the standard to be adopted by the jury must be one of current standards of ordinary decent people. While deciding the capability of material in question to corrupt the mind of people, the jury cannot take the help of expert opinion. However, Jury may utilize expert opinion to see whether the material in question has any literary, artistic, political or scientific value.[6] This means that once the jury has decided that the material in question is a prohibited material; expert evidences can be given for defense under section 4(1) of the Act. However, expert evidences were held inadmissible in the case of *D.P.P.* v. *Jordan*[7] where expert evidences were given to prove psychotherapeutic benefits of pornography because it is not related to science, literature, art or learning. However, the decision failed to take into account the last phrase of section 4(1) that deals with objects of general concern. This phrase may be used to include benefits of pornography like relieving tension or growth of body if there are any.

There are many legislations in the United Kingdom that prohibit publication of pornographic material. One of them is The Customs Consolidation Act, 1876. This legislation is considered to be one of the most efficient legislation in United Kingdom to curb pornography. It prohibits importation of indecent or obscene prints, books, cards, lithographs, engravings, photographs or other indecent or obscene articles in United Kingdom.[8] This Act does not have public good defense

---

1. Susan M. Easten, The Problem of Pornography, pp. 126-127, 1994.
2. Section 1(1) of Obscene Publications Act, 1964.
3. Section 2 of Obscene Publications Act, 1964.
4. 1972 AC 849.
5. (1973) 2 AC 435.
6. *R.* v. *Anderson*, (1972) 1 QB 304.
7. (1977) AC 699.
8. Section 42 of Customs Consolidation Act, 1876.

in contrast to section 4(1) of Obscene Publication Act, 1876 and defines obscene as filthy, loathsome, repulsive and lewd.[1]

Under section 170(2) of Custom and Excise Management Act, 1979, it is an offence to be knowingly concerned in attempting to evade the prohibition on indecent and obscene article imposed by section 42 of Customs Consolidation Act, 1876.[2] In the case of *Regina* v. *Forbes,* (2000),[3] Giles Javen Forbes was arrested at London Heathrow Airport in relation to a certain video casset labelled as 'Spartacus' that contained indecent photographs of children. He was charged under section 170(2) of Custom and Excise Management Act read with section 42 of Customs Consolidations Act. He denied having any knowledge that the material which he was carrying was prohibited material and therefore he contended that he should not be prosecuted for the material which he did not know to be prohibited. He contended that he thought that the cassettes which he was carrying are "The exorcist" and the "kidz" that are not prohibited material.

The House of Lords in this case held that the offence that is created under section 170(2) is the offence of being "knowingly concerned in any fraudulent evasion' of any prohibition with respect to the goods." Hence knowledge of evasion of prohibition is the main requirement of the offence. The fact that he bought two video films at Amsterdem Airport that did not contain any indecent picture of child but leaving those films in the lavatory of Heathrow Airport and then producing the receipts which appeared to relate to the videos that contained obscene material clearly denotes that the offender knew that he is involved in the evasion of prohibition against importation.

Post Office Act, 1953, prohibits sending a packet through the post which encloses any indecent or obscene print, painting, photograph, lithograph, engraving, cinematograph film, book, card or written communication, or any indecent or obscene article, or which has on the packet or its cover any words, marks or designs which are grossly offensive or of an indecent or obscene character.[4] However, the application of this Act is impractical because there are no means to check whether the material contained in the mail is prohibited or not. For example an obscene photograph can be mailed in an envelope to any person without exposing the content to the authorities. It is only when the authorities get to know about the obscene content they can start a prosecution but that is rare.

The Children and Young Persons (Harmful Publications) Act, 1955 has prohibited the circulation of comics which are harmful to children and young persons. This Act was enacted with the aim to prevent the dissemination of certain pictorial publications that is harmful to young children and young persons. According to this Act any book, magazine or other like work that is likely to fall into the hands of children or young persons and consists wholly or mainly of stories told in picture (with or without text) or being stories that depict the

1. *R.* v. *Bow Street Magistrates Court* ex parte *Nochyp Ltd.,* (1990) 1 QB 1.
2. www.lawcf.org/.../LCF%20briefing%20on%20obscenity%20laws%20%20%2024th%2...
3. (2001) UKHL 40.
4. Section 11 of Post Office Act, 1953.

commission of crime, the act of violence, or incidents of a repulsive or horrible nature in a manner that the work if taken as a whole would tend to corrupt a child or young person into whose hand the work material fall.[1] Hence, all hardcore pornography that depicts violence upon the person involved in the making of pornography is prohibited under this Act.

Under this act, mere possession of prohibited material with the intention to sell is also an offense. A person is required to print, publish, sell or let on hire the prohibited material or possess for the purpose of selling it or letting on hire.[2] However a defense is available to him that he has not examined the contents of the material and did not have any reasonable cause to suspect that the material was a prohibited material.[3] It is sufficient for the prosecution to prove that the defendant had in possession prohibited material and wanted it to be sold. The burden of proof to prove that the defendant has the knowledge that the material is obscene is shifted upon the defendant.

This Act also prohibits importation of prohibited material under this Act including any plate or photographic film prepared for the purpose of importing obscene material. The expression 'plate' includes block, mould, matrix and stencil and the expression 'photographic films' include photographic plate also.[4]

The Act adopts the definition of 'child' from section 107 of Children and Young Person's Act, 1933 where a child is defined to mean a person who is under the age of 14 years of age.[5] Hence, the persons who are above 14 years are not included within the definition of child.

Protection of Children Act, 1978 makes it an offence to publish, distribute or take an indecent photograph of a child.[6] Criminal Justice Act, 1988 makes even possession of indecent photograph of a child an offence.[7] Now the Sexual Offence Act, 2003, has illegalize possession of indecent and obscene material featuring children less than 18 years of age.[8] This Act includes persons who are above 18 years of age within the definition of child. Any such material if being exported may be seized under Police and Criminal Evidence Act, 1984.

Pseudo-Photographs

Pseudo-photograph means to include photos depicting a child in sexual activity who is actually not in existence. For example pornographic images created with the use of photo mixing software that depict a child engaged in sexually explicit act but actually prepared by using an adult's body and a child's face, can be called a pseudo-photograph.

1. Section 1 of Children and Young Persons (Harmful Publications) Act, 1955.
2. Section 2 of Children and Young Persons (Harmful Publications) Act, 1955.
3. Proviso to section 2 of Children and Young Persons (Harmful Publications) Act, 1955.
4. Section 4 and 5 of Children and Young Persons (Harmful Publications) Act, 1955.
5. Section 107(1) of Children and Young Persons Act, 1933.
6. Section 1 of Protection of Children Act, 1978.
7. Section 160 of Criminal Justice Act, 1988.
8. Section 45(1) of Sexual Offences Act, 2003.

In the case of *R.* v. *Bowden*,[1] the Crown Court in Cambridge convicted Bowden on 12 counts of making an indecent photograph of a child contrary to section 1(1)(a) of the Protection of Children Act, 1978. Section 1(1)(a) of Protection of Children Act, 1978 before being amended by Criminal Justice and Public Order Act, 1994, read:—

1 (1) it is an offence for a person—

(a) To take, or permit to be taken, any indecent photograph of a child.

After amendment it read:

1 (1) It is an offence for a person—

(a) To take, or permit to be taken or to make, any indecent photograph or ***pseudo-photograph*** of a child.

Hence, it is clear that pseudo photographs were added in Protection of Children Act, 1978 by the Criminal Justice and Public Order Act, 1994. Bowden Contended that the amended act makes an offense of making a pseudo-photograph and not making a photograph. The Court in this case clearly held that section 1(1)(a) of Protection of Children Act, 1978 as amended by Criminal Justice and Public Order Act, 1994 covers both making a pseudo-photograph and making copies of photographs by knowingly copying the photograph. The Court also stated that the word 'make' should mean to cause to exist, to produce by action or to bring about. Hence copying a photograph or downloading an indecent photograph from internet amounts to making a copy of an indecent photograph.

The ruling of Court in this case meant that the law enforcement officers were also committing offence in trying to make a copy of the contents of suspect's computer disk. That was absolutely not the intention of the legislature. Hence an amendment was brought by Sexual Offence Act, 2003 in the Protection of Children Act where a statutory defense was created which removed making photograph or pseudo-photograph for the purpose of prevention, detection or investigation of crime, or for the purpose of criminal proceedings.

In a subsequent case of *R.* v. *Smith and Jayson*,[2] Lord Justice Dyson, Mr. Justice Johnson and Judge Rhys-Davies considered the issue as to what constitutes making a photograph or pseudo photograph for the purpose of section 1(1)(a) of Protection of Children Act, 1978. Police made a search of Jayson's computer and found numerous images of sexual acts involving men with young girls, including images of rape. Jayson did not voluntarily download those images but those images were saved in the hard drive as cache. The cache was retrieved by the expert from the hard disk.

Smith got an e-mail in his inbox containing an attachment showing images of a naked girl taken by her mother. Smith opened the attachment but did not save the image in his computer nor did he delete those images from his mail account. He continued to ask for more images from the sender of that mail.

Both Smith and Jayson argued that browsing internet and viewing pictures does not amount to making of a photograph or pseudo-photograph under

1. (2000) 2 All ER 418.

2. (2002) EWCA Crim Law 683.

section 1(1)(a) of Protection of Children Act, 1978. But the prosecution argued that searching the internet and selecting images to view on screen and automatic storage in the temporary cache of the images amounted to 'making.' The Court applied mischief rule of interpretation and held that the mischief that the new Act intended to remedy was to regulate the reproduction of indecent material found on the internet. Hence, the Act of voluntary downloading an indecent image from the internet to the computer screen and opening an e-mail attachment containing an indecent material is sufficient to amount to 'making'. However, there should be adequate *mens rea*. The activity of the person involved must have been done with the knowledge that the image was or was likely to be an indecent photograph or pseudo-photograph of a child. In Jayson's situation, the act was a deliberate act because while browsing he has the opportunity to select photographs and in Smith's situation, the further communication between him and sender of the mail constitutes adequate mens rea.

In 2008, the Protection of Children Act, 1978 was further extended to include tracings and other works derived from photographs or pseudo-photographs by an amendment brought to it by Criminal Justice and Immigration Act, 2008.[1] The Coroners and Justice Act, 2009 made all sexual images showing minor (all children below 18 years) including non photographic images of child abuse. It prohibits possession of a prohibited image[2] of child which includes a pornographic image that must reasonably be assumed to have been produced for the purpose of sexual arousal[3] and is grossly offensive, disgusting or otherwise of an obscene character or an image that focuses solely or principally on a child's genitals or anal region[4] portraying the performance by a person of an act of intercourse or oral sex with or in the presence of a child or an act of masturbation by, of, involving or in the presence of a child or acts which involve penetration of vagina or anus of child with a part of a person's body or anything else or the performance of an act by a child of an act of intercourse or oral sex with an animal (whether dead or alive or imaginary) or the performance by a person of an act of intercourse or oral sex with an animal whether dead or alive or imaginary in the presence of a child.[5]

This Act also prohibits an image which is found in the possession of a person that forms part of a series of images but the question whether such an image is prohibited or not, has to be determined by reference to the image itself and if the series of images is such as to be capable of providing a context for the image, the context in which it occur in the series of images.[6]

The Court, in case of *R.* v. *Oliver, Hartrey and Baldwin*,[7] categorized indecent images of children into 5 categories. These 5 categories are:—

---

1. Section 69 of Criminal Justice and Immigration Act, 2008.
2. Section 62(1) of Coroners and Justice Act, 2009.
3. Section 62(3) of Coroners and Justice Act, 2009.
4. Section 62(6) of Coroners and Justice Act, 2009.
5. Section 62(7) a, b, c, d, e, f, of Coroners and Justice Act, 2009.
6. Section 62(4) of Coroners and Justice Act, 2009.
7. Times Law Report, 6 December 2002.

(i) Images depicting erotic posing with no sexual activity

(ii) Sexual activity between children, or solo masturbation by a child

(iii) Non-penetrative sexual activity between adult and children

(iv) Penetrative sexual activity between children and adults, and

(v) Sadism and bestiality

Lord Justice Rose opined that possession including downloading of artificially created pseudo-photographs and the making of such images is also an offence but it should generally be treated as being at lower level of seriousness than possession and making of images that involve real children. However, he also agreed that there may be situations when possession of pseudo-photographs becomes as serious as the possession of photograph of real children. He illustrated this situation with an example where the pseudo-photograph provided a 'particularly grotesque image' that is generally beyond the scope of a photograph. According to him, even if pseudo-photographs do not corrupt real children depicted in the photograph but these photographs are as likely as the real photographs to fall into the hands of, or to be shown to be vulnerable and may have equally corrupting effect.

Sentencing Guidelines in Cases of Pornograrphic Images Depicting Children

Certain guidelines were laid down in *R.* v. *Oliver,* case for determination of sentence in cases of pornographic images depicting children. These guidelines are very important and should be kept in mind by legislature including India while making laws relating to pornographic images.

"A custodial sentence of up to six months would generally be appropriate in a case where—

(a) The offender was in possession of a large amount of material at level (ii) or a small amount at level (iii); or

(b) The offender had shown, distributed, or exchanged indecent material at level (i) or (ii) on a limited scale, without financial gain.

A custodial sentence of between six and 12 months would generally be appropriate for—

(a) Showing or distributing a large number of images at level (ii) or (iii); or

(b) Possessing a small number of images at levels (iv) or (v).

In relation to more serious offences, a custodial sentence between twelve months and three years would generally be appropriate for—

(a) possessing a large quantity of material at levels (iv) or (v), even if there was no showing or distribution of it to others; or

(b) showing or distributing a large number of images at level (iii); or

(c) producing or trading in material at levels (i) to (iii).

Sentences longer than three years should be reserved for cases where—

(a) images at levels (iv) or (v) had been shown or distributed; or

(b) the offender was actively involved in the production of images at levels (iv) or (v), especially where that involvement included a breach of trust, and whether or not there was an element of commercial gain; or

(c) the offender had commissioned or encouraged the production of such images.

An offender whose conduct merited more than three years would merit a higher sentence if his conduct was within more than one of categories (a), (b) and (c) than one where conduct was within only one such category. Sentences approaching the ten-year maximum would be appropriate in very serious cases where the defendant had a previous conviction either for dealing in child pornography, or for abusing children sexually or with violence."[1]

These sentencing guidelines were amended by guidance from the sentencing advisory panel.[2] The sentencing guidelines of sentencing advisory panel are following:—

> "The Panel believes that sentencing for these offences should reflect the harm suffered by children who are abused and exploited by pornographers. Even an offender who has simply downloaded images from the Internet for his own use, without showing or distributing them to others, must bear some responsibility for the child abuse involved in making the images.

The Panel offers sentences a structured approach to assessing the seriousness of an individual offence and selecting the appropriate penalty. It proposes that the two primary factors determining the seriousness of an offence should be:

- the nature of the indecent material (from images of nudity or erotic posing to those depicting gross assault of children by adults, sadism or bestiality); and
- the extent of the offender's involvement with the material (from possession for the offender's personal use to the original production of images or widescale commercial distribution).

The Panel accepts that, in cases of showing or distributing indecent photographs, a prison sentence is normally the only option. Nevertheless, the Panel points out that community penalties requiring attendance at a sex offender treatment programme can be effective in preventing some offenders from committing further offences. Accordingly, the Panel advises that, when the offence is less serious, the offender's suitability for treatment should be assessed."[3]

Other Statutes

The indecent displays (Control) Act prohibits public display of material which is indecent which may cause offence or embarrassment to the public.[4] There are other Acts like Local Government (Miscellaneous Provisions) Act, 1982 that provides power to local authorities to regulate sex shops after taking into account the feelings of local people.[5] The Theatres Act, 1968 also prohibited direction of a

---

1. *R.* v. *Oliver*, Times Law Report, 6 December, 2002.
2. www.cps.gov.uk/legal/h_to_k/indecent-photograph-of-children/#RELEVANT_CASE-LAW
3. http://www.sentencing-guidelines.gov.uk/docs/press_15aug02.html
4. Section 1(1) of Indecent Displays (Control) Act, 1981.
5. Section 2 and section 3 of Local Government (Miscellaneous Provisions) Act, 1982.

play whose effect if taken as a whole is to deprave and corrupt the audience. However, if it can be shown that play is in the interest of drama, art, literature or learning, then direction of such play is permitted.

Section 2 of Theaters Act, 1968 defines an obscene play to mean if taken as a whole, its effect was such as to tend to deprave and corrupt persons who were likely, having regard to all circumstances, to attend it but the Act forbids from conviction for display of an obscene play if it is proved that the giving of performance in question was justified as being for the public good on the ground that it was in the interest of drama, opera, ballet or any other art, or of literature or learning.[1]

The Cinematograph (Amendment) Act, 1982 provides power to local administration to ban films or demand part of the film to be cut on the ground of offensiveness, the degradation of women or glorification of violence.[2] The Video Recording Act, 1984 also provides the appropriate authority, the power to censor video films if the content is found in violation of Obscene Publication Act by containing human sexual activity.[3] The Criminal Justice and Immigration Act, 2008 prohibits possession of images which depict extreme pornography commonly understood as violent pornography.[4] Extreme pornography includes acts which threaten a person's life, results, or is likely to result, in serious injury to a person's anus, breasts or genitals, involves sexual interference with a human corpse, or sex with an animal (dead or alive) and a reasonable person looking at the image would think that any such person or animal was real. Hence, this Act also bans the kind of pornography where no exploitation of workers may occur because the images in question are imaginary. Section 63(3) of this Act also defines pornographic images which means to include images of such nature that it must reasonably be assumed to have been produced solely or principally for the purpose of sexual arousal. It also requires the image to be grossly offensive, disgusting or otherwise of an obscene character.[5]

According to Human Revenue and Customs, United Kingdom the activities listed below are prohibited:—

Bestiality	sexual acts between humans and Animals.
Bondage	tying a person in an unnatural position for sexual gratification where the participant is unable to withdraw their consent (for example they are gagged).
Cruelty to animals	includes organized dog fighting, bear baiting, badger baiting, cock fighting. Also 'crush' material, which features humans stamping on vertebrates or

1. Sections 2(1) and 3(1) of Theatres Act, 1968.
2. The Cinematograph (Amendment) Act, 1982.
3. Section 4A of Video Recordings Act, 1984.
4. Section 63 of the Criminal Justice and Immigration Act, 2008.
5. Section 63(6)(b).

	standing on them with increased pressure until they are crushed.
Defecation	voiding excrement from the bowels.
Enemas	flushing the bowels with water, usually to drink the product or torture the victim.
Fisting (anal or vaginal)	inserting a fist in the anus or vagina for sexual gratification.
Insertion of an object	only where the insertion clearly inflicts pain.
Menstrual Blood	Sex between adults where the female is menstruating heavily and the blood is being smeared on the body or the used tampon is being sucked etc. This does not include post intercourse depictions where a small amount of blood can be seen on the participants.
Necrophilia	sexual intercourse with a corpse.
Sado-masochism	sadists achieve sexual pleasure through inflicting torture and humiliation upon another person masochists desire maltreatment as a means of sexual gratification.
Scatology	depictions indicating a general interest in excrement such as smearing or eating of excrement.
Urolagnia	the act of urination in the context of any of the following where a person is shown: urinating at the same time as they are engaged in a sexual act. The urination and sexual act must be seen at the same time. The sexual act includes those such as fellatio (oral sex) and masturbation which would not be obscene if shown without urination; smearing urine on themselves or another; urinating on another person; being urinated upon; drinking urine.
Violence (non-simulated)	scenes of actual violence or mutilation shown in an exploitative context where they are not part of a legitimate documentary. For example a compilation of newsreel footage concentrating solely on scenes of violence or mutilation. This would also cover scenes of actual sexual assault including rape.
Violence (simulated)	scenes of simulated sexual violence such as rape shown in an exploitative context where the activity is graphically depicted and clearly intended to

> appear non-consensual. This excludes scenes contained in serious dramatic films.[1]

The above mentioned activities more or less consolidate all the activities that are included within the purview of pornography. The above activities are not only limited to pornography but go beyond it and include all activities that can be considered to be obscene. There is no particular definition of materials that are indecent, filthy or pedophile. Hence the judges have to depend on dictionary definition of these words.

Dworkin (the modern supporter of pornography) agrees on the point that right to moral independence can be violated if the only ground for regulation is that the attitudes to sex found in pornography were demeaning, bestial, or otherwise unsuitable to human being of the best sort even if this were true or that others were disgusted and offended by them.[2] The activities mentioned in above table absolutely fall within the criteria provided by Dworkin for regulation.

Pornography under Common Law

A prosecution against pornographic material can be brought under the Common law of conspiracy to corrupt pubic morals.[3] The best part about prosecution of pornographic material under the common law is non-availability of defense of serious literary or artistic value in the common law.

In the case of *Shaw* v. *D.P.P.*[4] Shaw published a directory of prostitutes named *The Ladies Directory.* He was prosecuted under common law for corruption of public morals, under Obscene Publications Act, 1959 for publishing nude photographs in an obscene book and under Sexual Offences Act, 1956 for being a male living on the earning of a prostitute. The House of Lords upheld the conviction on the charge of conspiracy to corrupt public morals on the basis that when he published the directory, he was conspiring with the prostitutes. According to Lord Simonds, Courts have the power to enforce the supreme and fundamental purpose of the law to conserve not only safety and order but also the moral welfare of the state. The majority opinion of the Court upheld that the Courts have residual power superintend the offences which are prejudicial to public welfare. In this case the majority opinion was based upon the principle brought up by Lord Mansfield 200 years earlier, that the Courts are guardians of public morals and that they ought to restrain and punish whatever is *contra bonos mores et decorum*.[5]

After this case an anxiety occurred about the non-availability of statutory defense of public good that was available under section 4(1) of Obscene Publications Act.

---

1. Information obtained from www.hmrc.gov.uk
2. Ronald Dworkin, "Do we have a Right to Pornography" In a Matter of Principle, p. 354, 1986.
3. Attorney General's Commission on Pornography, Final Report 234 (1986) available at porn-report.com at 133.
4. (1962) AC 220.
5. www.cs.anu.edu.au/~james.popple.publications/articles/retroactive/6.html

In the case of *R.* v. *Khuller,*[1] the appellants were directors of a company that published a fortnight magazine *The International Times.* This magazine included advertisements inviting homosexuals to make contacts with others in order to engage in homosexual activities. The appellants were convicted on the grounds of corrupting public morals and conspiracy to outrage public decency. House of Lords dismissed their appeal on the first charge of corrupting public morals and said that even if *Shaw* v. *D.P.P.,* was wrongly decided the charge must stand until it is altered by parliament and it is not altered by the virtue of section 1(1) of the Sexual Offence Act. The Parliament if wanted to alter the common law of corrupting public moral, could have done so while passing this Act. Since the Parliament did not do so, then even if the offence which could have been committed by encouragement from advertises (homosexual act) is itself not illegal might amount to a conduct to deprave public morals under the common law of conspiracy to corrupt public morals.

However, the Court allowed the appeal on the second charge of conspiracy to outrage public decency as Lord Reid who gave a dissenting opinion in *Shaw* v. *D.P.P.,* was very critical about this offence. In the present case Lord Reid stated that such an offence was unknown to common law. However, the majority affirmed existence of such offence under common law but quashed conviction because the jury has been misdirected. Lord Reid also showed concern about the non-availability of public good defence in such offence and stated that to recognize this new crime would be against the whole trend of public policy followed by Parliament in recent times.

In *R* v. *Gibson,*[2] also the Court of Appeal recognized the offence of outraging public decency under Common law. In this case, Gibson was charged for outraging public decency by exhibiting at an art gallery a human earring made from a freeze-dried human foetus. The Court of Appeal followed Knuller where House of Lord affirmed that the offence of outraging public decency exists under common law and stated that the ingredients of such an offence are made out irrespective of whether or not the work also tends to corrupt and deprave those who see or hear it. There is no requirement under this offence to prove that corruption of minds of people has occurred.

The utilization of these common law offences by Courts has been criticized by jurists across the world for non-availability of public good defence and attack on the literary, political, scientific and social value of the material in question. However, the Courts have restricted themselves from upholding the conviction under these common law offences until and unless there is no specific statutory provision dealing with the situation in question.

---

1. (1973) 2 AC 435 (HL).
2. (1991) 1 All ER 439.

CHAPTER 5

ADJUDICATION OF PORNOGRAPHY IN INDIA

Similar to the laws prevailing in United States, United Kingdom and many other Countries there is no particular category of law in India that deals specifically with pornography. Pornography is governed by laws dealing with obscenity in India. It is considered to be more aggravated form of obscenity. This chapter analyses the law of obscenity in India covered under various enactments and regulations.

Legislations which prohibit Pornography:—The publication, sale or transfer of obscene or pornographic material is prohibited and punishable under various Acts.

Indian Penal Code:—Under sub-section (1) of section 292 of I.P.C, book, pamphlet, paper, writing, drawing, painting, representation, figure or any other object shall be deemed to obscene, if it is lascivious or appeals to the prurient interest or if its effects are such as to tend to deprave and corrupt persons who are likely, having regard to all relevant circumstances, to read, see or hear the matter contained or embodied in it. The application of this section does not extend to any book, pamphlet, paper writing, drawing, painting, representation or figure the publication of which can be proved to be justified on the ground of public good that is in the interest of science, literature, art or learning or other objects of general concern. The object which is kept or used *bona fide* for religious purpose and any representation sculptured, engraved, painted or otherwise represented on or in any ancient monument within the meaning of Ancient Monument and archeological sites and remains Act or any temple or car used for conveyance of idol or kept or use for religious purposes are also outside the purview of this provision.

Section 292 and section 293 of the Indian Penal Code were incorporated in the Indian Penal Code to give effect to International Convention for the Suppression of the Circulation of and Traffic in Obscene Publication signed at Geneva in 1923.[1] The definition of obscenity in section 292 is borrowed from the tests laid down in *R.* v. *Hicklin* and *Roth* v. *United States*. The first phrase if it is lascivious or appeals to prurient interest in borrowed from *Roth* v. *United States,* after 1969 amendment and the phrase 'such as to deprave and corrupt' has been borrowed form *R.* v. *Hicklin Test*.

Section 292(2)(c) specifically deals with people involved in pornography industry where obscene objects are produced. This sub-section prohibits taking part in a or receiving profit from any business in the course of which he knows or has reason to believe that any obscene objects are for any of the purpose

1. R.P. Kathuriya, Law of Crimes and Criminology, pp. 1804.

mentioned in above sub-sections, made, produced, purchased, kept, imported, exported, conveyed, publicly exhibited or in any manner put into circulation. Sub-section 2(d) makes it an offense to advertise or making known that such obscene objects may be procured from any person who is willing to engage in such act. This sub-section is very wide and covers middleman that procure girls through human trafficking who are used for the purpose of production of pornography. This subsection does not restrict itself to prosecuting these middlemen but it also attempts to punish those who advertise the sources from where the obscene material may be procured.

For example if Ramesh brings some girls from Chattishgarh for the purpose of making a pornographic video of those girls. He then makes a porn video of those girls. Suresh goes to the Market and tells Mahesh, Lovelesh, and Jignesh that a porn video of Chattisharh Girls is available by the name of Chattisgarh Dhamaka and the video may be procured from Ramesh for 200 Rupees. In this case, Ramesh and Suresh both can be prosecuted within this sub-section.

It is clear from an overview of section 292 that this section does not prohibit production of pornographic material for own use. For example, if a person produces pornographic images of his wife then it is not an offence within section 292 but if he produces such pornographic images for the purpose of sale or distributes, lets to hire, or publicly exhibits such images then he will be guilty of an offence within section 292. However, it is for the prosecution to prove that he prepared such video with the intent to sell.

Pornography and Obscenity

The word obscene was explained by Madras High Court in *Public Prosecutor* v. *Sabapathy,*[1] to mean anything offensive to chastity or modesty, expressing or presenting to the mind or view something that delicacy, purity and decency forbid to be expressed, impure as obscene language, obscene pictures, anything expressing or suggesting unchaste and lustful ideas, impure, indecent and lewd. Pornography was also defined by Supreme Court of India in 1965 to mean libidinous writing or anything of high erotic effect.[2] However, Allahabad High Court gave a very clear overview of pornography in *State* v. *Kunjilal,*[3] where it distinguished between obscenity and pornography as such. It said Pornography denotes writing, pictures etc. intended to arouse sexual desire. The Court no doubt accepted that both offend against public decency and morals but pornography is obscene in more aggravated form. The Court expressed in very clear terms that regarding pornography there can be no doubt that they would be obscene within the meaning of section 292. Hence, it is clear that all the pornographic material is prohibited by section 292 under Indian law.

Pornography is a crime because the definition of crime according to *Halsbury Laws of England* is "A crime is an unlawful act or default which is an offence against the public and renders the person guilty of the act or default liable to legal

---

1. AIR 1958 Mad 210.
2. *Ranajit Udeshi* v. *State of Maharashtra,* AIR 1965 SC 881.
3. AIR 1970 All 64.

punishment. While a crime is often also an injury to a private person, who has a remedy in a civil action, it is an act or default contrary to the order, peace and well-being of society that a crime is punishable by the state."[1] Pornography is an offence against public because it causes both moral and physical harm to the members of society and thus harmful for the well-being of society. This is also punishable under the various laws. Thus pornography is a crime not a right.

Objective Assessment Test

The test of objective assessment of the matter in question was introduced in *Samaresh Bose* v. *Amal Mitra*[2] case to remove subjectivity in the determination of obscenity of the matter that is imperative due to difference in perspective of different judges. Objective Assessment was defined in the case itself and means that the judge in the first place should try to place himself in the position of the author and from his point of view should try to understand what the author seeks to convey and whether the work has any literary or artistic value. The judge then would place himself in the position of a reader of every age group in whose hands the book is likely to fall and should try to appreciate what kind of possible effects the book is likely to have in the minds of readers. The standard of a reader is neither one of exceptional sensibility nor of one without any sensibility whatsoever.[3] The Court must bear in mind that average public does not consist of archbishops on the one hand and libertines on the other and neither a man of wide culture or rare character nor a person with depraved mentality should be thought of as being the reader of the obscene publication and also the effects of the publications must be ascertained on the ordinary member of society.[4] Based on the findings of above activities, the judge should decide whether the material is obscene or not.

Obscenity* v. *Art

Works of art are not usually considered as prohibited under section 292 but where obscenity and art are mixed together then the effect of art must be so preponderating as to throw obscenity into a shadow or the obscenity is so trivial or insignificant that it can have no effect and may be overlooked.[5] While determining as to whether the material falls within section 292 of Indian Penal Code, the judges have to see whether the material treats sex in a offensive manner to public decency and morality and likely to pander to lascivious, prurient or sexually precocious. The standards applicable must be national. Hence, obscenity may be justified and permitted in society if applying national standards; the material is not offensive to public decency or morality. Even if it is offensive to public decency or morality, if the effect of art is sufficient to obliterate the effect of pornography, then also it may be permitted in society.

---

1. B.M. Gandhi, Indian Penal Code, p. 7.
2. AIR 1986 SC 967.
3. *C.T. Prim* v. *State,* AIR 1961 Cal 177.
4. *Sreeram Saksena* v. *Emperor,* AIR 1940 Cal 290.
5. *Ranajit D. Udeshi* v. *State of Maharashtra,* AIR 1965 SC 881.

Section 293

Indian Penal Code treats sale of obscene material to young person differently and has a different provision for such offense. Section 293 of Indian Penal Code prohibits any person from selling, letting to hire, distributing, exhibiting, or circulating to any person under the age of twenty years any obscene object as is referred to in section 292 or offering or attempts to do so.

109th Law Commission Report recommended insertion of section 293A in Indian Penal Code for specifically concentrating on indecent display of obscene material along with the lines of Indecent Displays (Control) Act. It recommended that section 292 and section 293 shall also apply to any person who publicly displays an indecent matter that is offensive to reasonable persons from the point of view of decency.[1] However, these recommendations have not been accepted yet.

Mens Rea

Unless statutory provisions either clearly or by necessary implication rule out *mens rea* as to constitute part of the crime, nobody can be found guilty of an offence unless he is proved to have a guilty mind. So in absence of any proof that the owner, publisher, manager of a newspaper knew and ordered the publication they cannot be held guilty of the offence under section 292.[2]

The offense of obscenity as it was dealt with in *R.* v. *Hicklin* case is one of strict liability. In this case Justice Cockburn observed that if the material in question is *prima facie* obscene then it is immaterial whether the person committing such offense had any knowledge to commit it or not. It is noticeable that the *explanation* of obscenity in section 292 is borrowed from Hicklin test. So, it can reasonably be suspected that section 292 of Indian Penal Code embraces strict liability and does not require *mens rea*. The same position was upheld in the *Kailash Chandra Acharjee's* case[3] where the Court accepted that when material *per se* is obscene there is no requirement of any proof as to whether the publisher intended to corrupt the mind of person or not.

In a Malaysian Case, *Muhamed Ibrahim* v. *Public Prosecutor,*[4] that was decided in 1993, the Court held that to attract section 292 of the Malaysian Penal Code, which is *pari materia* to section 292 of Indian Penal Code, mere possession of obscene book for the purpose of sale is sufficient because the object of this provision is protection of members of society from books which have corrupting influence and *mens rea* and intention are not required as an ingredients of the offence. In this case Muhamed Ibrahim had copies of 'Book Tropic of Cancer' in his possession which was found under the counter of his shop by police officers. Muhamed Ibrahim could not read English Language. He was charged for possession of 65 copies of obscene books under section 292 of Malaysian Penal Code. He was convicted by lower Court and on appeal he contended that he has no knowledge of the nature of contents of the book. The Appellate Court dismissed

1. 109th Law Commission Report on Obscene and Indecent Advertisement and Displays, section 292-293 of Indian Penal Code, 12 (1985).
2. *O.P. Lamba* v. *Tarun Mehta,* 1988 Cr LJ 610 (P&H).
3. (1932) 33 Cr LJ 771.
4. (1993) 29 MLJ 289.

the appeal by applying Hicklin Test laid down in *R.* v. *Hicklin*, Case because according to this test it is sufficient that the tendency of the matter charged as obscene is to deprave and corrupt the minds that are open to such immoral influences and into whose hands the publication of this sort may fall.

However, a different view was earlier taken by Calcutta High Court. The High Court opined that word 'possession' referred to in section 292 means conscious possession and in that sense *mens rea* or guilty mind has not been dispensed with under the provision.[1] From 'conscious possession of the material' the Court meant possession with the knowledge that the material in question is obscene in nature. The Court illustrated this principle with example of a blind person who might be used to sell obscene books if the requirement of conscious position is excluded from the purview of section 292. Hence, all the surrounding circumstances had to be taken into account to determine the requisite *mens rea*. Even in a case where accused is a mere spectator of a blue film and does not have any role in public exhibition of the blue film, he cannot be held guilty of offense of obscenity.[2]

Let us consider the view of Supreme Court with regard to requirement of *mens rea* in the offence of obscenity. In case of *Ranjit D. Udeshi* v. *State of Maharashtra*,[3] the Supreme Court stated that first sub-section of section 292 does not make it necessary for knowledge to be there on part of the offender as in every case if knowledge of the same were to be prove, that would shift the balance in favour of accused. Hence the liability here is strict liability. Justice Hidayatullah, in Ranajit Udeshi case rejecting the necessity of proving *mens rea* in section 292 stated that section 292 does not make knowledge of obscenity an ingredient of the offense because first sub-section of section 292 unlike some other sections that start with words 'whoever knowingly, or negligently etc.' The difficulty of acquiring legal evidence of the offender's knowledge of the obscenity of the book has made the offense a strict liability one. However, absence of such knowledge may be taken in mitigation.

After analyzing the above positions of law it can be said that the prosecution need not prove whether the accused knew that the material is obscene or not. The mere fact that the material is obscene is sufficient to make him guilty of the offense however, it is necessary to prove that the accused had intention to sell, let to hire or publicly exhibit the matter in question.

Indecent v. *Obscene*

Generally all open lewdness, grossly scandalous and whatever openly outrages decency or is offensive and disgusting, or is injurious to public morals by tending to corrupt the mind and destroy the love of decency, morality and good order, is a misdemeanour indictable at common law.[4] However, Lord sands in *M'Gowan* v. *Lanmuir*,[5] observed that indecent and obscene are different. He

1. *C.T. Prim* v. *State*, AIR 1961 Cal 177.
2. *Dr. B. Rosaiah* v. *State of Andhra Pradesh*, 1991 Cr LJ 189.
3. AIR 1965 SC 881.
4. Dr. Harisingh Gaur, Penal Law of India, p. 2268, 2006.
5. 1931 SC (J) 10.

illustrated the difference as for a male bather to enter the water nude in the present of the ladies would be indecent, but it would not necessarily be obscene but if he directed the attention of a lady to a certain, art of his body his conduct would certainly be obscene. Hence there exist a difference between indecency and obscenity. Obscenity is prohibited under section 292 of Indian Penal Code but indecency is not. It is prohibited in the state of Tamil Nadu under section 292A in the form of indecent blackmailing.

As a whole

According to the earlier view of Indian Courts it is not necessary that the whole book must contain the prohibited material. The whole book may infringe section 292 even if it contains only one single passage that is obscene.[1] Even if the matter published is written by eminent writer or is composed in a style not easily understood by all[2] or the book is a medical one sold only to registered subscribers,[3] it can not mitigate the effect of infringement on section 292 of Indian Penal Code. This view reflects the fact that section 292 was adopted from *Hicklin's* case that permitted the books to be judged obscene on the basis of isolated pages. That is why courts followed Hicklin case for a long time.

However, after the independence with the impact of *Roth* v. *United States*, this prolong view of Courts was alterated. In the Case of *Ranajit Udesh* it was clearly mentioned that the offending book must be judged in its entirety. The dominant theme of the material has to taken into account and not the isolated pages of the book while determining the obscene nature of the book. However, the obscene matter must also be considered by itself and separately in order to find out "whether it was so gross and its obscenity so decided that it was likely to corrupt those whose minds are open to such immoral influence and into whose hands the book was likely to fall." This view of Supreme Court led to an amendment in 1969 in Indian Penal Code.

Japan and South Korea

In Japan, article 175 of the Japanese Constitution prevents pornography. The courts in Japan have been refrained from formulating an objective test for deciding that whether a particular material is obscene or pornographic or not. They have adopted very pragmatic approach in considering the fact that is a material pornographic or mere piece of artistic and literary work. The Korean Supreme Court has adopted the test of seeing the material in dispute as a whole and not in isolation. In *'Happy Sara'* case where a novel bearing the title of Revolting Slave containing two page descriptions of his sexual activities was under dispute, Korean Supreme Court refused to look the two pages in isolation and after analyzing the novel as a whole, refused to acknowledge the novel as pornography.[4] Hence the international approach prevalent in United States,

1. *Empress of India* v. *Indarman*, (1881) ILR 3 All 837.
2. *Public Prosecutor* v. *Markandeyulu*, AIR 1918 Mad 1195.
3. *Thakar Datt*, AIR 1917 Lah 288.
4. Pallabi Ghosal, Freedom of Art under siege in India available at, http://www.legalserviceindia.com/articles/re_ind.htm, accessed on 2nd November, 2001.

United Kingdom, Japan, Korea is to treat the effect of work in question as a whole and not in isolation.

However, after amendment of section 292 of Indian Penal Code in 1969, it is made very clear that where the work comprises of more than one item, if taken as a whole is capable of corrupting the minds of people. Cases that came up after the amendment like *Chandrakant Kakodar* case and *Samaresh Bose* case also accepted the requirement of judging the work in its entirety and not in separation.

Into whose Hands such Material is Likely to Fall

The Hicklin Test allows a material to be judged obscene even if it depraves and corrupts a particular class including unusually susceptible persons. If this view is considered to be proper then the books on sex education will also be considered obscene because these books may corrupt certain members of society. Hence, the effect of the material must be considered upon general public and average member of society, not upon unusually susceptible members of society.

In case of *Sukanta Halder* v. *State of West Bengal,*[1] also Calcutta High Court refused to follow the test of judging effect of obscene material on unusually susceptible person or particular class of society. It accepted 'average and ordinary person' test. According to the opinion of High Court the effect of the material must be judged on ordinary member of society for whom the material is meant for. He is not a man of 'wide culture' or 'rare character' or a person of depraved mentality.

The High Court of Bombay in case of *Ranjit D. Udeshi* pointed out that the person to be affected by the material in question must be an ordinary man *i.e.*, a man in street and none other than him. The Court ruled out the test of unusually susceptible person by holding that the person must not be a person of 'exceptional susceptibility.'

The Supreme Court of India, in the *Chandrakant Kakodar's* case observed that if the effect of books, articles and magazines on young and adolescents only is taken into account then the adults of the society will be deprived of the content they truly deserve. That is why the Court very categorically stated that it was only 'class of persons' and not the 'isolated cases' of the 'young and adolescents' which should be taken into account while determining the debasing and debauching 'effect of any work.'

As Hidayatullah, C.J. also remarked in *K.A. Abbas* v. *Union of India,*[2] that *"the test for judging a work should be that of an ordinary man of common sense and prudence and not an 'out of the ordinary or hypersensitive man.' If the depraved begins to see in these things more than what an average person would, in much the same way, as it is wrongly said, a Frenchman sees a woman's legs in everything, it cannot be helped."*

Finally an end has been put to this debate by the decision of Supreme Court in *Samaresh Bose* case where the Supreme Court after making reference to *Ranjit Udeshi* case and *Chandrakant Kakodar* case stated that it is not right to insist that an author must write in such a manner that the adolescents could not have come

1. AIR 1952 Cal 214.
2. (1970) 2 SCC 780.

into contact with sex. It is for the 'mature and adolescents' to judge the nature of material in question to the exclusion of adolescents.[1]

Hence, the position in India is now clear that the effect must be judged on 'average persons' of society. But even now the position is not clear as to what are those average person and how to judge whether the 'average person' of society would treat a work as obscene or not. Opinion of experts of literature may help the court in determination of obscene nature of material. Let's see whether courts also accept the opinion of experts as an aid in determination of obscenity or not.

Opinion of Literary/Artistic Experts

A judge has two options where he has to decide the obscene nature of the book. The first option is that he can read the whole book and based upon arguments advanced before him he may decide the question of obscenity and the second option is that he can take the help of expert opinion. However, Indian judiciary does not seem to be favourable to ease out the task of judges by allowing them to rely upon expert testimony in all cases.

In the case of *Ranjit Udeshi* this Court held that the delicate task of deciding what is artistic and what is obscene has to be performed by courts therefore, the evidence of men of literature or others on the question of obscenity is not relevant. In *Chandrakant Kakodar* case also the same principle was applied and expert testimony was not allowed. In both cases, the Supreme Court refused the admissibility of oral evidence in determination of obscene nature of work in question. However, in later case the Supreme Court provided an exception to the general principle of inadmissibility of expert opinion to cases where the Court is not conversant with the language of the work. However, even in such cases expert evidence are only admissible to determine whether the work in question has any literary or artistic merit. The question of obscenity can only be determined by Courts and expert testimony can not play any role in determination of obscene nature of the work.

In *Samresh Bose* v. *Amal Mitra*,[2] this Court observed that "In appropriate cases, the court, for eliminating any subjective element or personal preference which may remain hidden in the subconscious mind and may unconsciously affect a proper objective assessment, may draw upon the evidence on record and also consider the views expressed by reputed or recognized authors of literature on such questions as if thereby any of his own consideration and satisfaction to enable the court to discharge the duty of making a proper assessment." However, in this case also the Supreme Court did not hold that the Judges may rely upon expert testimony to hold a book obscene. It only stated that help of expert testimony can be taken for elimination of any doubt but it is only for the Courts to decide whether the work is obscene or not.

---

1. Inder S. Rana, Law of Obscenity in U.K. USA and India, p. 151
2. AIR 1986 SC 967.

Other Enactments

Criminal Procedure Code, 1973

Section 95 of Criminal Procedure Code prescribes the procedure by which any newspaper or book or any document containing any pornographic material can be forfeited. The provisions of this Act are discussed later in detail.

The Young Person Harmful Publication Act, 1956

Section 2 of the Act defines the meaning of Harmful Publication which is more or less similar to the definition of obscenity given in *R.* v. *Hicklin*. This Act prohibits 'publication of any book, magazine, pamphlet, leaflet, newspaper or other like publications which consist of the stories told with the aid of pictures or without the aid of pictures or wholly in picture being stories portraying wholly or mainly the commission of an offence or acts of violence or cruelty, or incidents of repulsive or horrible nature in such a way that publication of such material as a whole would tend to corrupt a young person into whose hands it might fall whether by inciting or encouraging him to commit an offence or acts of violence or cruelty or in any other manner whatsoever.'[1] Section 3 of the same Act punishes the offender with six months of prison or fine or both.

This Act covers pornography that depicts sexual violence against women and children portraying rape, sexual assault and like crimes. Comics, Cartoons and other story books in which a story is portrayed with the help of pictures are also dealt with by this Act. This Act also has a very specific feature of making it an offense of advertising any material which is prohibited by this Act. Section 3(c) of the Act that deals with penalties under this Act, makes the act of, 'advertising or making known by any means that any harmful publication may be procured from or through any person, an offense'. Production of prohibited material under this Act is also made an offense only if such production is done with the intent of selling the prohibited material.

This Act also provides the procedure of forfeiture of material falling within section 2(a) of the Act. Such power is conferred upon Government and similar to the power of forfeiture provided under section 95 of the Criminal Procedure Act. However, there is a difference between both the provisions. Section 95 of Criminal Procedure Code does not require consultation with law officer (Advocate General) of the state. However, section 4 of this Act makes it mandatory to consult with law officer of the state. Only after consultation with the law officer of the state, the Government can declare every copy of the material to be forfeited but only after declaring the grounds of forfeiture. After such an order is made in the official gazette of the state, any police officer may forfeit the material which is found anywhere in the territories to which the Act extends.[2] This Act also confers the power of destruction of any harmful material which is prohibited by the purview of this Act upon Courts. However, such an order can only be made after the accused has been convicted under this Act. After such conviction, any copy of the book or such material either in the possession of Courts or in possession of the

1. Section 2(a) of the Act.
2. Section 4(2) of the Act.

accused or in possession of any other person may be ordered to be destroyed by Courts.[1] Similar procedure of applying to High Court for removal of forfeiture has been provided in this Act as provided in Criminal Procedure Code and any offence committed under this Act is a cognizable offense.[2] Hence, this Act is an exhaustive provision to deal with circulation of sexually offensive pornography in India.

This Act has been adopted from English Act of Children and Young Person Harmful Publications Act, 1955. Most of the provisions of this Act are similar to the provisions of Indian Act. However, section 2 of the Children and Young Person Harmful Publications Act, 1955 provides a statutory defense to any person who 'prints, publishes, sells, and lets to hire, any work or has in possession for the purpose of sale or letting to hire any work which is prohibited under this Act.'[3] Such Persons may claim that he has not examined the content of the work and has no reasonable cause to suspect that it was one to which the Act applies.[3] However, such a defense is totally absent in Indian Law. Indian Law seeks to impose strict liability upon any person who is engaged in activities that are harmful for young person and may incite violence including sexual violence in society.

The English Act protects child and young persons both whereas Indian Act only covers Young persons. The definition of Child and Young Person in the English Act provides a child to mean any person who has not completed age of 18 years and a Young Person to mean any person who has completed age of 14 years but has not completed the age of 18 years.[4] Hence, this Act attempts to protect any person who is under the age of 18 years. However, Indian Law defines a Young Persons to mean a person who has not completed the age of 20 years.[5] Hence, Indian Law attempts to protect all persons who are under the age of 20 years. English Law also punishes import of material prohibited within the purview of this Act but Indian Law does not have any such provision within the Act. English Law is not only limited to prohibition of books, magazines and other like material but it also prohibits importation of photographic plates including block, mould matrix and stencil.[6]

The Customs Act, 1962

Section 11 of the Act provides that Central Government is empowered to put restriction on the import or export of goods to maintain decency and morality. Under this Act Maximum Punishment of 2 years can be given. Section 11(2) of the Act provides various grounds on which the Government can prohibit importation of goods in India. Ground (b) mentioned in section 11(2) of the Act provides the ground of maintenance of public order and standards of decency and morality. Hence, if Central Government is satisfied that importation of any material may

1. Section 3(2) of the Act.
2. Section 5 and 7 of the Act.
3. Section 2 of Children and Young Person Harmful Publications Act, 1955.
4. Section 5(2) of Children and Young Persons Harmful Publications Act, 1955 read with Section 107(1) of Children and Young Persons Act, 1933.
5. Section 2(c) of Young Persons Harmful Publications Act, 1956.
6. Section 4(b) read with section 5(2) of Children and Young Persons Harmful Publications Act, 1955.

affect the standard of decency and morality in India, then it may prohibit importation of such material either absolutely or subject to some conditions.

Post Office Act, 1898

Section 20 of the Act says that 'no person by post shall send any indecent or obscene painting, photograph, lithograph, card, book or any other indecent or obscene material.' The first part of the section covers the material which is posted inside the envelope or the packet and the second part of the section covers any words, marks, design of an indecent, obscene, seditious, scurrilous, threatening or grossly offensive characters that are present on the envelope or the packet in which the material is contained. However, the application of such provisions suffers from impracticality as post office cannot check what is contained inside every envelope or pack posted by it. It's only when any person brings into notice of a post officer that such a content is present inside the envelope or if the prohibited content is available on the cover of material being posted, the provisions of this Act can be taken recourse to. Section 23(2) empowers the officer-in-charge of post office or any person authorized on the behalf of Post Master General to 'open or unfasten any newspaper or any book, pattern or sample packet in course of transmission by post' only if he suspects that such material contains any material that is prohibited within the Act. The phrase 'officers of post office' is defined within the Act itself. According to section 2(e) of the Act 'officer of the post office' includes any person employed in business of the post office or on behalf of the post office.

In case of *Nathu Ram* v. *Secy. of State,*[1] Addison J. defined the word 'indecent' for the purpose of this Act. He took the help of new English oxford dictionary and defined indecent to mean unbecoming, highly unsuitable or inappropriate, contrary to the fitness of things, uncomely, inelegant in form and suggesting or tending to be immodest and offends against the recognized standards of delicacy and is suggestive or tends to obscenity. However, the judge did not define the term 'obscenity'. In absence of a clear definition of obscenity the judgment is not much of a significant value.

Indecent Representation of Women's Act, 1986

This Act was enacted with the aim of prohibiting indecent representation of women through the means of advertising or in 'publication, writings, paintings, figures, or in any other manner and for matters connected therewith or incidental thereto.'[2] This Act is drafted to deal with problems of indecent representation of women. This Act covers all sorts of pornographic images, drawings, paintings and figures where women are depicted in indecent manner. Section 2 of the Act defines indecent representation to mean 'depiction in any manner the figure of a woman, her form or body or any part thereof in such way as to have the effect of being indecent, or derogatory to, or denigrating women, or is likely to deprave, corrupt or injure the public morality or morals.' This provision does not define words such as 'indecent,' 'deprave' and 'public morality' and leaves it upon the judiciary to decide the meaning of these words. The word 'advertising' is defined by the Act

1. AIR 1930 Lah 552.
2. The Indecent Representation of Women (Prohibition) Act, 1986.

to include 'any notice, circular, label, wrapper, or other document and also includes any visible representation made by means of any light, sound, smoke and gas.'[1] Section 3 of this Act prohibits publication, exhibition or advertisement of indecent representation of women. Section 4 of the Act makes it an offense to 'produce or cause to be produced, sell, let to hire, distribute, circulate or send by post any book, pamphlet, paper, slide, film, writing, drawing, painting, photograph, representation or figure which contains indecent representation of women in any form.' Hence, by the application of this act, production, publication, exhibition and advertisement of indecent representation of a women is prohibited.

This Act also provides for public good defense to the offender. Section 4 exonerates the offender if the indecent representation of a woman can be proved to be justified on the ground that such indecent representation is in the interest of science, literature, art or learning or other objects of general concern or kept or used bona fide for religious purposes. Any such representation sculptured, painted or engraved upon an ancient monument, any temple and car used for conveyance of idol and the film to which provisions of part II of Cinematograph Acts are applicable, are also exonerated from prosecution.[2] Hence, indecent representation of body parts of women in medical books, Khajuraho paintings, indecent representation of a dacoit by depicting her completely nude in a movie that attempts to revolt against the exploitation of women or indecent representation of Bharat Mata by a famous painter in the name of Art are exonerated from prosecution within this Act. Any person contravening the provisions of this Act shall be punishable with maximum of two years of imprisonment or two thousand rupees, however, in case of subsequent conviction he may be punished with imprisonment up to 5 years and fine up to one lakh rupees.[3]

This section gives rise to many problems because in India, judges have the sole discretion to decide that a book or material is obscene or not. There is no definition of indecency itself in the Act then how a publisher does or author is expected to decide what is indecent and what is not. A publisher of the book cannot know that the publication is artistic or lascivious in the eyes of law. Its only when a prosecution has been started against him, he will get to know that the material is an indecent representation of women.

Information Technology Act, 2000

Section 67 of the Act says that "whoever publishes or transmits or causes to be published or transmitted in the electronic form, any material which is lascivious or appeals to the prurient interest or if its effect is such as to tend to deprave and corrupt persons who are likely, having regard to all relevant circumstances, to read, see or hear the matter contained or embodied in it, shall be punished on first conviction with imprisonment of either description for a term which may extend to five years and with fine which may extend to one lakh rupees and in the event of a second or subsequent conviction with imprisonment of either description for a term which may extend to ten years and also with fine which may extend to two

1. Section 2 of the Act.
2. Section 4 of the Act.
3. Section 6 of the Act.

lakh rupees." This explanation of word 'obscenity' of is also similar to the definition of obscenity by J. Cockburn in *R.* v. *Hicklin* case. The provisions of this Act are discussed later in detail.

Drugs and Magic Remedies Act

Section 3 of the Act prohibits any person from taking part into publication of any advertisement referring to any drug in terms that suggest or is calculated to lead the use of the drug for the maintenance or improvement of the capacity of human being for sexual pleasure.[1] Hence, this Act prohibits publication of indecent display of material that refers to sexual activities and has the capacity of offending people and capable of depraving and corrupting the minds of people who are likely to see, read and hear the matter in question.

Press Council Act, 1978

Section 13, 2(c), 14(1) and 14(2) empowers the press council to impose restrictions upon news agency, newspaper, journalist, editors who violate the norms of press council or the norms of decency of society.

Dramatic Performance Act, 1876

Section 3(c) of the Act prohibits any dramatic performance, a play, pantomime etc. in public place that is likely to deprave and corrupt the mind of persons present at the performance. Section 12 of the Act exempts any Jatras or performance of the same kind at a religious festival from the purview of this Act.

The provisions of this Act came into consideration in case of *State* v. *Baboo Lal*.[2] In this case Allahabad High Court stated that the play must be likely to deprave and corrupt the people to offend the clauses (a), (b) and (c) of the Act. It also stated that section 3(b) of the Act has become a nullity after the enactment of Constitution because Indian Constitution provides that restrictions can only be imposed if they are reasonable, however no such qualification for restrictions is mentioned within this Act. However, it is submitted that the fact that these plays are prohibited on the ground of depraving and corrupting the minds of people, which is a reasonable restriction imposed upon freedom of expression of screening the play, hence the provisions of this act do not infringe article 19(2) of the Constitution.

Bar of Prosecution

Where the Censor Board certifies a film as being fit to be exhibited, it will be a relevant fact in ascertaining whether or not the film is obscene. Such certificate is not conclusive and it will not debar from trying the case under this section. A certificate granted under section 6 of Cinematography Act does not provide an irrefutable defense to the accused who have been granted such certificate but it has to be taken into consideration by Court in trial for the offence under sections 292 and 293 of Indian Penal Code.

This preposition was laid down in the case of *Raj Kapoor* v. *State (Delhi Administration)*[3] where public prosecution was initiated on a private complaint against theater owner, producer, actor, photographer of 'Satyam Shivam

1. Section 3(b) of Drugs and Magic Remedies Act, 1954.
2. AIR 1956 All 571: ILR (1957) 1 All 399: 1956 Cr LJ 1143.
3. (1980) 1 SCC 43: AIR 1980 SC 258: 1980 Cr LJ 202.

Sundaram' for promoting punitive prurience, moral depravity and shocking erosion of public decency. The Court observed that though such certificate is not a piece of utter inconsequence but it is not infallible in its verdict. Even of issuance of such certificate, the Courts have the power to examine the film and judge whether its public display breaches public morals or depraves basic decency as to offend section 292.

The certificate given by Censor Board is very important because the presence of such certificate shows that such movie is not pornographic. A movie which is pornographic usually bears a Red XXX mark on it and no censor board certificate is shown before the beginning of the movie. The presence of such certificate ensures that the movie has been viewed by honourable members of Sensor Board and at least in their opinion the movie does not have any pornographic content. After considering the opinion of member of Censor Board the judge may himself view the content of the movie and form his opinion on the movie and the presence of censor certificate may add in the determination of pornographic nature of the content.

Making and Producing

Expression "make or produce" occurring in section 292 does not exclude printing from its ambit.[1] To make means 'create or manufacture'.[2] Printing is created with the use of machines and it is a man-made product. Hence, printing pornographic content is surely covered within the purview of section 292. However such making and production of obscene material must be proved to be done for the purpose of sale. Mere viewing of pornographic content does not amount to making and hence not punishable under this section.

Watching a Pornography Film at Home

The Law accepts that obscene content has the tendency to deprave and corrupt the mind of accused but it does not punish a person who watches the content in a private room. In the opinion of Rajasthan High Court that mere viewing obscene film at home on T.V. with VCR does not amount to an offence under section 292 because an offence under section 292 can only be made out when an obscene article is kept for sale, distribution, circulation and public exhibition.[3] It is only when the person viewing the content goes out of the door and calls his friends for public exhibition of the prohibited material; the offence under section 292 is committed.

The word 'exhibit' in section 4 of the Cinematograph Act, 1952 does not cover private exhibition of film. This section only deals with public exhibition of the film. Public exhibition means exhibiting a video to a group of persons. A private household if prepares a video film for itself or exhibiting a duly certified video of video film of *bona fide* members of family without having any kind of intention of public exhibition is not covered within section 4 of Cinematograph Act. Similarly a club preparing a public video itself for its *bona fide* members without intending

---

1. *Ravi. v. S.I. of Police*, 1989 Cr LJ (NOC) 49.
2. Dictionary definition.
3. *Jagdish Chavla v. State of Rajasthan*, 1999 Cr LJ 2562 (Raj).

or doing public exhibition in any form or a club collecting funds and purchasing duly certified video film for exclusive use of its *bona fide* members without intending or actually doing any public exhibition in any form and exhibition of films to restricted audience such as family members or their friends or their relatives are not covered under section 4 of the Act.[1]

Cinematograph Act, 1952

The power of Board of Film Censors under the Cinematograph Act, 1952 was explained in the case of *K.A. Abbas* v. *Union of India*.[2] In this case, the petitioner challenged the denial of Board of Film Censors for granting a 'U' certificate for his film 'Tale of Four Cities.' Board offered to give the certificate only on the condition that certain cuts were made in the film. However, the petitioner was not agreeable for such cuts in the movie. Board of Censors after examining the film can sanction the film for unrestricted public exhibition or it can sanction the film for public exhibition restricted to adults or direct such excisions and modifications in the film before sanctioning the film to any unrestricted public exhibition or for public exhibition restricted to adults and refuse to sanction the film for public exhibition.[3] In his opinion, motion pictures must be treated differently from other forms of art and expressions because it instantly appeals to both sight and hearing and has a great effect on children, immature and adolescents.

Under the Cinematograph Act, 1952, 'cinematograph' is defined to include any apparatus for the representation of moving pictures or series of pictures and the word 'adult' is defined to mean a person who has completed 18 years of his age.[4] After examination of the film, if the board finds that the film is suitable for unrestricted public exhibition, then it may grant a person who is applying for the certificate 'U' or 'UA'[5] certificate and if the film is not suitable for unrestricted public exhibition but suitable for public exhibition suitable to adults then 'A' certificate may be granted and if the movie is suitable for exhibition restricted to members of any particular profession or any class of person then 'S' certificate may be granted.

Deprave and Corrupt Mind

Courts in India, in various cases have clarified that obscene material must have the tendency to deprave and corrupt minds otherwise the material cannot be held to be obscene. If the tendency of the material in question is neither depraving to the ignorant nor corruptible to the innocent, then the material can not be held to be obscene.[6] A particular book containing pictures of positions adopted in sexual intercourse may not be obscene if it is being circulated to married couples only because in such case it will not have tendency to deprave and corrupt the

1. *M/s. Video Master* v. *Union of India,* AIR 1986 Bom 428.
2. (1971) 2 SCR 446.
3. Section 4 of Cinematograph Act, 1952.
4. Section 2(a) and (c) of Cinematograph Act, 1952.
5. If an endorsement of guidance of parents for children below 12 years of age is required, is needed under section 4(i).
6. *State* v. *Dinanath,* AIR 1956 Punj 85.

mind of readers but if is indiscriminately circulated to married and unmarried couples then it may have tendency to deprave and corrupt the minds of readers, therefore the book can be held to be obscene.[1] Hence it is necessary to look who is going to read the book to decide the capability of the book to deprave and corrupt its readers.

To constitute depravity, the publisher must take advantage of the curiosity of young men and women to know something about sex in such a way that the content arouses lustful thoughts and sensual feelings in the mind of reader.[2] Any matter that expresses or suggests 'unchaste and lustful' ideas and prepares to incite a reader to indulge in acts of indecency and immorality can be held to be obscene.[3] While considering the effect of material the effect must be taken as a whole and it must be seen that the 'dominant theme' and general character of the material tends to corrupt minds or not.[3] Sexual arousal, development of unchaste ideas and lustful thoughts must occur in the mind of reader if the effect of the work is taken as a whole.

When news of film stars and incidents happened in film are published in newspapers or magazines that do not contain any obscene or vulgar language and such printed material do not have any tendency to deprave and corrupt those whose minds are open to immoral influences, there is no offence under section 292.[4] A sociologist's account of valuable information about call girls despite having reference to sex does not have the tendency to deprave and corrupt the minds of accused because its object is to help eradication of evil of the prostitution.[5] Indecent object does not have tendency to corrupt and deprave. Film stars interviews in famous magazines and sociologist account of call girls may be filthy, disgusting or abhorable but they are not obscene.

In case of *Muhamed Ibrahim* v. *Public Prosecutor*,[6] on the issue of whether the book was capable of depraving and corrupting the mind of accused, the Court said that the book conveys the impression that casual and frivolous indulgence of the sexual instinct is something of no importance and nothing more than a joke. Hence, it corrupts the minds which are open to such immoral influences and into whose hands the publication of this sort may fall. Here portraying sex as insignificant activity is something that goes beyond indecency and can be termed as capable of depraving and corrupting the minds of those whose minds are open to such immoral influence.

Vulgarity

Vulgarity and obscenity are not one and same because a vulgar novel need not always deprave the morals of its readers.[7] Vulgar descriptions create feeling of

1. *State* v. *Girdharilal Popatlal*, AIR 1956 Bom 32: 57 Bom LR 952: 1956 Cr LJ 206.
2. *Ramamurti* v. *State of Mysoore*, 1954 Cr LR 1622; *State* v. *Girdhar Lal Popat Lal*, (1954) 57 Bom LR 952.
3. *State* v. *Thakur Prasad*, AIR 1959 All 49: 1958 All LJ 578: 1959 Cr LJ 9.
4. *P.K. Somanath* v. *State of Kerala*, 1990 Cr LJ 542 (Ker).
5. *Promila Kapur* v. *Yash Pal Bhasin*, 1989 Cr LJ 1241 (Del).
6. (1963) 29 MLJ 289.
7. *Samresh Bose* v. *Amal Mitra*, AIR 1986 SC 967: (1985) 4 SCC 289.

disgust and revulsion and boredom whereas obscenity has the effect of depraving, debasing and corrupting the morals of any reader whose mind is open to such immoral influence.[1] Mere showing a nude female in the film is not necessary to be obscene because it has to be decided by considering to a great extent the surrounding circumstances and the pose etc.[2] The Courts have to see the manner in which the nude female appears in the film and if the manner is such as to arouse unhealthy and lustful thoughts in the minds of viewers only then the movie can be held to be obscene.[2]

Many movies contain vulgar content such as slangs and vulgar songs. However, the vulgarity in dialogues of the movie or lyrics of the song is not a content which is obscene within the purview of section 292 because even though these dialogues of the movie or lyrics of the songs might offend certain viewers of the movies in society but they do not have the tendency to appeal to the prurient interest of viewers and lack the capability of depraving and corrupting their minds.

Interest of Art, Science, Literature etc.

The obscene material is exempted from prosecution if the material can be justified on the ground that such material is in the interest of science, literature, art or learning or other objects of general concern. In *Harnam Dass* case[3] the appellant pleaded before the Lahore High Court that his work involved 'paramount medicinal value' and therefore exempted from prosecution. Justice Falshaw observed in this case that the book in question was intended to give advice to married couples on how to regulate the sexual side of their life with a view to promote mutual happiness and health. He opined that such work of medicinal value must be written in plain language in order to fulfil their intended purpose. The Court in this case accepted the contention of appellant and acquitted him because the words used in the book were colourless, unimpassioned and quasi-scientific character and presented the intended purpose in a very serious manner throughout the book.

In *Sukanta Halder* v. *The State*[4] case, a sex magazine was in question which contained pictures of cohabiting couples found on walls of certain specified temples. The Court observed in this case that material depicted in the magazine had nothing related to science. The manner in which the pictures were published in the magazine was sufficient to arouse lustful and unchaste ideas in the mind of readers. Hence the material clearly fell within the purview of section 292 of Indian Penal Code.

Supreme Court had held that works of art are not usually considered as prohibited under section 292 but where obscenity and art are mixed together then the effect of art must be so preponderating as to throw obscenity into a shadow or the obscenity is so trivial or insignificant that it can have no effect and may be

1. *Samresh Bose* v. *Amal Mitra,* AIR 1986 SC 967: (1985) 4 SCC 289.
2. *Farzana Bi* v. *Board of Film Censors,* 1983 ALJ 1133.
3. Inder S. Rana, Law of Obscenity in USA, UK and India 162.
4. AIR 1952 Cal 214.

overlooked.[1] In case of *Samaresh Bosh* v. *Amar Mittal*,[2] Supreme Court held that opinion of experts can also be taken to judge whether the work in question has any literary or artistic merit or not. However, first he should place himself in the shoe of author of the material and assess whether the book has any literary merit. Only when he is unable to find out any literary merit in the work and has a reasonable doubt about the presence of literary merit in the work, he may consider resorting to expert opinion.

Film and Censorship

In case of *Body Art International* v. *Om Pal Singh Hoon*,[3] the Supreme Court held that scene of nudity and rape and the use of expletives were in aid of the theme of the film and they were not intended to arouse prurient or lascivious thought but revulsion against perpetrators and pity for the victim. The film carries a message that social evil is evil and it cannot be banned because it depicts social evil and the message conveyed by the film must also be applied to an individual scene depicted in the movie.[4] The court further observed that the scenes of humiliation, stripping naked, paraded, made to draw water from the well within the circle of hundred men, the exposure of her breast and genitalia is not intended to arouse sexual desire or lustful thoughts but intended to demean compelling the victim to do so.

There are certain incidents where pornographic scenes are shown in theatres in a movie which is not pornographic. These scenes are introduced in the movie in between and wholly unconnected to the main movie. In the Case of *Mohammed Rafi* v. *State*,[5] where the Court was dealing with similar sort of situation, it held that it can not be stated that the offending act of exhibiting a film containing the obscene scenes that are totally unconnected with the censored film shown in the theatre is actually justified by law or is *bona fide* believed by mistake of fact to be so justified. Hence, screening a CBFC certified movie with scenes totally unconnected with the movie is punishable under Indian Law.

Now Public Interest Litigation is also helping to fight against pornography. The Bombay High Court has also admitted a citizen's letter on offensive sex sites as public interest litigation. Justice Rajan Coacher admitted the application *suo moto* as writ petition and described pornography on internet as 'cultural pollution.' That website provided the whereabouts of sex-workers, agents, massage parlors, pick up joints in Maharashtra and other states.[6] However, Information Technology Act is not sufficient to deal with such situation because the servers of such kind of websites are located outside India and it is very difficult for the Government to check who the owner of such websites is.

---

1. *Ranajit D. Udeshi* v. *State of Maharashtra*, AIR 1965 SC 881.
2. AIR 1986 SC 967.
3. AIR 1996 SC 1846.
4. K.D. Gaur, Commentary of Indian Penal Code, pp. 704, New Delhi: Universal Law Publishing Company, 2006.
5. 1992 (3) Crimes 57.
6. http://timesofindia.indiatimes.com/articleshow/1171868083.cms

Cyber Café Owner's Liability

The law related to liability of cybercafé owners is not very well settled in India. If a customer downloads any obscene material for his own viewing on the computer assigned to him for surfing by the café owner, and the fact is known to the cyber café owner then it amount to an offence under section 292 of Indian Penal Code read with section 67 of Information Technology Act. However, if the knowledge could not be established then it would be difficult for the prosecution to charge the cyber café owner under section 292. However, he may be charged for abetment of offence in terms of facilitating the circulation and distribution and distribution of the material.[1] However, he may claim the defense of the restricted liability of intermediary but they have to show that they did not have any knowledge about the commission of the offence and they have exercised due diligence to prevent the commission of offence.

Huge amount of pornographic material is being produced more quickly and cheaply on new media including hard disks, floppy disk and CD-ROMs.[2] These pornographic materials include pictures, images, full motion videos and complete movies that are streamed over internet. Today, pornography is not only limited to books, images, websites, blogs but it has taken many new avatars.

Adult Softwares that include Adult Gaming Software, softwares containing pornographic images and software containing sexually violent acts of rape and assaults on girls and children are spreading pornography indiscriminately among children and adults. There are websites on internet that promote offensive and sick flash games that are purely pornographic in nature.[3] These games are available in 3D formats and the characters in the game are made to do sexually explicit acts on the direction of the player. Adult Games like 'Ass-hunter,' 'you the sperm' and strip that girl'[4] are extremely violent in nature and sufficient to encourage sexually offensive behaviour in their players that may be children of our society. These games are capable of appealing to the prurient interest of teenagers which are targeted by game making companies for selling their products.

These games and other like material contain pornography in electronic form. Pornography in electronic form is covered by the provision of Information Technology Act, 2000 as amended by Information Technology (Amendment) Act, 2008. This Act is the only provision in India that deals with offenses committed with the use of digital devices and drafted in very smart way. The provisions of this Act not only cover the offense of publication and transmission of obscenity on internet, attempts but also deal with other computer related offenses. This Act also sets liability for intermediary such as network service

---

1. Lekhesh Dholakiya, "Opinion on The Law of Pornography in India and the implication on Cyber Café Operators". Available at wwww.apiap.org/opinions/legal/opinion-the law-on-pornography-in-India-and-implication-on-cyber-cafe-operators
2. Dev Saif Gangjee, "Pornography on the internet and the Indian Penal Code" in Nandan Kamath, *Law Relating to Computers, Internet and E-Commerce*, pp. 260, Delhi: Universal Law Publishing Company, 2000.
3. http://www.bizarrevideogames.com
4. Games available at http://www.bizarrevideogames.com

providers, host websites and telecommunication companies for aiding and abetting or helping in publication or transmission of obscene content in electronic form.

Although there is not much clarity on the application of the provisions of Information Technology Act due to lack of extensive litigation involving provisions of this Act however, an attempt is made in the next chapter to explain the applicability of the provisions of Information Technology Act that cover pornography on internet.

The Information Technology Act

To understand the implications of this Act, first we should look at the aims and objective of the bill of The Information Technology Act, 2000. It says that it endeavours to "provide legal recognition for data interchange and other means of electronic communication, commonly referred to as electronic commerce, which involve the use of alternatives to paper-based methods of communication and storage of information, to facilitate electronic filing of documents with the Government agencies and further to amend the Indian Penal Code, the Indian Evidence Act, 1872, the Bankers' Books Evidence Act, 1891 and the Reserve Bank of India Act, 1934 and for matters connected therewith or incidental thereto.[1] Hence, this legislation is aimed to promote electronic commerce in a healthy environment by regulating transactions that occur in electronic format.

This law applies to crimes committed with the use of electronic means of communication. It also attacks crimes committed on cyber space. Hence this law attacks pornography in cyber world. Today, the main source of pornography is internet. Pornographic clipping, movies, pictures and images are downloaded from various websites on internet and being circulated all over the world at any place. The biggest problem created related to cyber porn is jurisdictional problem. A pornographic MMS can be uploaded in a small village in India and can be sold to any customer in the world with the use of internet websites. This Act lays down proper procedure to be followed in detection and prosecution of cyber crime. This law attempt to attack the problems related to cyberporn and provides a substantive law to deal with pornography.

The Act penalizes activities concerning damage to computer system, failure to furnish information and any such residuary activity that is related to use of electronic communication and amounts to an offence within the purview of The Information Technology Act, 2000.[2] Section 46 of the Act provides the power to adjudicate the offenses to an officer appointed by Central Government not below the rank of Director to the Government of India or an equivalent officer of the State Government. The adjudicating officer has to follow principles of natural justice and give reasonable opportunity to the accused and after such enquiry if he is satisfied that the person accused has committed any offense, then only he may impose such penalty and award such compensation as he thinks fit in accordance with provisions of this Act.[3]

---

1. The Information Technology Act, 2000.
2. Section 43 to 45 of the Act.
3. Section 46 of the Act.

This Act has several penal provisions that provides penalty for the offenses. Section 67 of the Act penalizes publication of information which is obscene in electronic form. This sections states that, "Whoever publishes or transmits or causes to be published or transmitted in the electronic form, any material which is lascivious or appeals to the prurient interest or if its effect is such as to tend to deprave and corrupt persons who are likely, having regard to all relevant circumstances, to read, see or hear the matter contained or embodied in it, shall be punished on first conviction with imprisonment of either description for a term which may extend to three years and with fine which may extend to five lakh rupees and in the event of second or subsequent conviction with imprisonment of either description for term which may extend to five years and also with fine which may extend to ten lakh rupees."[1]

This is clear from the provision of the Act that it borrows the definition of obscenity from section 292 of Indian Penal Court which borrowed it from the Hicklin Test. This Act also covers transmission of e-mail by one person to other person and affects personal privacy of a person. This Act also covers search engines, Internet Service Providers and Pornographic Websites. The offense is a cognizable and non bailable offense.

According to section 67, mere viewing of pornographic content on internet is not an offence but if you download it and transmit it to your friends then it is an offense. This section does not deal with making pornographic content or viewing pornographic content. Hence, viewing pornography on internet is legal in India. Even when a person transmits pornographic content to any person then the receiver of such content is absolved from any liability under law because section 67 only punishes any person who publishes, transmits or causes to be published such content. An argument can be advanced that the phrase 'causes to be transmitted' that is included by way of 2008 amendment in section 67 that may include a person who receives such content.[2] The argument is plausible because a receiver is a person who asks the transmitter to transmit the content; hence, he causes the pornographic content to be transmitted. However, the veracity of such argument is yet to be tested in Indian Courts.

The word 'any material' in this section may include audio files, text files, video files, images, animation that restored in websites, computers, Compact Disks and mobile phones. The word 'lascivious' means something that tends to excite lust.[3] The word 'appeals to' means 'arouses interest.'[4] The word 'prurient interest' means unusual sexual desire.[5] The word 'effect' means to produce or cause some change or event.[6] The word 'tend to deprave or corrupt' means to lead someone

1. Section 67 of the Information Technology Act, 2000 as amended by 2008 Amendment Act.
2. http://www.cis-india.org/advocacy/igov/it-act/short-note-on-amendment-act-2008.
3. Black's Law Dictionary, 7th Edn., p. 886.
4. http://www.thefreedictionary.com/appeal.
5. Black's Law Dictionary, 7th Edn., p. 1241.
6. Bryan A. Garner Edn. Black's Law Dictionary, 7th Edn., p. 532.

to become morally bad from being morally good."[1] The word 'person' here should refer to natural persons not juristic persons such as companies etc.

The matter in question must satisfy at least one of these conditions:—

1. It must tend to excite lust;
2. It must arouse interest in unusual sexual desire;
3. It must cause a person to become morally bad from being morally good.

Another important element of the statute is the requirement that the matter must tend to corrupt those persons who having regard to all circumstances are likely to read, see or hear it. For example if photos of human sexual activities are given in medical book specially prepared to educate young doctors and these photos are viewed by his young brother whose prurient interest is attracted by viewing such photographs, then this would not constitute an offence under the purview of this Act because the young brothers of the doctors are not person who are likely to read, see or hear the matter.

The word 'publishes' means to 'make known to any person'. This means that at least one person must be aware of the information that is published or understands the information. Hosting a website, visiting a website or indexing a pornographic content does not amount to publication of the content.[2]

The word transmission covers situations which are not covered by the word 'publication.' As soon as a pornographic content is conveyed from one person to other irrespective of whether the other person is made known or be aware of the content of the matter, the offence under this Act is committed.[2]

In case of *L. Parekh* v. *Dr. L. Parekh*,[3] an Orthopaedician, was convicted by a fast track court in Chennai, under various sections including section 67 of Information Technology Act, 2000. In this case, a complainant Ganesh complained to the police that the doctor has forced him to perform sexual acts with women and he has shot a pornographic film. The doctor circulated various copies of the pornographic CD's marked 'material on surgical procedure' that were sold in United States and France. He also prepared a website in United State to upload such content.

Section 67A was included by way of amendment in 2008 that makes it an offense to publish, transmit or cause to publish and transmit in electronic form any material that contains sexually explicit act or conduct. Punishment for this offense is higher than the punishment provided for distribution of obscene content in section 67. This section provides for imprisonment up to five years and fine up to 10 Lakhs on first conviction and imprisonment up to seven years and fine up to 10 Lakhs Rupees. By way of enacting this section, legislature has tried to carve out a section of obscene materials that contain sexually explicit act or conduct. Hence, the present section 67 now deals with all those materials that are obscene but do not contain sexually explicit act or conduct. Section 67A is enacted considering the fact that obscene materials that contain sexually explicit act and conduct in

---

1. Black's Law Dictionary, 7th Edn., p. 348.
2. www.asianlaws.org/library/cyber-laws/cyber-pornography-indian-law.pdf
3. www.indianexpress.com/news/sex-doctor-found-guilty-in-cyber-porn-case-270072.

electronic form are more severe in nature therefore warrants higher punishment. This is the reason behind difference of punishment between section 67 and section 67B.

Section 67B, which is inserted in Information Technology Act, 2000 by way of amendment in 2008, attempts to deal with online child pornography. It penalizes any person who publishes or transmits or causes to be published or transmitted material in any electronic form which depicts children engaged in sexually explicit act or conduct or any person who creates any text or digital images, collects, seeks, browses, downloads, advertises, promotes, exchanges or distributes material in electronic form depicting children in obscene or indecent or sexually explicit manner shall be punished on first conviction with imprisonment of either description for a term which may extend to five years and with fine which may extend to ten lakh rupees and for subsequent conviction imprisonment for seven years and fine up to ten lakh rupees.

The new Amendment makes available public good defense for offence committed within section 67, section 67A and section 67B and a new defence of *bona fide* heritage is also included. The expression children in this provision connotes to a person who is less than 18 years old. Section 67B. This provision makes creating any text or digital image, browsing, downloading and collecting child pornography an offence even if the person doing these acts does not have any intention to publish or transmit the obscene objects. Hence, this provision is different from section 292 of Indian Penal Code and section 67 of the Information Technology Act. So, the current position of law in India is viewing pornography on internet other than child pornography is an offence under Indian Laws.

Section 67B(e) also attempts to deal with production of internet child pornography directly. It makes an offense to record in electronic form own abuse or that of other pertaining to sexually explicit act with children. The consent of child in any of the offences mentioned in this section is made immaterial by the provisions. This provision deals with child pornography exhaustively and in an effective manner.

Section 67B does not mention anywhere about virtual child pornography or pseudo-images of children. We have already seen that virtual child pornography has been made offense in UK and England and this form of pornography is no less harmful than pornography that depicts exploitation of real children. From the plain reading of this section it is unclear whether drawings depicting children shall also be deemed to be prohibited by this section.[1] *Prima Facie*, this section seems to be an attempt of Indian Legislature to prohibit exploitation of real children and depiction of same by way of electronic means. The legislature has deliberately missed out 'pseudo-images' and virtual pornography from the purview of section 67B.

Pornographic Spamming

The offence of spamming pornographic content is covered under the Act. Section 67 of Information Technology Act covers publication and transmission of

---

1. http://www.cis-india.org/advocacy/igov/it-act/short-note-on-amendment-act-2008

obscene content in electronic form that also includes including sending unsolicited e-mails containing pornographic content to random receivers. The Act of pornographic advertising on internet by transmitting e-mails to the receivers is a huge problem. These spams impose filtering cost upon recipients because they have to spend their valuable time in reading the subject lines of those messages and deleting unwanted messages.[1] Even monitory costs such as money spent on installation of filtering software are also associated with the problem of spamming. Pornographic e-mail is being sent by both solicited and unsolicited e-mails. Unsolicited e-mails that are intended for millions of addressees in the form of mass e-mail, for example all the users of yahoo e-mail in India, or a particular user group for example students group e-mail IDs of students of National Law School of India University, or e-mail from businesses with which recipients have prior business relationship.[1] There have been enormous reports of internet users receiving unsolicited e-mails which often contain obscene language and amount to harassment.[2]

In United States, Can Spam Act was enacted in 2003 to deal with problem of internet spamming. The Act was enacted to control the assault of non-solicited pornography, which is clear from the name of the Bill 'Controlling the assault of Non Solicited Pornography and Marketing Act, 2003 from where the Act derives its full name. Section 4 of Can Spam Act amended Chapter 47 of title 18 United States Code by adding section 1037 which is following:—

"1037. Fraud and related activity in connection with electronic mail

(a) IN GENERAL.—Whoever, in or affecting interstate or foreign commerce, knowingly—

(1) Accesses a protected computer without authorization, and intentionally initiates the transmission of multiple commercial electronic mail messages from or through such computer,

(2) Uses a protected computer to relay or retransmit multiple commercial electronic mail messages, with the intent to deceive or mislead recipients, or any Internet access service, as to the origin of such messages,

(3) Materially falsifies header information in multiple commercial electronic mail messages and intentionally initiates the transmission of such messages,

(4) Registers, using information that materially falsifies the identity of the actual registrant, for five or more electronic mail accounts or online user accounts or two or more domain names, and intentionally initiates the transmission of multiple commercial electronic mail messages from any combination of such accounts or domain names, or

---

1. Peter B. Mags, "Abusing Advertising on Internet", p. 54 American Journal of Comparative Law, p. 385, 2006.
2. Address by Hon'ble K.G. Balakrishan, "National Consultation on enforcement of cyber law" available at www.supremecourtofindia.nic.in/.../National_consultation_on_Cyber_Law_31-1-10.pdf

(5) Falsely represents oneself to be the registrant or the legitimate successor in interest to the registrant of 5 or more Internet Protocol addresses, and intentionally initiates the transmission of multiple commercial electronic mail messages from such addresses,

or conspires to do so, shall be punished as provided in sub-section (b)."[1]

The provisions of Can Spam Act are efficient enough to deal with problem of online spamming of pornographic content. The provisions of this Act prohibit registering 5 or more e-mail address using information that materially falsifies the identity of actual registrant. This provision carves out an offense from the offense of transmission of pornography. This provision punishes that segment of offense of transmitting pornography where pornographic content is sent in the form of unsolicited e-mails to one or multiple receivers. It is submitted that similar provisions has to be made in India to deal with problem of online spamming of pornographic content. Any person who sends unsolicited pornographic e-mails to multiple senders must be punished with severe punishments.

Intermediary Liability

Section 79 of the Information Technology Act, 2000 declares that no person providing any service as a network service provider shall be liable under this Act and the rules and regulation that would be made under this Act for any third party information or data that is made available by him, if he is able to prove that the offence or contravention was committed without his knowledge or he has exercised all due diligence to prevent the commission of such offence or contravention.[2]

The explanation to this section defines 'network service provider' to mean an intermediary. The term intermediary is explained in the Information Technology (Amendment) Act, 2008 states that 'intermediary with respect to any particular electronic record means any person who or on behalf of another person receives, stores or transmits that record or provides any service with respect to that record and includes telecom service providers, network service providers, internet service providers, web-hosting service providers, search engines, online payment sites, online auction sites, online market places and cyber cafes.[3] It also defines 'third party information' to mean any information that is dealt with by a network service provider in his capacity as an intermediary.[4] The definition of intermediary includes any person who receives, stores or transmits electronic record of pornography. If Raj Sharma, a regular net user, stores a pornographic MMS on a file sharing website then the file-sharing website will be termed as intermediary and Rajesh complains to the management of file sharing website about availability of pornographic content on their website and the management instructs its employees to remove the content immediately. In this situation, if the MMS is downloaded from that website then the owner of this file sharing website will be

---

1. Section 4 of Can Spam Act, 2003.
2. Section 69 of the Act.
3. Section 2(1)(w) of the Information Technology (Amendment) Act, 2000.
4. Explanation to section 69 of the Act.

made liable under this Act unless he proves that he had no knowledge that the material was obscene or he had exercised all due diligence required to remove the pornographic content from the website as soon as possible.

The highlighting point of the Recent Amendment in Information Technology Act is that it includes Search Engines within the definition of intermediaries. We all are aware about the role of search engines in distribution of pornography over internet. Search Engines provide us information about the web-sites which store pornographic content in them. A layman in the world of internet gets to know about various websites offering pornographic content through a normal Google search or search on any of the search engines available on internet. Many search engines including Google also provide for specific searching such as images and documents.[1] A normal image search on www.image.google.com yields numerous pornographic images. After the amendment any search engine that provides information about pornographic website would be termed as intermediary and will be held liable for publishing obscene content on Internet. That is why Microsoft's search engine 'bing' and yahoo's search engine has blocked porn search on internet. Both the search engines have blocked sex searches on internet.[2] However, the most popular search engine on web has not blocked porn search on internet.[3] Google has option of safe search using which anybody can block sex search by setting his preferences. However, by deselecting safe search anybody can do sex search on internet. It is submitted that the not banning porn search on Google Search is completely illegal after enactment of 2009 Information Technology Amendment Act and Google can be prosecuted under the Act for publishing or causing to be published obscene material under section 67 of Information Technology Act.

According to section 79 an Intermediary will not be held liable if he proves that:—

(1) the offence was committed without his knowledge,

(2) or he has exercised due diligence to prevent the commission of such offence or contravention.

The term 'knowledge' means clear awareness of fact or circumstances.[4] For example if a person has signed up for an e-mail account provided by an e-mail service provider and transmitted pornographic material then the e-mail service provider will not be liable for the act of account maker because he did not have any specific knowledge about the misuse of the account. However, if any person has informed the e-mail service provider before the arrest of account maker about the misuse of the account by the account maker then the e-mail service provider would be liable. 'Due diligence' means the diligence reasonably expected from, and ordinarily exercised by, a person who seeks to satisfy a legal requirement or

1. www.image.google.com
2. Ed. Berridge, "Microsoft and Yahoo decide on Indian Porn Ban" available at http://www.theinquirer.net/inquirer/news/1567050/microsoft-yahoo-decide-indian-porn-ban
3. http://www.alexa.com/topsites
4. Black's Law Dictionary, 7th Edn., p. 876.

to discharge an obligation.[1] For example if a person has complained about the misuse of an account for spreading cyber-pornography to the e-mail service provider and the e-mail service provider has immediately verified the genuineness of the complaint and deleted the e-mail account but the account maker is arrested for misuse of e-mail account created by fictitious name for spreading cyber-porn by police officers, in such case the e-mail service provider will not be liable because he has exercised due care to prevent the misuse of the account.

Section 67 of the Information Technology Act, 2000 has been revised by Information Technology (Amendment) Act to bring in line with Indian Penal Code and other laws and to link it up with section 79 with respect to liability of intermediary.[2] The insertion of section 67C in the Information Technology Act, 2000 seems to suggest the same. Section 67C penalizes intermediaries who do not preserve and retain information as may be specified for such duration prescribed by Central Government and knowingly contravenes the provision of this Act.[3] This section helps in collection of digital evidence against the perpetrators of offense of distribution of pornography over internet. For example if Raj Sharma has enlisted pornographic MMS on a website but deleted the content from the hard drive of his computer and in the process of investigation the police finds no evidence from his computer or internet browser, then digital evidences may be procured from the website or internet service provider within the period specified by the Central Government.

Section 79 was substituted by Information Technology (Amendment) Act, 2008. The new section 79 exonerated intermediary from liability if the function of intermediary is limited to providing excess to a communication system which information made available by third parties is transmitted or temporarily stored or the intermediary does not initiate the transmission, does not select the receiver of the transmission and he does not select or modify the information contained in the transmission provided that intermediary has not conspired or has not abetted in the commission of the unlawful Act or after receiving actual knowledge from appropriate authority about commission of unlawful act, he did not fail to expeditiously remove or disable access to that material on that resource without vitiating the evidence in any manner.[4] By the way of amendment the grounds of exoneration of liability are increased. Now to claim exoneration of liability, the intermediary has to prove that he did not initiate the action or he does not select the receiver or did not modify the information. If the grounds for exoneration of liability have been followed by intermediary then the intermediary will not be liable for any third party information, data or communication link made available or hosted by them.

Section 75 of the Act attempts to resolve the giant problem of jurisdiction attached to commission of offenses in Cyber world. The first sub-section of section 75 states that "the provision of this Act shall apply to any offense or

1. Black's Law Dictionary, 7th Edn., p. 468.
2. www.mit.gov.in/download/summary-final.doc
3. Section 67C of the Information Technology Act, 2000.
4. Section 79 of Information Technology Act, 2000.

contravention committed outside India by any person irrespective of his nationality". However, the requirement to this application is that the act constituting the offence or contravention must involve a computer, computer system or computer network located in India. Hence, if an MMS is uploaded in India and downloaded in any part of the world then the downloader can be prosecuted under this Act.

Section 67, 67A, 67B and 67C does not cover any book, pamphlet, paper, writing, drawing, painting, representation or figure in electronic form if there is any public good defence available with the accused which means that if he is able to prove that such pamphlet, paper, writing, drawing, painting, representation or figure is in the interest of science, literature, art or learning or other objects of general concern, or if it is kept for *bona fide* religious purpose.[1] Hence, even publisher or transmitter of obscene material which is prepared in electronic forms like e-books, e-magazines, and blogs can avail public good defense under the Information Technology Act.

Under this law, the cyber café owners would also be held responsible if any of his client watches pornography in his shop. Now a police officer ranked inspector or above has the power to arrest any person, if he is satisfied that person has published and transmitted pornography over internet.[2] The police officers have been provided with the powers to enter into any house without permission to check resident's computers.

In the *Avnish Bajaj* v. *State* case, the Managing Director of an internet website, Bazee.com, that carried a listing which offered for sale a video clip shot on a mobile phone depicting two children of a school in a sexually explicit act, was prosecuted for an offence under sections 292 and 294 of Indian Penal Code and section 67 of Information Technology Act, 2000. This website used to provide an online market for buyer and seller to interact with each other. Ravi Raj, a fourth year student of IIT Kharagpur posted an MMS video on this website for sale. The listing of video on the website took place inspite of filters operating on the website that could have removed word sex and sexual. 8 transactions of the video clip took place before the deactivation of the listing.

From the side of Avnish Bajaj, Arun Jaitley and Sidharth Luthra argued that the video clip was not displayed in the website but only listed in the website without any intervention from the website and the revenue generated by such listing is not a profit under section 292 of Indian Penal Code but it is an income generated by company which is not an accused in this case. The counsel for the State argued that section 292 of Indian Penal Code does not cover only overt acts but illegal omissions also within the meaning of sections 32, 35 and 36 of Indian Penal Code. He further contended that the website committed illegal omission by not providing adequate filters and the fact that the profit is earned by the M.D. is evident from the bank statement.

The Supreme Court opined that the listing of MMS video amounts to obscenity under section 292 of Indian Penal Code because it attracts the prurient interest and

1. Exception to section 67A.
2. Section 78 of Information Technology Act, 2000 as amended by Information Technology (Amendment) Act, 2008.

if taken as whole is sufficient to deprave and corrupt the minds of people who are likely to read, hear or see it. The Court refused to agree with the submission of counsel of the petitioner, that the accused did not do any overt act to attract section 292, because according to Supreme Court, the offence under section 292 is attracted when the prosecution is able to prove that a person has "publicly exhibited or in any manner put into circulation" or "had in his possession" the obscene objects. The fact that the video was listed on the website amounts to "possession" and the fact that the website was accessible on internet amounts to public exhibition of the obscene material. According to Supreme Court ruling in Ranajit Udeshi Case, section 292 does not warrant the prosecution to prove *mens rea* as to whether the seller has knowledge that the material was obscene or not but it mandates that the seller must have *mens rea* to sell the object. The Court stated that the website company BIPL is guilty of violation of section 292 keeping in view the strict liability imposed by this section on the ground that it failed to install proper filters.

On the issue of whether Bazee.com caused publishing of obscene material in electronic form for the purpose of section 67 of Information Technology Act, the Court opined that the fact that the obscene material was transmitted to 8 people across the countries and listed on the website to be accessed publicly amounts to publishing of obscene material.

In this case a *prima facie* case under section 292 of Indian Penal Code and 67 of Information Technology Act, 2000 is made out against the company, Bazee.com. On the issue of liability of petitioner under section 292 of Indian Penal Code , the Court stated that there is no provision of automatic liability of the director where the company is arraigned as an accused. The fact that section 85 of the Infromation Technology Act provides for liability of director in case of offence committed by Company but absence of any such provision in Indian Penal Code, explains the intention of parliament that it wanted to exonerate the director from the liability of offences committed by Companies under the Indian Penal Code unless the prosecution is able to make out a case against the accused in his individual capacity. In the present case, there are no sufficient evidence to prove that the petitioner was involved in the commission of offence in his individual capacity. Hence, the petitioner can not be held liable under section 292 of Indian Penal Code, however, he can be held liable for violation of the provisions of section 67 of the Information Technology Act, 2006 because section 85(2) of the Act makes a director guilty of an offence under this Act if the act is done by him with his knowledge or neglect.

In the case of *Maqbool Fida Hussain* v. *Raj Kumar Pandey,*[1] online auction of a painting depicting a nude woman created by a famous painter was challenged as sale, distribution, publishing of obscene material under section 292 of Indian Penal Code and section 67 of Information Technology Act, 2000. The Supreme Court, in this case opined that the painting was not obscene under the definition of section 292 because it is neither lascivious nor does it not appeal to prurient interests. In the words of the Court, the painting does not have capacity to arouse sexual

1. 2008 Cr LJ 4107: (2008) 2 JCC 1433 http://indiankanoon.org/doc/1191397/

interest in perverted inordinate persons or would not morally corrupt a person viewing it. The painting does not have the tendency to embarrass an average person due to the presence of artistic touch.

Cyber Café Regulations

The introduction of new rules to regulate cyber café depicts the concern of Indian Government about the circulation of pornography through cyber cafes. These cafes are available in almost every corner of every streets in India including small towns. The price for accessing internet from these cyber cafes is very cheap (less than 4 rupees/ hour) which attracts net surfers towards these cafes. These cafes also facilitate production of pornography.

A recent scandal in Rawalpindi proves it. A person in Rawalpindi set up an internet café by constructing small cabin wide enough to accommodate a couple, installed lights inside the cabin, put a screen door with locks on inside and hid cameras inside the lights of the cabin. Customers who came as couples went inside the cabin, viewed dirty websites and did dirty things. The Activities of these couples were recorded by hidden Cameras by the Cyber-café owners and later converted into CDs and DVDs only to blackmail those couples. The Copies of the CDs and DVDs were sold in Dubai and many European Countries in very expensive prices. Someone delivered those CDs and DVDs to the houses of couples depicted in the CDs and DVDs and as a result 3 girls committed suicide, one was killed by her father and two were divorced.[1]

Such incidents have caused anxiety amongst Governments all over the world. A need to regulate cyber café was also felt in India. Cyber café regulation in India is state centric model as exact regulation differs from state to state consequently affirmed by difference in regulatory framework that work upon the instructions and mandated policies contained in notifications by executive agencies of State Governments.[2] State Centric Model of Cyber Café regulations mean different rules and regulations made for cyber café situated in different states.

In certain states Government agencies make delegated legislations including rules and regulation to regulate cyber café. These delegated legislations draw their authority from section 90 of Information Technology Act, 2000. This section empowers the Government to make rules for the matters that come within the Act. These rules provide framework for the precautions against the use of internet for illegal activities in cyber café and a procedure for mandatory record keeping.[2] The framework includes mandatory registering of customers and requirement to show valid ID proof.

In Union Territory of Delhi, police has asked cyber-café owners to allow the surfers to surf the net only if they have a valid identity proof and if any cyber café owner violates this rule, they he may be punished within section 188 of Indian Penal Code which punishes disobedience to order duly promulgated by public

1. http://www.jang.com.pk/jang/apr2004-daily/28-04-2004/editorial/col3.htm
2. Raman Chima, "The regulation of internet with relation to speech and expression by the Indian State", full article available at http://papers.ssrn.com/sol3 papers.cfm?abstract_id=1237262.

servants.[1] The Mumbai model that mandates all cyber café owners to take permission from police before the establishment of cyber café and pay a particular fee does not derive its authority from any central enactment but from Bombay Police Act.[2] These rules and regulations seems to suggest that Indian Legal Authorities are showing appropriate concern for publishing and distribution of pornography and other related crimes with the use of Internet Cafes.

Cable TV

Cable TV has expanded to smaller towns and villages now. It is affordable and provides varieties of entertainment. Sometimes adult pornographic content is transmitted through cable television. Appropriate actions are taken against the cable TV operator under the law whenever broadcasting of such content is reported.[3] However, such content is controlled by the broadcasting companies that broadcast such pornographic content. Clause (o) of rule 6(1) of the Cable Television Network Rules, 1994 provides that no programme shall be carried on the cable service which is 'unsuitable for unrestricted public exhibition. Hence, no cable programme, which is unsuitable for unrestricted public exhibition such as movies that are given adult certificate, can be broadcasted by cable TV operators. However, sub-rule (5) of the Cable Television Network Rules, 1994 also provides that programme unsuitable for children shall not be carried at times when large number of children are viewing. A harmonious construction of both the rules can be taken to provide that programmes that are suitable for unrestricted exhibition as certified by CBFC but unsuitable for children due to some other reason may be telecasted or transmitted when large numbers of children are not viewing them. In the opinion of Bombay High Court, only films sanctioned by Central Board of Film Certification as suitable for unrestricted public exhibition can be telecasted or transmitted on cable television and this does not violate viewers right to view adult content because they are always free to view such content in cinema hall, VCR, and by means of DVDs and VCDs.[4] It is submitted that the view of Bombay High Court is appreciable because adult's right to view adult content must not cause to deprave and corrupt children. Broadcasting of adult content on television even in hours when children are least likely to view it, can not guarantee that no children that are attempted to be protected by the provisions of this Act are not going to view the adult content section.

Bombay High Court has issued a directive in a writ petition filed by some consumers who objected to the obscene content shown on some of the channels. The directive mandated that only films certified by Censor Board be shown on the movie channels.[4] This case was issued in case of *Pratibha Naitthani* v. *Union of India*,[5] where the petitioner got aggrieved by telecast of adult and obscene films

1. http://www.hindu.com/2006/07/22/stories/2006072227630300.htm
2. Raman Chima, "The regulation of internet with relation to speech and expression by the Indian State", full article available at http://papers.ssrn.com/sol3/papers.cfm?abstract_id=1237262
3. www.timesofindia.indiatimes.com/india/crackdown-on-obscenity-Cable-guys-strike-back.articleshow/1914123.cms
4. *Pratibha Naitthani* v. *Union of India*, AIR 2006 Bom 259.
5. AIR 2006 Bom 259.

shown by the electronic media and obscene photographs in print media and filed a writ petition before Bombay High Court. The affidavit filed by Joint Commissioner in this case reveals the problem associated with distribution of pornography on TV channels. The Joint Commission stated that channels broadcast programmes via satellite and it is practically impossible for police to take any action against cable TV operators or TV channels.

This is a welcoming move because pornographic movies do not have any censor certificate. Hence, it would not be possible for the channel to screen pornographic movies. Other than pornographic movies the television channels today broadcast rape and sex scenes, music videos where half naked girls dancing and making gestures that almost resemble with a girl performing pornography and sex talks by experts of sex related illness.

The above information is only about the content that is transmitted through authorized satellite channels. However, there are many local television channels that are run by local TV cable operators. These cable operators screen blue films (hardcore pornographic film) at nights on the demand of the customers.[1] It is very difficult to prosecute these operators because these cable operators have connection with police and politicians.

Telecast of 4 films that were telecasted by television channels out of which two did not have any Censor Board Certificate were prosecuted in the case of *R. Basu* v. *National Capital Territory of Delhi* under section 7 of the Indecent Representation of Women (Prohibition) Act, 1986 and sections 292/293/294 of Indian Penal Code.[2] The Chief Metropolitan Magistrate in this case observed the role played by cable TV operators in circulation of obscene content on television. He observed that viewing of such content would not be possible until the cable TV operators broadcast the signals of these channels. The High Court very clearly stated that the according to the established position of law in this regard, no movie that does not have a CBFC certificate can be telecasted *via* Satellite Channels. Hence, the movies without any CBFC certificate that were telecasted by television channels can not claim immunity from section 292 of Indian Penal Code. It also observed that Legislature has made an attempt to deal with the problem of obscenity by enacting Cable Television Regulations Act and various statutory safeguards to deal with this problem are made available within the Act and the Rules. The Television channel operators and cable TV operators are bound by these rules.

It is true that cable TV operators are the ones who are responsible for viewing of obscene content on television. They can stop telecasting of obscene content by closing down the signals of TV channels that broadcast such obscene content.

---

1. S.B. Balakrishnan, City Cable Operators telecast porno films, Times of India, (31-5-1996).
2. 2007 Cr LJ 4254.

CHAPTER 6

PORNOGRAPHY AND FREEDOM OF SPEECH

Freedom of speech is treated as a fundamental right available to every citizen of the country by many countries in the world. However, restrictions upon this right vary in different countries. This chapter deals with treatment of pornography under the right of freedom of speech in United States, United Kingdom and India.

United States

First let us consider the status of pornography as speech in American law from where India has borrowed the concept of freedom of speech and incorporated into article 19(1)(a) of the Constitution. The concept of freedom of speech was included in American Constitution as first amendment in 1791.[1] First Amendment states that, "Congress shall make no law respecting an establishment of religion, or prohibiting the free exercise thereof; or abridging the freedom of speech, or of the press; or the right of the people peaceably to assemble, and to petition the Government for a redress of grievances.[2]" It is visible from the text of the amendment that it only protects freedom of speech and not expression. Pornography can only be protected under the first amendment to the United States Constitution if it amounts to speech. So, the question which is going to be dealt with now is whether pornography is speech or not?

Pornography is regarded as conduct rather than speech by various scholars. The reason given for such recognition is the fact that it also involves actors that are engaged in sexually explicit activities. If pornography is accepted to be a conduct rather than a speech then the question is whether it can enjoy the protection of first amendment of constitution because first amendment only prohibits speech and not conduct. However, there are incidents where conduct has also been treated as a form of speech. The conduct of protesting amounts to exercising the right of free speech. Political conduct such as wearing black arm-bands in hand for protest is also accepted as utilization of free speech principle.[3] Hence, it can be argued that the mere fact that pornography is a conduct is not sufficient to exclude it from the definition of speech. Now we are going to examine whether pornography which involves sexual conducts must be treated as speech or conduct?

---

1. David Smith, Time Line: A history of Free Speech available at <http://www.guardian.co.uk/media/2006/feb/05/religion.news
2. First Amendment to United States Constitution.
3. *Tinker* v. *Des Moines Independent Community School District,* 393 US 503 (1969).

Cass Sunstein, an American Legal Scholar, argued that pornography is not really speech because the 'message' of pornography is communicated indirectly and not through rational persuasion.[1] Normally all newspapers, books and magazines where opinions of writers are expressed, exercise the right to freedom of speech through rational persuasion. These writers express their opinion in a certain fashion and invite for comments on their opinions. However, in pornography, the pornographers exercise their right of free speech (in case they have one) without considering the element of rational persuasion through mere conduct. Frederick Schauer, a distinguished professor in law, argues in the same way that pornography should receive no protection because it is "designed to produce a purely physical effect." He also argues that pornography is only a tool of sexual arousal and does not communicate ideas to constitute speech.[2] His argument is based on the fact that pornography is used by purchasers as an aid to masturbation that indicates that it is a tool of sexual arousal. Catharine MacKinnon, the high-profile critic of pornography, argues, 'in pornography, consumers are not consuming an idea any more than eating a loaf of bread or consuming the ideas on its wrapper or the ideas in its recipe.[2] All these views of scholars promote the preposition that pornography can be termed as conduct of pornographers devoted for sexual arousals of its viewers but it is not an activity. However, these scholars tend to ignore the fact that pornography is also being circulated in the form of books, magazines, sex stories and in virtual format where no actors are involved. In these forms of pornography, only ideas about sexual activities are communicated from the minds of pornographers to the purchaser of pornography through the medium of these writings. Hence, it can be said that pornography is also about communication of ideas to the readers in whose hands the material may fall.

It can also be argued that the problem of pornography lies in the fact that it communicates powerful ideas and statements about the degradation of workers involved in the making of pornography and the legitimization of their degradation and abuse along with achieving sexual arousals.[3] Pornography certainly has communicative content in it. Authors of pornographic books certainly convey their ideas about sexual activities to the readers of the book. Hence it can be accepted that pornography amounts to speech.

However, the fact that pornography may amount to speech does not necessarily mean that it is protected by law under first amendment because not all forms of speeches are protected by first amendment. Seditious Speeches[4] and inflammatory speeches directed to incite or likely to incite imminent lawless action[5] do not enjoy protection of first amendment of American Constitution.

1. Cass R. Sunstein, "Pornography and the First Amendment," 1986 Duke Law Journal 589, 616-17 (1986).
2. John M. Kang, "Taking Safety Seriously, Using Liberalism to Fight Pornography," 1(15) Michigan Journal of Gender and Law 1, 2008.
3. Attorney General's Commission on Pornography, Final Report 234 (1986) available at porn-report.com., at 92.
4. *Schenck* v. *United States,* 249 US 47 (1919).
5. *Bradenburg* v. *Ohio,* 395 US 444 (1969).

In *Roth* v. *United States*,[1] the Supreme Court rejected the argument that obscenity is protected under the free speech principle. Justice Brennan stated that obscenity is materials that are produced to arouse lustful thoughts and if it is without social values then no first amendment exemptions can be claimed. The Court went behind the intention of the framers and found that the framers of first amendment never intended to protect every form of utterance or expression like materials which have no social importance but it intended to assure 'unfettered interchange of ideas' for the promotion of social and political changes desired by people. In *Paris Adult Theatre* v. *Slaton*,[2] the Court accepted that it is well established that obscenity is not protected within first amendment. In *Miskin* v. *United States*,[3] also the Court held that Hard Core pornography that includes material on sadomasochism, homosexuality and lesbianism and therefore offensive to community does not come within the area of constitutionally protected free speech. Hence, in United States obscenity does not enjoy full protection as free speech.

In the case of *Stanley* v. *Georgia*,[4] there was a conflict between right to privacy and right to freedom of speech. The Court did weigh both rights and concluded that private possession of obscene material is constitutionally protected. According to the opinion of Justice Marshall in this case, 'if the first amendment means anything it means that a State has no business telling a man, sitting alone at his house, what books he may read or what films he may watch.' This preposition is problematic because we have already seen that regulation of a material that is capable of depraving minds must not only be limited to publishing but reading, viewing, making it must also be prohibited as both have same harmful effects. Individual right to see adult content is not regulated but individual's right to see that adult content which can deprave and corrupt his mind and thereby becoming threat to society is prohibited by law.

However, the Courts in United States have also adopted liberal attitude towards obscenity. In the case of *Ashcroft* v. *Free Speech Coalition*,[5] the Court struck down the provisions of Child Pornography Prevention Act, 1996, because it violated first amendment as it prohibited pornography even if it did not depict an actual child. In the opinion of Justice Kennedy, "Government must not be allowed to control thoughts to the extent of impermissible end. The right to think is the beginning of freedom, and speech must be protected from the Government because speech is the beginning of thought." However, in the case of *United States* v. *Williams*,[6] the Supreme Court of United States upheld a federal statute that prohibited pandering of child pornography. The Court clearly stated that first amendment does not protect offers to engage in illegal transactions. Pornography that involves illegal transactions between producers of child pornography and purchasers is not protected under the first amendment.

---

1. 354 US 476: 1 Law Ed 1498 (1957).
2. 413 US 49 (1973).
3. 383 US 502 (1966).
4. 394 US 557 (1969).
5. 535 US 234 (2002).
6. 553 US 285 (2008).

Pornographer's freedom of speech is the loss of speech of others. The aim of first amendment is to promote freedom of speech whereas the aim of pornography is to silence women.[1] Hence, pornography and freedom of speech share different aims and objectives.

In the case of *Jenkins* v. *Georgia*,[2] the appellant, a manager of theater was charged under section 26-201 of Georgia Obscenity Law for knowingly exhibiting a picture 'Carnal Knowledge' that contained an act of sexual intercourse, lewd exposure of sexual organs, a lewd appearance in a state of partial or complete nudity and lewd, careless and indecent fondling of another person. The Court applied contemporary community interest test as laid down in *Miller* v. *California*,[3] case and held that the picture can not be found to depict sexual conduct in a patently offensive way and it is within the protection of First and Fourteenth Amendment to the United States Constitution. It also observed that first Amendment to US Constitution does not protect the commercial of 'Hard Core' pornography.

In absence of distribution to juveniles or obtrusive exposure to un-consenting adults, the first and fourteenth amendments prohibit the state and Federal Governments from attempting wholly to suppress sexually oriented materials on the basis of their allegedly 'obscene contents'[4] This reflects liberal approach of Courts in United States towards pornography.

United States of America Passed Communication Decency Act, 1996 that was struck down in *ACLU* v. *Reno*,[5] In this case, 9 justices of United States Supreme Court voted to strike down the anti-indecency provisions of Communication Decency Act, 1996 because it violated first Amendment of United States Constitution that protects freedom of speech. The Act imposed criminal sanctions upon any person who knowingly uses an interactive computer service to send any specific person or persons under age of 18 or to display any person under 18 years of age any comment, request, suggestion, proposal, image or other communication that in context depicts or describes in terms patently offensive as measured by contemporary community standards sexual or excretory activities or organs. The majority opinion held that CDA is overtly broad (a classification evolved by Courts in United States to hold obscenity statutes unconstitutional) because it prohibits distribution of speech that the adults are entitled to receive and address to one another under the guise of protecting such distribution of speech to children. Hence the current position of law on United States to regulate pornographic speech is, the law regulating pornography must not be overtly broad that means it must aim to regulate the amount of speech which can be reasonably regulated under the law.

---

1. Attorney General's Commission on Pornography, Final Report 234 (1986) available at porn-report.com at 108.
2. 418 US 153 (1974).
3. 413 US 25 (1973).
4. *Paris Adult Theater* v. *Slaton*, 413 US 49 (1973).
5. 521 US 844 (1997).

United Kingdom

United Kingdom does not have a Constitution. So, it does not have constitutional protection to freedom of speech. The protection of free speech in United Kingdom has developed through common law and statutory provisions.[1] United Kingdom incorporated article 10 of European Convention of Human rights and the right to free speech which is guaranteed in this article in its domestic law in Human Rights Act, 1998 which became enforceable on 2nd October, 2000.

Article 10 of European Convention of Human Rights Act guarantees that everyone has a right to freedom of expression. The right of freedom of expression means freedom to hold opinion and freedom to not only receive information and ideas but also to impart those information and ideas without any interference from the state and without any boundaries.[2] However, this freedom has certain restrictions such as this freedom does not bar the state from requiring licenses from broadcasting agencies, television or cinema enterprises.[2] No public authority can act incompatibly with a right in the convention.[3] Public Authority is defined to include Courts tribunals and any person whose functions are of a public nature.[4] This Act guarantees freedom of expression, which is not expressly mentioned in United States Constitution. Hence, if it can be proved that pornography is a part of expression then it may enjoy freedom of expression under this Article.

Other than the above restriction on freedom of expression, the right can also be subject to such formalities, conditions, restrictions or penalties as are prescribed by law and are necessary in a democratic society, in the interests of national security, territorial integrity or public safety, for the prevention of disorder or crime, for the protection of health or morals, for the protection of the reputation or rights of others, for preventing the disclosure of information received in confidence, or for maintaining the authority and impartiality of the judiciary.[5] This provision gives the power to legal authorities to prohibit pornography on the ground of prevention of morals. However, there has been no litigation under this section on the issue of imposing restriction on pornography in the name of protection of morals, hence the position of law in this regard is unclear.

Section (1) of the Human Rights Act states "the Convention rights" means the rights and fundamental freedoms set out in—

(a) Articles 2 to 12 and 14 of the Convention,

This means that article 10 of the convention which guarantees freedom of expression is adopted in the domestic legislation of United Kingdom by way of Human Rights Act.

The common law protection given to freedom of speech and statutory protection to freedom of speech is already dealt with in the chapter titled adjudicating pornography in United Kingdom.

---

1. Eric Berendt, Freedom of Speech, p. 39 (2005).
2. Article 10(1) of European Convention of Human Right.
3. Section 6(1) of Human Rights Act, 1998.
4. Section 6(3) of Human Rights Act, 1998.
5. Section 10(2) of European Convention of Human Rights.

India

In the case of *Maneka Gandhi* v. *Union of India,*[1] the Supreme Court of India held that the freedom of speech and expression has no geographical limitation and it carries with it the right of a citizen to gather information and to exchange thought with others not only in India but abroad also. The right of freedom of speech that is enshrined in Indian Constitution is very wide and efficient. In India, Freedom of Speech and expression is guaranteed by Indian Constitution in 1950. Article 19, (1)(a) of Indian Constitution provides every citizen a right to freedom of speech and expression. However, clause 2 of the same article imposes reasonable restriction on the freedom of speech on the ground of maintenance of public order, decency or morality or in relation to contempt of court, in the interest of sovereignty and integrity of India, the security of state, friendly relations with Foreign States, defamation or incitement to an offence.

In certain circumstances the social interest in public order may require reasonable subordination of free speech and expression; so the question that is to be asked is should the restrictions imposed on the exercise of the rights under Arts. 19(1) be reasonable in view of all the surrounding circumstances?[2] Article 19 embodies that there should be balance between freedom of speech and the restrictions imposed on it. The balance requires that no restriction can be put on freedom of speech except by law which should have reasonable or relevant ground in relation to fundamental right. The offence of obscenity is related to public order, decency or morality and if reasonable restrictions have been imposed as enacted under sections 292, 293 and 294 then it cannot be said that these provisions violate fundamental rights enshrined under article 19 of the Constitution.[3] Hence, it is clear that the restrictions imposed must be reasonable one. Article 19(2) of the Constitution also permits only reasonable restrictions to be imposed by law. The word 'reasonable' gives scope for the judiciary for exercising the power of judicial review. Any law that seeks to restrict freedom of speech and expression can be scrutinized by judiciary to check whether the restrictions imposed upon the exercise of right are reasonable or not. The judiciary has scrutinized various laws affecting freedom of speech. For example in *Kishori Mohan* v. *State of West Bengal,*[4] a law punishing the utterances deliberately tending to hurt the religious feelings of any class was scrutinizes by judiciary and it was held to be valid as it is a reasonable restriction aimed to maintaining the public order.

The judgment of Supreme Court in *Shri Chandrakant Kalyandas Kakodkar* v. *The State of Maharashtra,*[5] recognized that freedom of speech can not be a ground for obscenity if there is no social purpose or protection of the interest of community. This view was also upheld in *Samresh Bose* v. *Amal Mitra.*[6] The view is perfect

1. AIR 1978 SC 597.
2. *Virendra* v. *State of Punjab,* AIR 1957 SC 896.
3. *Kamla Kant Singh* v. *Chairman/ Managing Director, Bennett Colman and Company Ltd.,* 1988 (1) Crimes 106 (All).
4. AIR 1972 SC 1749.
5. AIR 1970 SC 1390: 1970 Mah LJ 46: 1970 Cr LJ 1273: (1970) 2 SCR 80.
6. AIR 1986 SC 967: 1986 Cr LJ 24: (1985) 4 SCC 289.

because as we have seen earlier that article 19 requires that there should be balance between freedom of speech and restrictions imposed on it. As we have seen that various reports have come out with the conclusion that pornography incites people to commit sexual crimes and thus pornography is harmful in general to the society. Hence, the possible harm justifies and requires restrictions to be imposed on it. In a recent case of *T. Kannan* v. *Liberty Creations Ltd.*,[1] the Madras High Court has said that there should be a substantial allowance for freedom thus leaving a vast area for creative art to interpret life and society with some of its foibles along with what is good. Art and literature include within themselves, a comprehensive view of social life and not only in its ideal form. Hence, the form of pornography that can be justified on the ground of having artistic values can be deemed to be protected within the right of freedom of speech and expression.

Decency and Morality

Decency

The meaning of word decency varies according to age, culture and alike things of the audience. In common law, this word is used in the sense of obscenity and conveys the idea of offending against the recognized standards of property.[2] Decency is defined as propriety of action, speech, dress etc.[3] Decency is becomingness and it is what is not indecent, immodest or obscene.[4]

Morality

The term morality can be used descriptively to refer to a code of conduct put forward by a society or some other group such as religion or accepted by individual for her own behaviour or it may be used normatively to refer to a code of conduct that given specified conditions would be put forward by all rational persons.[5] K.T. Shah, one of the member of Constituent Assembly was very critical of usage of the term 'morality' in the Constitution because of its vagueness and difficulty to define it. He wanted it to be defined or to be dropped together.[6]

Obscenity which is offensive to modesty or decency is not within constitutional protection given to free speech or expression because article dealing with the right itself excludes it. Article 19 is intended to assure expression of free opinions to change political or social conditions or for the advancement of human knowledge and this freedom is absolutely subject to reasonable restrictions which may be imposed in the interest of public decency and morality. Section 292 is a form of such restriction because law of obscenity seeks no more than to promote decency and morality.[7] Henkin stated that laws against obscenity are rooted in traditional notions of morality and decency; hence the moral foundation of these

1. 2007 (2) MLJ 1015: AIR 2007 (NOC) 1734 (Mad).
2. Durga Das Basu, Commentary on Constitution of India, 6th Edn., p. 125.
3. Black Law Dictionary, 6th Edn., p. 405.
4. Kagzi, The Constitution of India, 6th Edn., p. 1126.
5. http://plato.stanford.edu/entries/morality-definition/
6. P.K. Ray, "Law of Decency and Morality as Restraints on Freedom of Speech and Expression" p. 8.
7. *Ranjit D. Udeshi* v. *State of Maharashtra*, AIR 1965 SC 881.

laws must be regarded while considering the constitutionality of such laws.[1] However, it was decided not to define the term.

The concept of obscenity and decency changes according to time and place. These concepts differ from countries to countries depending upon the standards of morality of contemporary society in different countries.[2] For example, in United Kingdom 'Lady Chatterley' lover' was not considered obscene but in India it could not pass the obscenity test.[3] Hence, the test should be whether a class and not an isolated case into whose hands the book, article, story falls suffer in their moral outlook or become depraved by reading it or might have impure and lecherous thoughts aroused in their minds.[4] Hence the morality which matters is class morality or positive morality or shared morality and the moral outlook of readers.

Child Pornography

Child pornography is a different issue and must be treated differently because physical and mental health of nation is determined largely by the manner in which it is shaped in the very early stage.[5] It is realized everywhere that children must be brought up in an atmosphere of love and affection and under the tender care of parents to attain emotional, intellectual and spiritual ability and acquire self confidence and self respect for realization of role that they have to play in the nation building process.[5] There are provisions in our Constitution that empowers the Government to make special provisions regarding children.[6] Section 67B of Information Technology Act is an example of such special provision. This provision makes it an offense to view child pornography on internet whereas viewing adult pornography is not an offence in India. This section is enacted with the object that child pornography is different from adult pornography and needs special attention.

Freedom of Press

In Norms of Journalistic Conduct,[7] norm number 17 lays down 3 tests to check whether a material can be published or not—

1. Is it vulgar and indecent?
2. Is it a piece of mere pornography?
3. Is its publication meant merely to make money by titillating the sex feelings of adolescents and among whom it is intended to circulate or does it constitute an unwholesome exploitation for commercial gain?

Other considerations include whether the picture is relevant to subject matter of the magazine which means whether its publications serves any preponderating

---

1. P. Devlin, The Enforcement of Morals, p. 22 (1968).
2. *Samaresh Bose* v. *Amal Mitra,* AIR 1986 SC 967.
3. *Ajay Goswami* v. *Union of India,* AIR 2007 SC 493.
4. *Shri Chandrakant Kalyandas Kakodkar* v. *State of Maharashtra,* AIR 1970 SC 1390: (1969) 2 SCC 687.
5. *Laxmikant Pandey* v. *Union of India,* AIR 1984 SC 469: (1984) 2 SCC 244.
6. Article 15(3) of Indian Consitution.
7. http://presscouncil.nic.in/norms.htm

social or public purpose in relation to art, painting, medicine, research or reform of sex.

In case of *Doordarshan* v. *Anand Patwardhan*, JT 2006 (8) SC 255: AIR 2006 SC 3346, 3 tests were laid down for judging whether the material infringes section 292 of I.P.C.:—

(1) whether the average person, applying contemporary community standards would find the work taken as a whole appeals to prurient interest

(2) whether the work depicts or describes in a patently offensive way sexually explicit conduct specifically defined by the applicable law

(3) whether the work taken as a whole lacks any serious artistic or literary value.

These tests are similar to *Roth* v. *U.S.* Test. Based on these three tests any material that is published by press or any material that is broadcasted on news television channels can be judged as obscene.

In the case of *Ajay Goswami* v. *Union of India*, the petitioner brought into notice of the Court, prevalent indecent and vulgar advertisements in the newspaper having the captions like "Centre of Attention," "Double Jeopardy," and "Butt of Course." He challenged the freedom of speech granted to press in regard with the information provided by them about masturbation, ejaculation and penetration usually discussed by sex experts in the column of newspaper by objecting the indiscriminate circulation of these materials to the child. However the Supreme Court dismissed the writ petition citing *Unites States* v. *Playboy Entertainment Group Inc.* 529 U.S. 803 (2000) where it was said that State can only prohibit a particular expression of opinion if it can show that its actions are caused by something more than a mere desire to avoid discomfort and unpleasantness that always accompany an unpopular view point. The Court refused to regulate the content in question because these contents may arouse lustful desire only in children and unusually susceptible person. For some adults it may be a cause of unpleasantness or discomfort. A material cannot be judged obscene on its effect on unusually susceptible person and an average reader for whom the work was written would not be depraved and corrupted by the matter. Therefore the content in question is well protected under article 19 of Indian Constitution.

Difference between Freedom of Speech in India and USA

The case laws on freedom of speech decided in United States are not much helpful to enunciate the scope and effect of article 19(1)(a) and 19(2) of Indian Constitution because, in India, the right to freedom of speech and expression has limitations. Article 191(a) is subject to article 19(2) that provides for reasonable restrictions.[1] The question of whether the restrictions imposed is reasonable or not is completely upon the Courts to decide and the Courts must *prima facie* presume the law made in respect of the matters referred to in article 19(2) to be constitutionally valid, the restrictions imposed to be reasonable.[2]

1. *Santokh Singh* v. *Delhi Administration*, AIR 1973 SC 1091: (1973) 3 SCR 533.
2. Seervai H.M., Constitutional Law of India, 4th Edn., p. 710 New Delhi: Universal Law Publishing Co. Pvt. Ltd., 1991.

The difference between freedom of speech as enshrined in Indian Constitution and American Constitution was explained by Douglas J. in *Kingsley Corporation* v. *Regents of the University of New York,*[1] where a motion picture titled 'Lady Chatterley's Lover' was denied a license to be screened because "its subject matter was adultery and it was presented as right and desirable for certain people under certain circumstances", under the provisions of New York Educational Law that made it "unlawful to exhibit, or to sell, lease or lend for exhibition at any place of amusement for pay or in connection with any business in the state of New York, any motion picture film or reel (with certain exceptions not relevant here), unless there is at the time in full force and effect a valid license or permit therefore of the education department."[2] The law also provided that a license shall issue "unless such film or a part thereof is obscene, indecent, immoral, inhuman, sacrilegious, or is of such a character that its exhibition would tend to corrupt morals or incite to crime."[3]

Justice Douglas stated that United States does not have a provision in Constitution for reasonable regulation of the press such as India has included in its Constitution, that is why an argument can not be sustained that censorship in the interest of morality can be permissible in United States. That is why he held that Law to be unconstitutional as it violated first amendment to the Constitution which protects free speech without any restrictions. Indian Law permits censorship of freedom of speech on the grounds of morality under article 19. Hence any law which is made to regulate freedom of press in India can be upheld on the ground of State protecting morality but not in United States.

Free Speech and the Internet

The regulation of cyberspace in relation to free speech is a very difficult task. Internet websites are huge in numbers and it is not possible to keep an eye on the content of every website. According to digital libertarian philosophy, the nation state has no right to regulate any matter relating to the internet and in fact they can not do so, even if they wish.[4] This makes it explicitly clear that regulation of speech on internet is totally impossible.

Indian Constitution protects free speech and expression under article 191(a) of the Constitution that provides a right to freedom of speech and expression to every citizen. However, article 19(2) provides for reasonable restrictions upon such freedom on the ground of sovereignty and integrity of India, the security of state, friendly relation with foreign state, public order, decency and morality, as well as with relation to contempt of Court, defamation and contempt of Court.

According to D.D. Basu, legislations that impose restrictions on freedom of speech can be curtailed only if:—

1. 360 US 684 (1959).
2. McKinney's N.Y. Laws, 1953, Education Law, 129.
3. McKinney's N.Y. Laws, 1953, Education Law, 122.
4. Raman Chima, "The regulation of internet with relation to speech and expression by the Indian State", full article available at http://papers.ssrn.com/sol3/papers.cfm?abstract_id=1237262.

(a) It must be imposed by law:

(b) Such law must be made by the 'State'.

(c) Such law must be valid.

(d) The restriction must be proximately related to any of the grounds specified in the limitation clauses put in place by article 19(2)(6), which here would specifically be those grounds mentioned by article 19(2).

(e) The restriction imposed by the law must be reasonable.[1]

The word 'law' is explained in article 13(3)(a) of the Indian Constitution that states " 'law' includes any Ordinance, order, bye-law, rule, regulation, notification, custom or usage having in the territory of India the force of law." Hence, restrictions can be imposed by any ordinance, order, bye-law, rule, regulation, notification, customs or usage but they must be made with authority provided to the legislature by the Constitution.

Internet has varieties of communication methods including e-mail, video chat and chat-rooms. All these methods are capable of transferring electronic messages, pictures, movies, video clippings. With the evolution of group ID facility, an e-mail can be sent to enormous number of people with just one click. Thousands of people converse on internet in various chat rooms and exchange varieties of ideas and thoughts. They also exchange images, stories and video clippings without any check on the nature of the content.

It has become very easy to gain information on a particular topic with the evolution of search engines. For example, typing 'porn' on Google search engine produces more than 174, 000,000 results. These websites are impossible to be monitored by any Government agencies. There are many websites on the internet that provide adult content. Many of them have specific instructions which has to be followed before entering into the website.

Many adult websites contain warnings regarding possibility of availability of content that is not suitable for the minors and ask the surfer to confirm that he is more than 18 years old. However, most of the adult websites have no mechanism to ensure that the person entering their website is actually more than 18 years old and end up providing indiscriminate access to every one irrespective of their age. However, when the net user wants to purchase some content available on the website then he is asked to verify his credit card account but by then it becomes too late because the net user had accessed most of the adult content available on the website which is sufficient to deprave and corrupt the mind of the net user.

Internet Regulation in India

Supreme Court of India has accepted that the protection of free speech as enshrined in Indian Constitution in article 19(1)(a) extends to all possible media of communications. In case of *Life Insurance Corporation* v. *Manu Bhai Shah*,[2] Justice Ahmadi opined that the right to freedom of speech under Indian Constitution "includes the right to propagate one's views through the print media or through

1. D.D. Basu, p. 2136.
2. AIR 1993 SC 171: (1992) 3 SCR 595.

any other communication channel including radio and television." The 'phrase any other means' is not limited in its scope and followed by the word 'including'.

Even in the case of *Secretary, Ministry of Information and Broadcasting* v. *Cricket Association of Bengal,*[1] also Supreme Court agreed that right to communicate includes communication through any means of media including print or electronic, audio-visual advertisement, movie or speech. In a recent case also, Supreme Court's view that any person is free to impart, receive and seek information in any form of media of his own choice is sufficient to include internet as a means of communication which is well covered within the protection granted to free speech under article 19(1)(a) of Indian Constitution.[2] Hence, it can be said that right to freedom of speech under Indian Constitution includes right to propagate one's views through internet also.

Now it yet remains to see how much of reasonable restrictions can be imposed on internet by the legislature. After the recent amendment in Information Technology Act, 2000, section 69A was introduced in the Act. This Act took away the power to ban porn websites from the Government and conferred this power wholly upon the Courts to decide whether the porn websites are liable to be banned on the ground of decency and morality as provided in article 19(2). Before this Amendment Government could have made a legislation banning pornographic website for preventing incitement to the commission of a cognizable offence that included obscenity which is a charge liable to be imposed against porn websites. However, the new provision limits the power to block these websites only to protect sovereignty and integrity of India, defense of India, security of State, friendly relation with foreign states and public order. The newly introduced provision nowhere talks about banning porn websites on the ground of obscenity and therefore takes away the power to ban websites including desibaba.com and savitabhabhi.com as viewing those websites are not capable of inciting a public order problem such as riot.[3]

However, banning websites is still possible by the Government if it is possible to interpret the word 'public order' in a manner that it means to include an obscenity. If it can be proved that obscenity is a public order offence, then the publishing of these websites will become commission of an offense relating to public order and the Government will have power to block the websites.

Public order crime means "crime which involves acts that interfere with the operations of society and the ability of people to function properly *i.e.,* it is behaviour that has been labelled as criminal because it is contrary to shared norms, social values and customs."[4] A crime of publication of pornographic websites on internet is absolutely a behaviour which is contrary to shared norms

---

1. AIR 1995 SC 1236.
2. *Director General, Directorate General of Doordarshan* v. *Anand Patwardhan,* AIR 2006 SC 3346: (2006) 8 SCC 433.
3. http://timesofindia.indiatimes.com/india/Govt-cant-ban-porn-websites-for-obscenity/articleshow/5558110.cms
4. www.naavi.org/cl_editorial_0_edit_feb_2_2010_savita_2htm

and social values of society. Hence publication of pornographic websites may be considered commission of offence relating to public order and it can be prohibited by the Government.

Censor Board is not able to resolve the problem of pornography because almost all new films are released simultaneously on DVD and after sometime they are released on satellite channels and also viewed on camera phones and internet websites.[1] So, even if an Adult certificate is granted to a movie, it is extremely difficult to say that the viewing of such movie is going to be restricted to Adults only.

Chief Justice of India has also realized the need to ban porn website immediately.[2] According to him blanket ban on all porn websites is not feasible but distinguishing between Network Service Providers, website operators and individual users for the purpose of placing liability for wrongful Acts is important to impose liability for wrongful acts.[2] Hence an overhauling of present position of law is required to set the extent of ban that can be imposed upon porn websites and also to set up distinct liabilities upon Network Service Providers, website operators and other individuals.

Forfeiture

Section 95 of Code of Criminal Procedure provides procedure of forfeiture of obscene material. This section provides that if any newspaper, or book or any document appears to the State Government to contain any matter the publication of which is punishable under section 292 and section 293 of Indian Penal Code, then the State Government may by notification declare that every copy of the issue of the newspaper containing such matter, and every copy of such book or other documents to be forfeited to the Government. However, it is imperative to the Government to state the grounds of its opinion. After such declaration is passed, any police officer may seize the material and any magistrate may authorize a police officer to enter upon and search for the prohibited material in any premise where any copy of such issue or any such book or other document may be or reasonably suspected to be.[3]

The next section of the Code of Criminal Procedure provides the mechanism of obtaining an order to set aside such declaration of forfeiture. However, such an application can only be made to High Court. Any Person who has any interest in any newspaper, book or other newspaper, book or other document can make an application to the High Court within 2 moths from the date of publication of declaration of forfeiture in Official Gazette. It is not necessary that the person applying for such declaration must be the author, producer or publisher of the material. Any person who can show any kind of interest may apply to set aside

1. http://www.genderit.org/upload/ad6d215b74e2a8613f0cf5416c9f3865/SearchHistory.pdf
2. www.timesofindia.indiatimes.com/india//urgent-need-to-ban-porn-websites-chief-justice-of-india/articleshow/5520211.cms
3. Section 95 of Code of Criminal Procedure, 1973.

forfeiture. However, he has to prove that the material so declared to be forfeited does not contain any matter prohibited under section 292.[1]

In case of *Manish Jani* v. *State of Gujarat*,[2] the petitioners contended that the notification issued by Gujarat Government under section 95 banning display, sale and distribution of any kind of use of the book named 'Jinnah-India, Partition and Independence written by Jaswant Singh has infringed their fundamental right to read comprehend and criticize its content which is covered within the write of freedom of speech and expression guaranteed by article 19(1)(a) of Constitution. They further contended that even if they do not agree with the opinions expressed in the book but they have the right to read, understand and express their free opinion about the book.

The declaration of the Government was challenged on the ground that the Government did not express any opinion on the contents of the book as to how the contents of the book are 'misleading to the public' and 'against public tranquility and interest of the state.'

The Court analyzed the notification that denoted that 'it has come to the notice of the Government of Gujarat about publication of the book.' This notification does not denote that Government is aware of the content of the book and it is not discernible from the text of the notice that in what manner the content is objectionable and against the interest of the state. Section 95 requires the state to form an opinion based on reasonable grounds that have to be stated in the notification issued under section 95. Since, this was not done in this case, so the notification was set aside.

In this case the Court did not deny that the fundamental right to freedom of speech allows any person to challenge its violation in the form of challenging bans imposed upon books that he has right to read. Hence even if reasonable restrictions have been imposed in the form of sections 95 and 96 but fundamental rights to freedom of speech protects a person from devoiding him of the content which he is entitled to.

---

1. Section 96 of Code of Criminal Procedure, 1973.
2. Criminal Misc. Application No. 9865 of 2009.

CHAPTER 7

SOLUTION, ENFORCEMENT AND RECOMMENDATION

General Solution to the Problem of Pornography

Following Guidelines of Journalistic Norms

Newspapers must follow the guidelines that are made for them and mentioned in the norms of journalistic conduct. Such guidelines are also made for TV serial producers and owners of TV channels so that the distribution of pornographic content through these channels could be regulated.

Programmes like "Midnight Hot' which were being shown on Fashion TV were banned for broadcasting obscene content on television. The television channel named Fashion TV itself has been banned for 9 days for broadcasting pornographic content including showing topless women.[1] These incidents indicate that the Government of India has realized the need of preventing broadcasting of pornographic content on television. These incidents indicate that the guidelines are not being followed by television channel operators and programme creators and a committee must be formed to ensure that these guidelines are followed by those channels properly.

Pornography Cell

Specialized police forces to deal with problems of piracy and pornography must be established. These problems are not inferior to the problems of terrorism and drugs-smuggling. The money involved in terrorism and drugs smuggling is earned through piracy and pornography. The involvement of Dawood Ibrahim in the piracy business is the proof of the bondage between pornography, piracy and terrorism.[2] Pornography cells must be created in the same manner cyber cells are created to deal with the problems of pornography.

Enforcing Anti-trafficking Laws

Pornography and sex trafficking have a very strong linkage with each other. Women and children who are trafficked in India have been exposed to unprecedented vulnerabilities and commercial exploitation of these vulnerabilities has become an organized crime in India.[3] These women and children are trafficked for forced prostitution, sex tourism, circuses, beer bars and pornography.[3]

---

1. http://timesofindia.indiatimes.com/india/Govt-bans-FTV-for-nine-days-for-showing-women-topless/articleshow/5671786.cms
2. http://timesofindia.indiatimes.com/india/Film-piracy-funding-terror-US-thinktank/articleshow/4237371.cms
3. Dr. Intezar Khan, "Child Trafficking in India: A concern", available at *india.gov.in/allimpfrms/alldocs/12262.pdf.*

Special Acts such as Goa Children's Act deal with problems of trafficking in a very effective manner. The provisions of this Act are very helpful to curb pornography. Sections 2(i) and (ii) that define 'sexual assault' and 'grave sexual assault' cover almost every type of sexual exploitation by defining the terms to cover sexual touching of body parts of children, showing pornographic pictures to minors, all types of intercourse including oral, vaginal and anal and making children pose for pornographic videos and photos. Section 3(i) imposes an obligation on state to ensure that the children are protected from all forms of sexual exploitation. Section 8(10)(c) imposes obligation on hotels and other establishments having internet facility to ensure that no child has access to any internet facility that is not fitted with filters and contains objectionable matters not suitable for children. Section 8(14) makes it mandatory to report to appropriate authority pornographic pictures of children if found by developer of such pornographic pictures.

Such laws must be made by the legislatures of all states to protect sex-trafficking of children so that raw material supply to pornographic industry in India could be effectively stopped.

Cybercafé Regulation

Cyber Cafés are not only a place for facilitating distribution of pornographic content but also serve as a tool for facilitating terrorist activities and providing easy access to cyber criminals. We have already seen that cyber cafés have been used in preparation of pornographic content and other crimes such as blackmailing and piracy by criminals in Pakistan. There is thus a strong need to regulate cyber cafes to curb the problem of pornography in India.

Cyber Cafes are included in the definition of 'intermediary' in Information Technology Act, 2000.[1] They are entitled to avail the defenses available to them under the Information Technology Act, 2000. That also means the several liabilities that can be imposed upon intermediaries can also be imposed upon Cyber Café operators. The need for regulation of cyber café is strongly felt after recent terrorist attacks in which information between the terrorists were transferred with the use of cyber café by protecting their anonymity. That is why many states have enacted regulations for cyber café.[2]

However, the presence of these regulations is not sufficient to curb the problems of facilitation of pornography, terrorism and other computer related fraud. A Central Authority to monitor the activities of cyber café and ensure the compliance with regulations made by government must be established.

Banning Camera Mobiles

The first step that should be taken towards dealing with pornography is to ban camera phones in schools. The Delhi Public School MMS case and AIR Force Bharati School case are examples of situations where the students have used

1. Section 2(na) of The Information Technology Act, 2000.
2. For example Karnataka has its own Cyber Café regulations in which cyber café is defined as "Any premises where the Cyber Cafe Owner/Network Service Provider provides the computer services including internet access to the public".

mobile cameras to prepare pornographic videos of their schoolmates. The banning of camera phones inside school campuses may also help in curbing the problems like 'sexting' and MMS circulation.

Installing Filtering Software's

Content Control Softwares that are also known as filtering software provide very feasible solution to prevent access to pornography from users of internet including children. Safe Eyes, Cyber patrol and filter parks are amongst the top ten content filtering softwares designed to filter online content.[1] In Cuba, filtering is done at a national level and certain websites are blocked all over country.[2] Though in India, there is no need of national filtering of internet but parents, network providers in Schools, colleges Universities, Corporates and Government Departments may install these filtering softwares to prevent pornography from being circulating in their network.

Making Complaints

The main reason behind blossoming of pornography is the lack of interest in making complaints to the authorities by the people. There are laws which mandate a person aware of an offence to inform the authorities on commission of offence[3] but these laws are useless until people actually feel bound by them and follow them.

Normally people forbid themselves from complaining because they fear that they will offend someone or their voices will not be heard by the authorities. For example, a cable TV customer fears from reporting the transmission of adult content by his Cable TV operator because he fears that if his identity is revealed then he will never get a cable connection. A child victim of pornography may fear from revealing the commission of crime due to fear from revelation of his identity in public that may create trouble for his future and career.

The police authorities must ensure that the complainant's complaint is addressed and redressed properly. The law must also admit anonymous FIR and place it at the same pedestal as other FIRs so that the people who fear from reporting the pornographic content may report it to the authorities.

People must report distribution of adult content if they see it distributing on websites like amazon.com and ebay.com etc. to the concerned authorities and every such website must provide a complaint redressed mechanism either in the form of customer care service or in the form of complaint section.

Solution to Porn Spamming

Many a times when we surf the internet, we encounter websites that promote adult content, even if we do not intend to open them. Sites like beatfiltering.com introduce adware while surfing internet through those websites for bypassing IP address. An adware is a form of spyware that collects information about the user in order to display advertisements in the web browser based on the information

---

1. http://internet-filter-review.toptenreviews.com/
2. http://www.rsf.org/IMG/pdf/rapport_gb_md_1.pdf
3. Section 39 of Criminal Procedure Code, 1973.

it collects from the user's browsing patterns.[1] These adwares are mostly harmless but sometimes they also contain addresses of pornographic websites and ask for personal information.

Sometimes we provide our personal information including e-mail address to trusted website for creating an e-mail account and this personal information is stolen from these websites by the means of hacking or sold illegally to porn sites. These sites then start sending e-mails to the receivers containing pornographic content. Such e-mails are known as Unsolicited Commercial E-mails (UCE).

In such cases, if a person receives a spam containing adult content, the law prohibits further communication with the sender of such messages in order to facilitate further transmission of such mail.[2] Hence, the receiver must not reply to the sender of the mail and should search for any link which indicates to 'unsubscribe'. But this is not a fool-proof solution to the problem of porn spamming. The act of unsubscribing to the e-mail address indicates that your e-mail address is functional. Hence, the pornographers may sell the details of your functional e-mail address in higher prices to others. The buyer of such functional e-mail address may continue spamming to your e-mail account. Hence, the best way is to complain your Internet Service Provider or the Internet Service Provider of the sender so that they may block such spamming. To find out the ISP of the sender, look at the domain name of the email address of the sender. For example, in brajesh420@gmail.com, the domain name is gmail.com. A complain can be made to gmail.com about the misuse of their e-mail address and gmail.com is bound to interrogate into the misuse of their e-mail address according to the laws related to intermediary liability, as provided under section 79 of Information Technology Act, 2000. If they fail to interrogate the complaint and deactivate such e-mail account then a liability may be imposed upon them.[3]

Blocking of Pornographic Content for Local Users

Search Engines such as Google may block search of words like 'hardcore sex', 'porn' and other like words in their search engines. Microsoft's search engine Bing blocks out pornographic content for local users. For example, when a user types 'sex', 'XXX'or 'porn' in the search box, then the search engine displays a message like, "your country or region requires a strict Bing Safe Search Setting, which filters out results that might return adult content".[4] However, many other search engines do not follow the same and display content and information of websites that return adult content.

The pornographic content on internet is huge in amount. It is impossible to regulate or prohibit the pornographic content that is present on internet. However the access to such content can be prohibited if the all search engines follow the same way which is followed by Bing Search Engine. Any net user gets to know

---

1. Webopedia.com/TERM/adware.html
2. 'it amounts to cause to be transmitted in section 67 of Information Technology Act, 2000.
3. Obscenitycrimes.org/pornspam.php
4. www.deamonnews.org/internet/2950-pornography-filters-in-india-have-little-impact.html

about most of the adult content by the results which are returned by search engines. If all search engine block search of adult content then access to pornography in India can be restricted to a large extent.

There are content filtering softwares available in the market such as maxnet and Ihug. An e-mail-user may turn off loading of images from the web in the e-mail account without permission. These features are available in Gmail. Norton Internet Security Software also contains features such as spam filtering, website blocking and personal firewall. These features can be used to prohibit porn viewing on internet. While working on a Local Area Network, a proxy server with content filters such as Squidguard and densguardian can be installed. These programmes work by maintaining a blacklist for banned sites and also by creating specific criteria such as limiting the size of files that can be downloaded from the internet or blocking sites with particular extensions.[1]

Recommendations

Mere Viewing of Adult Pornography must also be Penalized

In the first chapter of the book we have seen that moral harm is also harm and pornography causes moral harm to its viewers including children. It is a fallacy in Indian Law that viewing child pornography is an offence but viewing adult pornography is not an offense. The offense of pornography is based on the capability of material that is able to deprave and corrupt the minds of people who are likely to read, see or hear it. Viewing pornography on websites certainly has the capability of depraving the person who is viewing it. Watching it on the internet is not a self regarding activity of a person because a person who is depraved and corrupted by viewing such material is a threat to society. We have seen reports in the first chapter that settles that sex offenders are encouraged by viewing such content to commit sexual offences.

Even if viewing pornography is considered a self regarding activity then also there is nothing in Indian Law which prevents the state from making a Law that affects the self regarding activity of a person. The state has the power to utilize the tool of law for parenting the members of society. State is a guardian of its citizens. The presence of section 377 in Indian Penal Code is an example of state's power of law-making on self regarding activity which penalizes unnatural intercourse. Unnatural intercourse between two people is a self regarding activity; even then the law penalizes it. Similarly viewing pornography is also a self regarding activity, the law must penalize it.

Not only is an amendment required in Information Technology Act, 2000 but also in section 292 of Indian Penal Code. The Code does not prohibit making a pornographic video not for the purpose of sale or with the intent of public exhibition. Mere possession of such video must be penalized by law under Indian Penal Code. Indian law prohibits both killing someone else and suicide. It is incomprehensible that it is a crime to deprave someone but if someone wants to be depraved then he is permitted to do so.

---

1. www.createtit.co.nz/index.mvc?ArticleID-152

No Definition of Pornography

No law in India defines what pornography is. Even if pornography is treated as aggravated form of Obscenity by Indian Courts[1] but the punishments for pornography and other associated crimes are similar in nature. For example, if a person beats a child and creates a pornographic video of a child depicting anal, vaginal and oral intercourse and distributes in the market and a person who has written Lady Chatterley's Lover are entitled to same punishment under Indian Law. There should be a separate category of law dealing with offense of pornography. Special provisions must be made for the offense of distribution of hardcore pornographic content and punishment for such offense must be higher than punishment for distribution of obscene content.

If it is not possible to make separate provision for the offense of pornography then certain amendments must be done in the explanation of obscenity given in section 292 of Indian Penal Code. The explanation of obscenity given in section 292 is a mingle-mangle of words that are vague and uncertain. Words like 'prurient interest' have not been defined in the code and it is tough to demarcate what is prurient interest and how it is distinguishable from other interests of mankind.

It is not clear as to what is meant by the words 'deprave' and 'corrupt.' There are no specific criteria to determine whether an object have the tendency to deprave and corrupt the mind of persons who are likely to read, hear or see it. It is completely left upon the Courts to determine the tendency of an object and the judges in India are free to determine the tendency based on their own perception of decency, morality and freedom. The Legislature must attempt to lay down specific criteria such as whether the work depicts sex in bad light, whether the work depicts sexual assault and whether it dehumanizes and degrades human being. Based on these criteria the judiciary must determine the tendency of an object.

109th Law Commission Report of India received a comment that definition of obscenity in Indian Penal Code must be reframed so as to provide that matter which is capable of arousing lustful thought, action or sensation should be regarded as obscene.[2] Though the need for such amendment in the definition was rejected by the Law Commission but this definition must be included in section 292. Even if this definition does not provide any special help to the judiciary in determination of obscenity, it at least is not a hotchpotch of words having uncertain meanings.

Hence, either the words such as 'prurient interest', 'deprave' and 'corrupt' must be defined in the Code itself or the whole definition of obscenity in Indian Penal Code must be substituted to make it clear.

Community Standard Test

Section 292 of Indian Penal Code nowhere talks about community standards. Community Standards are very important criteria to judge the effect of an object

1. *Samaresh Bose* v. *Amal Mitra,* AIR 1986 SC 967: 1986 Cr LJ 24.
2. 109th Law Commission Report on Obscene and Indecent Advertisement and Displays, section 292-293 of Indian Penal Code, 12 (1985), at 10.

on the people who are likely to read, hear or see it. The test of community standard must be added in section 292, which must be reframed as, "if the effect of any one of its item if taken as a whole, applying contemporary community standards, such as to tend to deprave and corrupt person who are likely, having regard to all circumstances, to read, see or hear the matter contained or embodied in it."

Even though community standard can not be defined by way of definition and we have to rely upon judges to guide us what are the community standards of society but addition of test of community standard in section 292 is very important because a material may be obscene in India but not in the United States on the basis of community standards. For example, the book named 'Lady Chatterley's Lover' was not considered obscene in United Kingdom but it was considered obscene in India. This fact clearly indicates that community standards are very important in determination of obscene content in India. There are other examples also which indicates the importance of community standards. The depiction of 'Shiva- Lingam' may arouse lustful thoughts and appeal to prurient interests of a Nigerian, Pakistani or Chinese but it is certainly not capable of arousing lustful thoughts and appealing to prurient interests of a Shaivite in India. Hence, in India, the depiction of 'Shiva-Lingam' cannot be adjudged obscene applying cotemporary community standards.

One more thing has to be kept in mind while considering the test of community standard. The community standards that are taken into consideration must be contemporary. Community Standards are not static and bound to change according to place and time. Those standards must be national and not regional as applied in United States.[1] Indian Culture is shared culture of different religion and divided in many regions that have their different regional standards. If regional standards are made applicable then it will become a cumbersome task to determine the obscene nature of the material. Hence, the best thing is to apply national standards in determination of obscene nature of the object.

The Community Standard test must not only be added in section 292 of Indian Penal Code but also in section 67 of Information Technology Act, 2000 that deals with online pornography. Newly developing websites are able to create verities of content with the help of animation softwares that are capable of creating forms of pornography that is way beyond the imagination of ordinary member of society.[2] To decide the obscene nature of such content, recourse must necessarily be taken to community standard of society.

Power of Officials

The search and arrest powers given to police officers are without any definite guidelines and may be misused.[3] The Act gives very wide powers to officers not below the rank of inspector to arrest anybody on the suspicion of commission of offense on internet However; it does not clearly identify the conditions in which

1. *Kahm* v. *United States*, 300 F 2d 78 (1962).
2. For example www.boiledalive.com
3. Sudhir Shah, India: Cyber Law, New Information Technology Legislation, 11 (7) International Company and Commercial Law Review 3 (2000).

the officers should act. In absence of laying down such conditions police officers are not sure when and where they should arrest a person found committing offense in cyber world. Specific guidelines must be laid down with respect to arrest of persons involved in cyber crime.

In absence of proper guidelines, occurrence of misuse of section 67 of Indian Penal Code is visible in India. There have been instances where this provision must have been invoked but was not had invoked and where it must not have been invoked but was invoked.[1] An example was seen in Delhi where section 67 was misused by Police Officials and a person was wrongly charged under it. Mr. Avinash Bansal complained that one Mr. Rohit was making abusive telephone calls and sending filthy SMS messages containing words such as 'motherfucker', 'fucking' and 'fuck.' On the basis of this complaint an FIR was registered against the accused and he was sent to Tihar Jail.[1] However, there is no offense which is made out against the accused in this case within section 67 of Information Technology Act. Section 67 of Information Technology Act punishes publishing or transmitting or causing to be published in the electronic form, any material which is lascivious or appeals to the prurient interest or if its effect is such as to tend to deprave and corrupt persons. The messages sent by accused to the complainant may be abusive and filthy but they are not capable of arousing the prurient interest of the complainant. These messages are only capable of encouraging feeling of anger and anxiety and not unchaste and lustful ideas in the mind of complainant. Hence in this case there was no need of introducing section 67 of Information Technology Act.

The above case clearly reveals the possibility of problems that can occur due to lack of proper guidelines and training of police officials. Hence there is an imperative need of laying down proper guidelines with respect to power of officials while investigating offenses under Information Technology Act.

Storing of Obscene Material

Section 67 could be amended to include storing of the pornographic content also. There are online files sharing websites like *www.file4share.com*, *www.rapishare.com* and *www.filesharing.com* that provided unlimited sharing space over internet. Most of the pornographic content is stored on filesharing websites and the link to such websites is provided on pornographic websites. A person interested in downloading such content has to follow the link and go to file-sharing websites where the content is stored.

The present section 67 can punish the file-sharing website for making available the pornographic content to net users because such act of file storing on website may amount to publication of material. However, this provision does not cover storing of pornographic material in electronic form by a person. For example if pornographic content is found stored in my hard drive then I will not be liable either under section 292 of Indian Penal Code or section 67 of Information Technology Act, 2000.

1. http://www.neerajaarora.com/blatant-misuse-of-information-technology-act/

Courts in United States have stated accepted browsing and storing pornographic content is covered within the purview of word 'making.'[1] Section 292 of Indian Penal Code makes it an offense to 'make and produce' obscene material for the purpose of sale, hire, distribution, public exhibition or circulation. However, in India, obscenity in electronic form is covered within Information Technology Act. This Act does not make it an offense to 'make and produce' obscene material other than creation of child pornography. It has been argued earlier also that adult pornography is no less harmful than child pornography. It is submitted that 'creation of adult pornography' in electronic form must also be made an offense under Information Technology Act. Hence an amendment must be done in section 67 of Information Technology Act to reframe it as 'whoever creates, any text or digital images, collects, seeks, browses, downloads, advertises, publishes or transmits or causes to be published in the electronic form, any material which is lascivious or appeals to the prurient interest or if its effect is such as to tend to deprave and corrupt persons who are likely, having regard to all relevant circumstances, to read, see or hear the matter contained or embodied in it, shall be ....'

Punishment

The offence of pornography is covered under section 292 of Indian Penal Code. The definition of offence of obscenity is similar in Indian Penal Code and Information Technology Act. However, the punishment in both the provisions for the offense of distribution of obscenity is different. This situation creates specific advantage to the criminal who are distributing pornography other than by electronic means because those who distribute pornography by mediums other than electronic means would rather be prosecuted under Indian Penal Code and would receive lesser punishment.

Any person if prosecuted under Indian Penal Code would receive imprisonment not exceeding two years and fine not extending two thousand rupees on first conviction. It is submitted that the amount of fine under this section is too less considering the huge profit involved in pornography business. Hence the amount of fine must also be increased in section 292 of Indian Penal Code and the period of imprisonment must be increased to keep it at par with the amount of fine and period of imprisonment mentioned in section 67 of Information Technology Act.

Introduction of New Offences

The Information Technology Act extends the applicability of certain offences under Indian Penal Code to Electronic Media and overlooks a lot of new offences.[2] The Information Technology Act, 2000, is primarily meant to be a legislation to promote e-commerce. It is not very effective in dealing with several emerging cyber crimes like cyber harassment, defamation, stalking and so on.[3] These crimes are

1. *R.* v. *Smith and Jayson,* (2002) EWCA Crim 683.
2. Pawan Duggal, "Cyber Crime in India" Roderic G. Broadhurst, Peter N. Grabosky, cybercrime, 187.
3. Gopika Vaidya-Kapoor, 'Byte by Byte' available at http://www.rediff.com/search/2003/feb/18crime.htm

associated crimes of pornography. Morphed images of teenagers are created by stalking on their public profiles on internet where the teenagers upload their profiles. The offences like cyber defamation and criminal intimidation are committed after preparation of pornographic images, video or photographs of the victim. Those who post personal information about themselves on job and marriage websites or social networking websites are the one who become prospective victims of 'cyber-stalking'.[1]

The problem of porn advertising is not only limited to internet. It has also spread its legs in the market of mobile phones. Pornographic Content is being advertised by way of mobile spamming. Most of the porn websites on internet have mechanism of registering mobile number of users. These websites also receive mobile numbers of receivers of mobile spam through cyber stalking, hacking and illegal sale of information. Then they send advertisement of pornographic content which is available on their website. The uninterested receivers treat those advertisements as nuisance but interested receivers buy such content and go on to the extent of showing such pornographic content to children.[2]

Section 292(c) of Indian Penal Code punishes any person who advertises or make known by any means whatsoever that any person is engaged or is ready to engage in any act which is offense under this section or any such material can be procured from or through any person. The solution to problem of pornographic advertising can be solved by enacting a similar provision in Information Technology Act. The insertion of new provision in Information Technology Act would penalize offense of advertising pornographic material in electronic form via internet or MMS services. It can be argued that offense of advertising pornographic material can be said to be covered within section 67 of the Act within the words 'causing to be published.' However, section 67B that deals with publication and transmission of child pornography in electronic form also includes the same phrase 'causes to be published.' The presence of 'advertising' in section 67B separately[3] which is absent in section 67 clearly indicates that legislature did not attempt to prohibit advertising of adult pornography. However, the veracity of such argument is not yet tested by Indian Courts. In any case, enacting a provision to deal with advertising porn in the manner it is enacted in section 292 of Indian Penal Code would only serve the purpose of giving more clarification to the invalidity of pornographic advertising in India.

Recommendation on Section 292

Section 292(1) of the Indian Penal Code which deals with definition of obscenity reads 'For the purpose of sub-section (2) a book, a pamphlet, paper, writing, drawing, painting, representation, figure or any other object, shall be deemed to be obscene.......' However, section 292(2)(a) of Indian Penal Code that

1. Address by Honorable K.G. Balakrishnan, 'National Consultation on enforcement of cyber law' available at www.supremecourtofindia.nic.in/.../National_consultation_on_Cyber_Law_31-1-10.pdf
2. http://news.oneindia.in/2009/09/08/up-teacher-accused-of-showing-porn-to-students.html.
3. Section 67B(b).

deals with punishment reads as 'whoever sells, lets to hire, distributes, publicly exhibits or in any manner puts into circulation.... any obscene book, pamphlet, paper, drawing painting, representation or figure or any other obscene object whatsoever .....'

In the above paragraph it is clear that legislature seems to have committed a glaring error in not including the word 'writing' in section 292(2)(a) of Indian Penal Code that deals with punishment. It cannot be possible that an object shall be deemed to be obscene but the sale is not. Distribution and circulation of it is not made an offense under section 292(2)(a) of Indian Penal Code that prohibits sale, letting to hire, distribution, public exhibition and circulation of obscene material. However, it can be argued that the phrase 'any other obscene object whatsoever' covers pornography in written form also.[1] Such a view is plausible but it is better to insert the word 'writing' to avoid any sort of confusion that may arise in future due to absence of word drawing in section 292(2)(a) of Indian Penal Code.

Jury System

A suggestion was made to the Law Commission of India about the introduction of jury system in trial of charges of obscenity. The suggestion was based on the assumption that at present judges are taking too liberal a view of the law.[1] However, the Law Commission rejected the necessity of jury system because they did not think that judges are taking too liberal view of section 292.

A series of cases including *Chandrakant Kalyandas Kakodar* v. *State of Maharastra*[2] and *Maqbool Fida Hussain* v. *Raj Kumar Pandey*,[3] case seems to suggest that judges are taking too liberal view of section 292. In the case of M.F. Hussain the Supreme Court went on to demarcate Indian society as a tolerant society. In words of Supreme Court, 'Our culture breeds tolerance-both in thoughts and in action.' Justice Sanjay Kishan Kaul who laid down judgment in this case accepted that he has penned down the judgment for encouraging greater tolerance. Now there is no other proof necessary to show that the judges in India are taking too liberal view of laws relating to pornography.

Hence, it is a better option to introduce jury system to decide the obscene nature of material. A jury is best fitted to determine the contemporary community standard and judge a book on the basis of this.

Expert Evidence

A recommendation was made by Law Commission of India in 42nd Report on Indian Penal Code about insertion of sub-section (3) to section 292 of the Indian Penal Code for admission of expert evidence in following words:—

> "(3) Where, in any prosecution under this section, the question is whether the publication of any book, pamphlet, paper, writing, drawing, painting, representation of figure is in the interest of science, literature, art

1. 109th Law Commission Report on Obscene and Indecent Advertisement and Displays, section 292-293 of Indian Penal Code, 12 (1985), at 10, 11.
2. AIR 1970 SC 1390: 1970 Cr LJ 1273.
3. 2008 Cr LJ 4107: (2008) 2 JCC 1433.

or learning or other object of general concern, the opinion of experts as to scientific, literary, artistic, academic or other merit may be admitted in evidence."[1]

This provision makes it optional for the judges to take opinion of experts if the publisher or distributor of obscene content claims any public good defense. The Supreme Court of India has also accepted that recourse may be taken to the opinion of expert evidence to determine the scientific, literary, artistic, academic or other merits of the material in question.[2] Hence, insertion of such provision will not contravene the existing position of law.

Opinion of experts on ground of merits of material in question becomes very important in situations where the Court itself is not conversant with the language of the book. In such an eventuality opinion of experts to determine the question of obscenity also becomes relevant. Hence, in situations where the Court is not conversant with the language of the material in question, recourse to expert evidence must be taken and a provision in this regard must be inserted in Indian Penal Code. Hence a new subsection must be inserted that should read as,

"Where in prosecution under this section or under 67 of Information Technology Act, the question is whether the publication of any book, pamphlet, paper, writing, drawing, painting, representation of figure is in the interest of science, literature, art or learning or other objects, or where the language of the such material is one the Court is not conversant with and the question is whether such material is obscene or not, the opinion of experts can be taken recourse to."

Such a provision may also provide substitute for need of establishing jury system in case of judging obscenity or literary merit of the work. A preference must be given to admission of expert evidence to determine both, the obscene nature of content and the literary merit of work. However, such a view will render the work of judges meaningless and also contravene the established position of law that it is only the job of judges and only judges to determine whether the work is obscene or not.[2] Hence, the amendment proposed in the manner provided in above paragraph is the best option that does not contravene with existing position of law also.

A tribunal system that is established to determine the question of obscenity of a work is also a workable solution in India. The opinion of experts may be taken independently or through establishment of a tribunal consisted of various experts. In this system the question of obscenity is determined by independent tribunals which consist of experienced members of the bar or solicitors, and also of persons qualified in the fields of literature, education and the social sciences.[3]

However, it is important to see that the members of tribunal follow the criteria given in obscenity Laws in India to decide obscenity. This Tribunal must not only be sought reference to in cases where the prosecution against a book has been

---

1. 156th Law Commission Report on Indian Penal Code, 424 (1997).
2. *Samaresh Bose* v. *Amal Mitra*, AIR 1986 SC 967.
3. Vishnu D. Sharma and F. Wooldridge, The Law Relating to Obscene Publications in India 22(4) The International and Comparative Law Quarterly 632, 645 (October, 1973).

initiated but in cases where a publisher suspects his book to be obscene too. In cases where a publisher suspects that his book may be obscene and thus prohibited within the purview of section 292 of Indian Penal Code, he may make an application to the tribunal to judge whether the book is obscene or not.

Blackmailing

There have been increasing cases in India where the pornographers have made obscene video clips of girls and blackmailed them for their dirty deeds. Recently two youths were arrested in Jaipur for allegedly blackmailing a girl after obtaining obscene MMS.[1] In Goa also, a girl allegedly committed suicide after her obscene MMS became public and she was being blackmailed.[2] A 26 year old businessman lured a girl and made her obscene MMS only to blackmail her in Ahmedabad.[3] These incidents show the gravity of the offense of blackmailing after preparation of obscene content.

An amendment was recommended by 156th Law Commission Report to check the menace of blackmailing by publication of scurrilous or grossly indecent matter in the media.[4] Such an amendment is in force in the state of Tamil Nadu. This Amendment must be made in Indian Penal Code, so as to include printing, exhibition, distribution, circulation of any picture or any printed or written document which is grossly indecent or scurrilous and intended to blackmail.

Addition of Mens Rea

The Penal Code should be amended to permit a defense where the person accused of disseminating an obscene article did not know or he did have a reasonable cause to not know, of its obscenity. Many illiterate stallholders have been convicted in the past despite the absence of such knowledge and literate people may also lack knowledge of the obscenity of a work due to existence of many regional languages in India.[4] The current section 292 in Indian Penal Code does not have any role for *Mens Rea*. Hence, a blind person circulating pornographic material may be prosecuted under this section without having any intention to sell pornographic content or without having any knowledge that the said material is obscene!

Manner of Use of the Obscene Material

Section 292 does not deal with the manner in which the book or drawing or painting is advertised. A nude depiction of Bharat Mata may arouse lustful thoughts and unchaste ideas if it is advertised in the section of supermarket where *Playboy* and other such filthy magazines are being advertised. However, if the same depiction is shown in an Art Gallery then there is possibility that such depiction will not appeal the prurient interest of people viewing it. The manner

---

1. http://timesofindia.indiatimes.com/city/jaipur/2-arrested-for-blackmailing-college-girl-over-obscene-MMS/articleshow/5102245.cms
2. http://ibnlive.in.com/news/blackmail-suspected-in-goa-suicide-over-obscene-mms/63609-3.html
3. http://timesofindia.indiatimes.com/city/ahmedabad/Man-held-for-blackmailing-girl-with-MMS/articleshow/5107640.cms
4. 156th Law Commission Report on Indian Penal Code, (1997), at 425, 646.

in which the material is advertised indicates the intention of publisher, distributor or exhibitor of obscene content. It was expounded by Warren C.J. in his dissenting opinion in the Kingsley Books case, where he stated that "there is totally lacking any standard in the New York statute for judging the book in context. The personal element basic to the criminal law is entirely absent. In my judgment, the same object may have wholly different impact depending upon the setting in which it is placed. Under the statute, the setting is irrelevant. It is the manner of use that should determine obscenity. It is the conduct of the individual that should be judged not the quality of art or literature."[1] This opinion of Warren C.J. clarifies the need of considering the manner of advertising and the conduct of publisher, distributor and exhibitor in determination of obscene nature of the material. Hence, section 292 of Indian Penal Code must be amended to include conduct of accused as a ground of judging obscenity.

Problems with Law Enforcement against Internet Pornography

Identification

The biggest problem with enforcement of internet pornography laws is the problem of identification of accused, victims and the perpetrators of such crime. Huge amount of pornographic material is available on numerous porn websites on internet. There is nobody to complain about the production, distribution and circulation of pornography on internet. The perpetrator of crime of pornography can be anyone situated anywhere in the world.

Nowadays India has also become a victim of the crime committed in the cyberspace[2] The most difficult thing is to identify the culprit. As the net can be accessed from any part of the globe, the field is wide open for hackers, pornographers and stalkers. At present, there are an estimated 198 million net connections.[3] However, identity of distributor of pornographic content can be tracked using IP address. An IP address is a 32-bit number that identifies each sender or receiver of information that is sent in packets across the Internet.[4] However, identification of IP address cannot serve any useful purpose if the server of the website is located outside. India. The applicability of Information Technology Act extends to offenses in which the computer servers involved in commission of offenses is located in India. Recently, Satyam, one of the men behind creation of porn website savitabhabhi.com has declared in a blog that he is going to shift the server of his website to European country so that Indian Law would not be held applicable on them and their identity could be protected.[5] Hence pornographic content may easily be distributed by pornographers in India by locating there servers outside India and Indian Law is unable to stop it.

---

1. *Kingsley Books Incorporation* v. *Brown*, 354 US 436 (1957).
2. Krishna Kumar, Cyber Laws-Intellectual Property and E-Commerce Security,2001.
3. 'The virus of Cyber Crime,' available at < http://www.hindu.com/businessline/2000/05/31/stories/043139ma.htm
4. Internet Protocol Version 4 available at http://searchwindevelopment.techtarget.com/sDefinition/0,,sid8_gci212381,00.html.
5. Read Satyam's Comment at http://blogs.timesofindia.indiatimes.com extraordinaryissue/entry/the-assassination-of-savita-bhabhi

The digital medium of internet provides the convenient shield of anonymity and fake identities. Errant persons are encouraged in their offensive behaviour if they think that they will not face any consequences.[1] This is premier reason behind the emergence of numerous porn websites everyday on internet.

Criminal Identification mechanism such as identification of IP address or using cyberspace architecture such as Cookies are not apt tool for identification of culprits of pornography because all IP address and Cookies become irrelevant in case where the culprit distributes and circulates pornographic content while browsing internet from cyber café. It is also not possible to identify the creator of pornographic websites from tracking down the information behind domain name such as credit card no or address of firm because usually the address on Credit Card is fictitious.[2]

There is always a possibility that the end-users who upload content on porn websites upload it through fake identities and proxy server locations to misguide the investigating agencies.[3] There are many websites such as beatfiltering.com that provide facility of bypassing IP address. Most of the social networking websites and email providers do not have any identity verification mechanism to check the veracity of information provided by profile maker or e-mail user. These facts contribute to the problem of enforcements of laws related to pornography.

Jurisdiction

The world of internet is different from the real world. It does not have any boundaries. The fact that Internet is a world made up of cables, telephones lines, satellites and computers, passwords and electronic data renders it difficult to establish the place of residence of the defendant or cause of action of the suit that are traditional basis for fixing jurisdiction as even a childish act may create confusing issue of jurisdiction in the world of internet.[4]

Criminal laws of every country usually operate over a particularly demarcated territorial jurisdiction but porn websites can be created and the content in them can be uploaded anywhere in the world. The problem of jurisdiction is the most important problem in the world of laws dealing with internet pornography. Even if the identity of the website makers is obtained after electronic trail, the problem of identification of jurisdiction still remains. For example, if the police officers in India discover after tracking down the IP address of a famous pornographic website that the source of such website is located in a Gulf Country, even then police have to face several difficulties in proceeding against the maker of such website who is residing in that Gulf Country.

1. Address by Honorable K.G. Balakrishnan, 'National Consultation on enforcement of cyber law' available at www.supremecourtofindia.nic.in/.../National consultation_on_Cyber_Law_31-1-10.pdf
2. Don Gossselin, *Java Script,* p. 406.
3. Address by Honorable K.G. Balakrishnan, 'National Consultation on enforcement of cyber law' available at www.supremecourtofindia.nic.in/.../National_consultation_on_Cyber_Law_31-1-10.pdf
4. K. Vishnu Konoorayar, "Regulating cyberspace: The emerging problem an challenges", *Cochin University Law Review* (2003) available at http://papers.ssrn.com/sol3/papers.cfm?abstract_id=994574

Under section 75 of Information Technology Act, 2008, any person or persons irrespective of their nationalities who commit offence under the Information Technology Act outside India, provided the act or conduct constituting the offence or contravention involves computer, computer systems, or computer networks located in India, can be prosecuted by Indian Courts. This provision attempts to resolve the problem of jurisdiction related to internet pornography but this provision does not serve any useful purpose in case where India does not any extradition treaty with the citizen of a country whose citizen has to be prosecuted under this Act. If a person cannot be extradited to India, there is no benefit of having such provision of universal application of provisions of Information Technology Act. To make such provisions workable and practicable, India should have extradition treaties with as many countries as possible.

The problem of jurisdiction is not to be resolved even if Indian signs extradition treaty with every country in the world. Even if the true address of the host website is known, an Indian court cannot punish the offenders who are in a foreign country because the publication of obscene materials may not be an offence in the country where the server of the host web site is situated. The criterion for punishment varies from countries to countries. For instance in USA the obscenity test is based on the 'contemporary community standards' of the nation.[1] There is no barrier to publish any material which matches their contemporary community standards.[2] Hence a citizen of the United States cannot be prosecuted for distributing obscene material on internet under Indian law even if the server of the receiver is located in India because material in question is not obscene applying contemporary community standards of his country. The difference in India's community standard and US community standard creates huge problem of jurisdiction even when the server is located within India and a US citizen offender tries to distribute content in India.

Training of Officials

The police investigating net crimes are not trained in collecting digital evidences. At present, the staff, used to handling routine crimes, is not competent to handle complex economic offences. In the future, apart from falling under the penal provisions of the current laws, Net-related crimes will have many features. The police should, therefore, be equipped to tackle this new form of crime. Cyber Crime Occur in the world of One and Zero that renders it impossible for an ordinary person understand the depth of the problem in such circumstances.[3]

Lack of International Co-operation

Police forces worldwide need to mobilize to tackle the estimated $104bn global business of internet crime menace but money, manpower and expertise varies

---

1. *United States* v. *Kennerly*, 729 F. 2d 780.
2. Donald T Stephen, "Obscenity Online: A Transnational Approach to Computer Transfers of Potentially Obscene Materials." 82 Cornell Law review, pp. 905, 916, 1997.
3. David J Davis, "Criminal law and the Internet: The Investigator's Perspective", Criminal Law Review 49 (1998).

wildly from country to country.[1] The Absence of Co-operation and integration between police forces and law enforcement agencies all over the world renders enforcement of internet pornography laws difficult.

The need of such international Cooperation was strongly felt in the conference organized by Central Bureau of Investigation on International Police Cooperation on Cyber Crime where the Director of CBI accepted that bad actors are exploiting internet for dissemination of pornography including child pornography and asked for effective international Cooperation between Law Enforcement Agencies and Private Sector Entities such as Internet Service Providers.[2] It is necessary to have such international cooperation to deal with problem of internet pornography.

High Cost of Security

Demand for security solutions is influenced by the costs of switching between cyberspace securities products on the market.[3] The security equipments are so costly that newly established firms with less capital forbid themselves from using them. Hence, these firms, universities or any other local area net users become easy victim of porn spamming. The high cost of tracking software, payment to software engineers who are well trained in electronic tracking of internet offenders are amongst the various factors that contributes in problems of enforcing internet laws.

Cost Deterrence

The cost deterrence principle plays an important role in commission of cyber crime. The cost of distributing pornography over internet is less than distributing it using internet. Cyber theft involves less resources and less risk thus people would commit it more. For example for distributing pornographic images of nude girls one requires to develop those images on photographic paper but for distributing them on internet there is no need to develop those images. These images can be transferred via e-mail from any kind of electronic device where these images are stored.

Internet has provided a medium to criminals where criminals can commit a crime in the cyber space and have its impact in the real world with less expense and with less manpower compared to the real world.[4] The statistics show that the crime on the net is exploding at 4.2% every week.[5] These statistics reveals why pornography on internet has become blooming business and growing day by day.

Enforcement of Decision

Now we come to the biggest problem which is associated with internet pornography. Even if, the identity of offender is tracked, the party had established

---

1. Nick Heath, 'Cyber Crime: 'The Global Battle' available at <http://www.silicon.com/research/specialreports/datalockdown/0,3800014480,39240486,00.htm.
2. http://cbi.nic.in/speech/dcbi_cybercrime_20090326.php
3. Brian Collins and Robin Mansell, "Cyber Trust and Crime Prevention: Synthesis of the State-of-the-Art Science Reviews" available at http://www.lse.ac.uk/collections/media@lse/pdf/Synthesisofthesciencereviews.pdf
4. Neal Kumar Katyal, "Criminal Law In Cyber-space" 149 *University of Pennsylvania Law Review* 1006, 1013 (2001).
5. Web page statistics at<http//:www.intergou.org/publicadministration/information/latestweb-stats.html> visited on 22/09/2001

jurisdiction to try a case, and the court had delivered a judgment, everything becomes superfluous if the decision of Court is not enforceable. If India does not have a treaty with a country where the decision has to be enforced, then the decision is meaningless. In the absence of a treaty it will not be possible to enforce the injunctive provisions of an order in the court of a different sovereign.[1] Hence, it is clear that enforcement of internet laws is not practical until India has treaty with other countries to enforce its decisions.

Solutions to the Problems of Enforcement of Internet Pornography Laws

Special Courts

Supreme Court Justice V.S. Sirpurkar has emphasized on the point of creating special courts for cases related to cyber crime which would be decorated by trained judges in cyber law.[2] These trained judges would be better able to appreciate the evidence. Thus expedite remedy would be achieved. These Special Courts will also serve as a tool for easy enforcement of internet pornography laws.

Special Training for Police

There is need to train police officials so that they can collect and apprehend the evidence in a well effective manner. Police Department of Mumbai, Chennai and Bangalore had already progressed in this regard. Cyber Police station should be established that would eliminate the need of transferring cyber cases from local police station to headquarters.[3] Establishment of Cyber Cell is welcoming move. It must be established in every state. Cyber labs must be created to deal with problems that occur in collection and investigation of digital evidences.

Technical Regulations

Regulation of I.P. addresses to prevent pseudo anonymity[4] and also regulating software manufacture will increase the probability of getting caught. Government should order the telecom companies to regulate I.P. address so that the identity of a website owner could be exposed easily.

Advancing Technology

Insisting upon mechanism which ensures electronic tracing of computer signals to locate offenders is a better way to curb internet offences.[5] Encouragement of G.P.S technology and offender alert mechanism would bring enormous change in manner of investigation.

---

1. Vishnu Konooryaar, "Regulating Cyberspace: Emerging Problems and Challenges", full article available at http://papers.ssrn.com/sol3/papers.cfm?abstract_id=994574
2. Special courts for cyber crime sought, available at < http://www.hindu.com/2009/02/09/stories/2009020954070400.htm
3. Jaidev Hemmadi, "A special Police Station to keep tab on Cyber Crime", available at < http://www.indianexpress.com/news/a-special-police-station-to-keep-tab-on-cyber-crime/405275/
4. Neal Kumar Katyal, "Criminal Law In Cyber-space" 149 *University of Pennsylvania Law Review* 1006, 1013 (2001), at 10.
5. Neal Kumar Katyal, "Criminal Law In Cyber-space" 149 *University of Pennsylvania Law Review* 1006, 1013 (2001), at 11.

Facilitating Research

Government should increase the research in field of digital infrastructure.[1] Instead of digital passwords, sequential image identification or oral passwords should be encouraged. Palm or fingerprint recognition is also one of the solutions.

Ban on Websites

The government can place bans on websites that are famous for circulating pornographic content over internet. A blanket ban on all such websites would not be a better option because it may cover genuine websites that spread awareness about STDs. It is also important to distinguish between intermediaries such as Network Service Providers, website operators and individual users for the purpose of placing liability for wrongful acts. Imposing equal liability upon every one of them would be comparable to punishing the persons who build roads for the rash and negligent driving of other persons who operate vehicles on those roads.[2]

However, there is always a possibility that users of services provided by intermediaries such as internet service providers and website owners may upload pornographic content without the knowledge of those who run the particular website. In such situations the investigators need to stay abreast with the latest developments in web-based applications to quickly identify the actual perpetrators instead of going after an intermediary.[2]

For example, if Raj Sharma uploads pornographic content on a famous website and the website takes appropriate measures to delete that content from the website but if Government bans the website in between for presence of pornographic material on website using any mechanism that prohibits publication of website on internet if pornographic material is present on website, then it would be detrimental for the development of e-commerce in India. So, the Government must check whether the porn site is exclusively designed to distribute pornography over internet. If a porn site is exclusively designed to distribute pornography on internet then it must be banned at any cost and for other website which temporary store pornographic content, other regulatory measures such as imposition of fine or imprisonment must be resorted to in absence of due diligence in place of blanket ban.

Establishment of Cyber Regulation Tribunal

The Cyber Regulations Appellate Tribunal (CRAT) has been established to hear and decide disputes related to internet offenses. These tribunals will serve the purpose of expeditious resolution of disputes related to liabilities of intermediary. However, the composition of this tribunal should reflect the technological and judicial expertise needed to resolve such disputes. Persons serving on the tribunal need to be familiar with the latest developments in the field of Information Technology while also being alert to policy concerns and the need to ensure the free flow of information in society.[2]

---

1. Neal Katyal, How to Fight Computer Crime, http://www.nytimes.com/2002/07/30/opinion/how-to-fight-computer-crime.html
2. Address by Honorable K.G. Balakrishnan, 'National Consultation on enforcement of cyber law'

Unification of Laws

Information Technology Act is not exhaustive to deal with problems of pornography. For example Indian Penal Code, Communication Decency Act, Information Technology Act, Data Protection Act, Criminal Procedure Code are some of the various laws that deal with different aspects of pornography. Due to presence of numerous laws dealing with pornography, confusion arises in relation with their applicability. There must be a law dealing with pornography exhaustively. A separate Code on pornography laws must be prepared to deal with growing problem of pornography.

Creation of World Commission

The problem of internet pornography is not going to be resolved with the effort of one country only. The need of an international organization monitoring internet activities is very much required in the present scenario. Separate International Cyberspace Convention and enforcement mechanism are needed for such initiative.

The European Union, the International Chamber of Commerce, the World Trade Organization and the World Intellectual Property Organization have already realized the need for international cooperation to fight with internet offenses and taken steps in this direction by drafting common standards for the E-commerce.

Recently the European Union has drafted a Convention on Cyber Crime.[1] The convention is drafted with the aim of fostering cooperation with the other State parties to the convention. It is suggested that the world community must also try to standardize the laws on cyber crime by constituting a commission on cyberspace, which shall enforce these norms at the international level where each State party to the convention will be required to file yearly report of compliance and in case of dissatisfaction with reports it can give directions to the State to comply with the convention and if the parties do not comply with the convention within the stipulated time, the Internet flow to that country can be blocked.[2]

This suggestion is very attractive and workable. This commission will also have to be empowered with proper enforcement authorities and all the State parties to the convention must provide proper cooperation in regulation of internet offenses by such commission. There must be a separate department in the commission to deal with internet pornography and all the powers and enforcement mechanism available to the commission must also be made available to this department.

---

1. Preamble to the convention, http://conventions.coe.int/Treaty/EN/Treaties/html/185.htm

CHAPTER 8

CONTRACTUAL ASPECT OF PORNOGRAPHY CONTRACTS*

Introduction

Pornography industry has undergone rapid proliferation over the time. The economic realities of this industry have necessitated the need to address various contractual aspects governing this industry so that the financial and legal interests of various role players are protected and furthered. Like any other large industry, the adult entertainment industry requires the protection by the judicial system in order to ensure that the tremendous financial value invested into its business is not sacrificed as a result of broken promises, faulty expectations, or criminal sanctions.

The murky aspect of the commodity on sale *i.e.* 'sexual performance on camera' has been subject of universal condemnation. Such sexual indulgence is considered as a social deviance and would encourage ills such as prostitutions and extra martial social encounter. This has created a barrier to legal sanctions of the industrial practice.

This paper is an attempt to address legal barriers in recognition and enforcement of pornography contracts. The purpose is not to make a normative argument against enforceability but to outline the irreconcilability of the enforcement of adult film contracts and how can it be resolved.

Various doctrines such as public policy prohibitions on contractual sexual exchanges stand as roadblocks to contractual enforceability of adult entertainment contract and address various points of conflict that arise in its enforcement. In order to preserve the contractual framework for unmarried cohabitation and respect extensive precedent prohibiting sexual consideration, courts must be willing to trumpet a countervailing public policy favouring the enforcement of adult film contracts. Enforcement of such contracts will require the court to carve out substantial exception in the light of existing laws that make these contracts void on the ground of public policy. If the State is willing to recognize the adult entertainment industry as legitimate, non-criminal entity, there would seem to be a strong public policy in favour of allowing individuals in this industry to have recourse to the same legal protections as are available in any other.

---

* Submitted by Neeti Shikha, Assistant Lecturer Stanafield College Singapore, LLM (University College London). The author has also worked as a Teacher/Research associate at Chanakya National Law University, Patna.

If such agreements are not enforceable, an industry of immense economic value might be legally sacrificed for the sake of doctrinal consistency. In the absence of enforceability, an industry providing significant financial benefit to the State and its citizens would be alienated from the legal system, and concerns over coercion and abuse in the industry would be exacerbated by the inability of performers to protect their monetary and corporal interests.

In the end, some suggestions are advanced as potential resolutions to the problem of enforceability. In order to shield industry contracting from criminal prohibition without obliterating any meaningful utility of prostitution statutes, courts must be able to distinguish convincingly pornography from prostitution in a manner that takes into account their differing relationships to disease, drugs, and violence. An effective differentiation would both enable courts to justify their statutory applications as upholding the governmental interests behind the criminalization of prostitution, and furthermore, allow them to enforce these interests without creating substantially counterproductive statutory loopholes.

Pornogrophy Industry – A Murky Reality

Over the past thirty years, the adult entertainment industry has rapidly evolved from a small underground industry into a mainstream industrial monolith.

In the mid-1970s, a federal study estimated the total retail value of all hardcore pornography to be between $ 5-10 million in the United States.[1] By contrast, current estimates of industry revenues have skyrocketed to somewhere in the range of $ 4-12 billion.[2] This is roughly equivalent to the amount spent on professional sporting events, music, or the mainstream box office.[3] Technological innovations have made production and distribution of pornography contents easier and quicker with privacy and anonymity.

Contracts in the adult film industry can be highly appealing to all parties, as they can both serve the long-term business needs of producers and protect often-vulnerable performers from both financial and physical mistreatment. Logistical nightmares are common in adult filmmaking, as screenplays fail to arrive and performers often do not show up on the set,[4] and contractual commitments provide producers greater predictability in the production process. For the

1. Eric Schlosser, The Business of Pornography, U.S. NEWS & WORLD REP., Feb. 10, 1997, pp. 42, 44.
2. FREE SPEECH COALITION, A REPORT ON THE ADULT ENTERTAINMENT INDUSTRY, http://www.freespeech coalition.com/whitepaper05.htm ($ 4 billion estimate); Steve Kroft, Porn in the U.S.A., CBS NEWS, Sept. 5, 2004, http://www.cbsnews.com/stories/2003/ll/21/60minutes/main585049.shtml ($ 10 billion); Nicola Simpson, *The Money Shot: The Business of Porn,* CRITICAL SENSE, Spring 2005, at 11, 11 ($ 12 billion).
3. Steve Kroft, Porn in the U.S.A., CBS NEWS, Sept. 5, 2004, http://www.cbsnews.com/stories/2003/ll/21/60minutes/main585049.shtml ($ 10 billion)
4. *See* Schlosser, *supra* note 5, p. 47. Also *see* Schlosser, *supra* note 5, pp. 32-33; *id.* at 13 ("In the pornography business, the performer *is* the product, and a staggering amount of work goes into promoting the product.").

performers, contracts can potentially help prevent the physical and psychological dangers that pornography opponents have insisted are inherent in adult film production.[1] Contracts in the adult entertainment industry can ensure that performers are not coerced into engaging in sexual acts to which they have not previously consented by stating the scope and duration of their performance before filming commences.[2] Furthermore, contracts can give greater assurance that actors at the very least will be compensated for these performances. Contracts in the adult film industry thus have the potential to mitigate risks undertaken by all parties to production.

However, despite the growth of this industry, the surprising absence of any written court opinion addressing the issue of enforceability has substantially diminished the practical effectiveness of industry contracts. The potential reason for this absence that the legal system and the adult film industry have historically been extremely hostile towards each other and there is a general distrust of the legal process that may accordingly dissuade legal action. Further, despite the

---

1. For an authoritative example of the radical feminist critique of pornography, *see* generally ANDREA DWORKIN, PORNOGRAPHY: MEN POSSESSING WOMEN (1989); CATHARINE MACKINNON, ONLY WORDS (1993). It should be noted that Dworkin and MacKinnon do *not* believe that contracts can prevent sexual coercion in pornography, because female performers are inherently subordinated by a patriarchal society regardless of actual consent. *See* Andrea Dworkin, *Against the Male Flood: Censorship, Pornography, and Equality*, 8 HARV. WOMEN'S L.J. 1, 25-26 (1985) (proposing a model anti-pornography ordinance which provides that contractual consent does not negate a finding of coercion). In contrast, pro-pornography feminists such as Wendy McElroy strongly support the use of contracts to protect against coercion.

   This, of course, is not to say that contracts are a panacea to fraudulent and coercive practices in the adult film industry, as unequal bargaining power and a lack of legal knowledge will undoubtedly shape the terms and conditions of the contract. *See*, e.g., Counterclaim at 7, *Cobra Video, LLC* v. *Lockhart*, No. 06cv0293-J(LSP) (S.D. Cal. Mar. 8, 2006) (alleging that the defendant, an underage adult film actor who desired to break his contract, was forced to disclose his true age when the president of the film company threatened that "he could get the courts to force [the defendant] to continue making productions"). However, at the very least, the negotiation and solemnization of the contract in writing clarifies the expectations of all parties prior to shooting. Unequal bargaining power could, in theory, be ameliorated through the unionization of adult performers, but such efforts remain difficult as the Screen Actors Guild excludes such performers from membership and their independent-contractor status precludes their protection under the National Labor Relations Act.

2. *See* Margot Rutman, Exotic Dancers' Employment Law Regulations, 8 TEMP. POL. & CIV. RTS. L. REV. 515, 519 (1999) (noting that, because adult film performers are excluded from the Screen Actors Guild, "they cannot exert pressure on the offenders like mainstream actors and actresses"); Holly J. Wilmet, Naked Feminism: The Unionization of the Adult Entertainment Industry, 7 AM. U.J. GENDER SOC. POL'Y & L. 465, 468-69 (1999) ("The courts have become an active partner in the continuing financial exploitation of adult entertainers ... by legally classifying various types of... entertainers as independent contractors, and thus denying these workers protection of the labor laws enacted for their benefit."); *see* also 29 U.S.C. § 157 (2000) ("Employees shall have the right to self-organization, to form, join, or assist labor organizations, to bargain collectively through representatives of their own choosing, and to engage in other concerted activities for the purpose of collective bargaining or other mutual aid or protection." (emphasis added)). Furthermore, even if adult performers were able to unionize, any collective bargaining agreements could face the same problems of enforceability as individual contracts to the extent that they compensate sexual exchange.

potential ability of contracts to alleviate economic uncertainty and sexual coercion, the industry generally has been skeptical of the enforceability of its own contracts.

Need for Contractual Protection

As we have discussed above that distrust and scepticism have prevented judicial clarification of contract enforceability, the perceived inability of both producers and performers to challenge unfulfilled promises has correspondingly persisted.

Hence, it is gathered that the perceived unenforceability furthers judicial reticence, judicial reticence reciprocally furthers perceptions of unenforceability, leaving an unstable field of legal obligations despite the existence of industry contracts. Without judicial guidance, parties to a contract whose enforceability is uncertain are left unable to discern reasonably the permissibility of breach or the availability of legal redress. Although there is a general recognition of the potential benefits of contractual employment, the lack of judicial attention and the accompanying legal unpredictability have undermined the ability of contracts to provide the benefits they promise. Hence, it is seen that litigation over contractual disputes is beginning to arise, and courts must inevitably address the difficult question of enforceability.

Without contractual protections, the scope of sexual performance will remain largely at the whim of directors and coercion to perform undesired sexual acts would be facilitated by the lack of any assurance of payment and submission to the director's demands. The contractual rights of the players will be put at stake. The inability of either performers or filmmakers to enforce their contractual obligations would have significantly detrimental ramifications for all facets of the adult entertainment industry as well as the economic vitality of the States.

Public Policy as Road Block to Enforcement

The law governing the rights of pornography participants is confused, and few women manage to recover some of their dignity through the legal process. In general, the legal process governing pornography contract is vague. The tenets on which a contract for pornography is tested is vague and looms in favour of public policy and a general conception that such contracts must not be recognised and that the participants of such contracts have neither right to enter nor any remedy for the frustration of the contracts.

The principle that contracts with some implication of prostitution are unenforceable on public policy grounds has received broad support both in courts and in contract jurisprudence nationwide. Indeed, a well-known tenet of contract jurisprudence is that contracts are unenforceable to the extent they rest upon sexual consideration because such contracts involve the type of prohibited economic sexual exchange underlying the statutory ban on prostitution. The explicitly sexual nature of the consideration in adult film contracts would certainly be subject to the scrutiny of this contractual principle, and courts' willingness to invalidate contracts with a far more attenuated link to prostitution creates a possibly insurmountable obstacle for the enforceability of adult film contracts.

The invalidation of contracts based on sexual consideration has deep roots in American jurisprudence. For centuries, American courts have made clear that there is a strong public policy interest in discouraging contracts for sexual relations, and parties continuously have been prohibited from trading sexual services in exchange for contractual promises.[1]

This makes extension of protection of law to such participants difficult. It must be realized that there are instances where women complain of being drugged, being coerced, and being offered money for sex by pornographers.[2] Many of the women who complain are not legally adults, which should give one pause in automatically assuming their culpability.[3]

Further, enforcement of pornography contract can be avoided is popularly known as bare defense. This aspect, almost universal to cases involving reality porn, is the presence of alcohol.[4] In theory, those who contract while seriously intoxicated may annul or ratify their contracts as minors can, but the law often puts more hurdles in their way. Any delay in disaffirming a contract entered into when inebriated may be enough to defeat the claim ,[5] especially if the facts quickly come to light.[6] Additionally, any action that affirms the existence of the contract will make it valid.[7] However, for the courts to allow the drunk to void their contracts, "the drunkenness must have been such as to have drowned reason, memory, and judgment, and to have impaired the mental faculties to such an extent as to render the party *non compos mentis* for the time being."[8] Further, some courts have laid dwn that if one is not induced to intoxication by the party one

1. *See* ELISHA GREENHOOD, THE DOCTRINE OF PUBLIC POLICY IN THE LAW OF CONTRACTS: REDUCED TO RULES 201 (Chicago, Callaghan & Co. 1886) ("Any promise in consideration of illicit intercourse or calculated to encourage immorality is void.").
2. In *Capdeboscq* v. *Francis*, the plaintiffs allege that Joseph Francis and the musician Snoop Doggy Dogg gave the plaintiffs alcohol, pressured them to pose naked for the cameras, and then reneged on plaintiffs' repeated requests not to appear in any videos. See Ex. A to Notice of Removal, at 2, *Capdeboscq* v. *Francis*, No. Civ. A. 03-0556 (E.D. La. Feb. 21, 2003). Another group of underage women allege that, after showing their breasts to the camera, they were lured to a hotel room and paid to engage in sex acts for the video. See Compl. and Demand for Jury Trial, at 7-9, Francis, No. 5:03CV260 (N.D. Fla.).
3. *See* generally *Capdeboscq*, 2003 U.S. Dist. LEXIS 8989; *Lane*, 242 F Supp 2d 1223; Doe, No. 01-12450 (Civ. Dist. Orleans 2002).
4. *See* Memorandum in Support of Motion to Dismiss Pursuant to Fed. R. Civ. P. 12(b)(6), *Capdeboscq* v. *Francis*, No. Civ. A. 03-0556 at 9-12 (E.D. La. May 2, 2003) (arguing that, even if Calvin Broadus supplied minors with drugs and alcohol, it does not lead to civil liability); Ken Hegan, supra note 11, at 64 (party held in a room with no furniture save a beer keg). Intoxication was not plead in *Lane*, 242 F. Supp. 2d 1205, but that may stem from Ms. Lane's picture being taken while she was driving a car, and such a position would amount to an admission of driving under the influence. *Lane*, 242 F Supp 2d 1209.
5. *See* Case *Threshing Machine*, 111 NW 604 ("If the defendant was so intoxicated as not to understand what he was doing when the notes were signed, he should have disclaimed liability thereon within a reasonable time after recovering his senses.").
6. In *Hauge* v. *Bye*, 201 NW 159 (N.D. 1924), "the plaintiff discovered all the facts which he claims entitled him to disaffirm and avoid the settlement on the morning after it was made," *id.* at 162, but waited two years to do so. *Id.* at 160.
7. See *Curry* v. *Stewart*, 368 P 2d 297 (301) (Kan. 1962) (determining that an individual who followed the terms of a contract for three months after signing it ratified it by implication).
8. *Martin* v. *Harsh*, 83 NE 164 (Ill. 1907)

with contract, it must be obvious that one is inebriated.[1] Also, English common law held that voluntary intoxication was not a defense to a contract action, and few modern courts have accepted it when pled.[2] It is only the significant solicitation and harassment of one who is inebriated makes a contract voidable,[3] which is suggested by inadequate consideration.[4]

Effects of Non Recognition and a Possible Solution

If courts desire to avoid the consequences of refusing to enforce adult film contracts, they cannot do so without substantially altering existing law. Next Part of the paper reflects upon the specific roadblocks to enforceability presented by the current state of contract doctrine.

As contracts in the expanding adult film industry become increasingly utilized and contractual disputes edge into the purview of courts, courts must inevitably confront the limitations of governing precedent.

In pornography contracts, a rescission is far less desirable to the pornographer than the photographed party. The pornographer has to return all tangible and intangible goods received as a consideration and also all rights to the image. Furthermore, if a court feels that an extended delay has financially harmed the non-rescinding party, the court may not allow for full restitution. The court might also use its powers in equity to require no restitution on the part of a minor or intoxicated person if the court deems it just.[5]

Let's pause here and think of the damage in today's time of advanced media and wide internet usages. Calculation of damages and determining real and future loss will always remain a challenge. As many of these cases come forth once the videos are in circulation,[6] this argument may be too late.

Further, anyone who can reasonably claim contractual inability due to infancy or intoxication, may be behoved from filing a declaratory judgment against the

1. See *Hauge* v. *Bye*, 201 NW 159 (161-62) (N.D. 1924).
2. *See* Lionel Sawyer & Collins, Nevada Gaming Law, *Creer* v. *Active Automobile Exchange, Inc.*, 121 A 888 (891) (Conn. 1923). Even in Nevada, where gambling contracts are generally enforceable, there is no hope of collecting a gambling debt from a minor. *See* Lionel Sawyer & Collins, Nevada Gaming Law 281 (3d ed. 2000).
3. In *Thackrah* v. *Haas*, 119 US 499 (1886), the court found: "Defendants, at the time of transfer hereinafter mentioned, knew the plaintiff was and for two months had been in that condition [essentially blind drunk]; that while he was in that condition the bank through its officers pursued, harassed and goaded him ... in order to extort from him a transfer." Id.. Compare with Exhibit A to Notice of Removal, Capdeboscq, No. Civ. A. 03-0556 (alleging that minors were offered intoxicants).
4. *Kendall* v. *Ewert*, 259 US 139 (1922), suggests that a broad disparity in value is evidence that a contract should be voidable. The intoxicated party in *Kendall* v. *Ewert* sold land for $ 700 that was quickly re-sold for $ 18,000.
5. E.g., *Thackrah* v. *Haas*, 119 US 499 (502) (1886) ("The plaintiff, without any fault of his, being unable to repay the consideration of the fraudulent transfer, equity will not require him to do so.").
6. Even more insidiously, they are also pirated on the internet. Girls Gone Wild is a common search on the Gnutella peer-to-peer network. For more information on Gnutella, *see* Jacob Strahilevitz, Charismatic Code, Social Norms, and the Emergence of Cooperation on the File-Swapping Networks, 89 Va. L. Rev. 505, 517 (2003).

pornographers most likely to have been photographing to prevent dissemination of one's image. Courts are willing to return property taken from a minor by fraud without making the deceiver pay interest.[1] However, to avoid a contract is to forgo a suit for damages resulting from the contract; to do so would be to affirm the contract.[2] This again is a contradiction that emerges from non-recognition of pornography contracts.

For contracts in the adult film industry to be enforceable, they must overcome the substantial obstacles posed by the contractual doctrines of illegality and public policy. Although these doctrines were developed in the common law, the principle finds its reiteration in many legal system. These statutes provide that a contract without a "lawful object"[3] is void and unenforceable in its entirety.

Conclusion

Although this paper discusses the existing roadblock in enforceability of adult film contracts, its purpose is not to make a normative argument against enforceability. Rather, the objective of the paper is to outline the irreconcilability of the enforcement of adult film contracts with the furtherance of interests expounded by courts in related areas of law and the implications of non-recognition of such contracts. Courts cannot condone and facilitate adult entertainment industry practices without substantially compromising their interest in discouraging prostitution *via* a reasonable application of criminal statutes. Similarly, the industry's employment contracts may not be validated without diverging from centuries-old precedent in a manner inconsistent with public policy. If courts want to uphold the illegality of prostitution, proscribe sexual consideration in cohabitation agreements, and foster a lucrative adult entertainment industry, they must alter doctrinal approaches to these issues.

The contractual rights of the parties can be protected from criminal prohibition without obliterating any meaningful utility of prostitution statutes only if courts are able to distinguish convincingly pornography from prostitution in a manner that takes into account their differing relationships to disease, drugs, and violence. An effective differentiation would both enable courts to justify their statutory applications as upholding the governmental interests behind the criminalization of prostitution, and furthermore, allow them to enforce these interests without creating substantially counterproductive statutory loopholes.

---

1. *See*, e.g., *Waldrep* v. *Merkle*, 38 F Supp 165 (173) (W.D. Okla. 1941) (regarding the theft of an estate from a family of child heirs).
2. See *J.I. Hass Co.* v. *Jones-Teer*, 755 F 2d 1264 (1267) (6th Cir. 1985). Furthermore, even in courts friendly to cases against Girls Gone Wild, unjust enrichment has been a failure as a legal theory. *Capdeboscq* v. *Francis*, No. Civ. A. 03-0556, 2004 WL 463316, at 2 (E.D. La. Mar. 10, 2004). It may therefore be difficult to get anything more than the "going rate" for such a performance; the Screen Actors' Guild states that a principal in a low-budget production outside of New York or Los Angeles gets four hundred and sixty-six dollars for a day's work. See Screen Actors' Guild, Low Budget Rate Sheet, at http://www.sag.org/sagWebApp/CMS/Documents/Tables/CheckRates-LowBud.htm (last accessed May 23, 2010). In light of SAG guidelines, the five hundred dollars offered Brian Buck for his role in Shane's World seems more than reasonable.
3. *CAL. CIV. CODE* § 1550 (3) (West 1982).

However, if the courts are unwilling to put forward a favorable public policy or are unable to differentiate effectively pornography from prostitution, any remaining desire to enforce industry contracts would require a wholesale revaluation of the role of sexual exchange in our legal system and society at large.

It is submitted that a safe analogy can be drawn from the State action on the constitutional mandate to prohibit use of alcohol and the regulation of the alcohol industry simultaneously in various countries such as India. At one side, where the Constitution suggests the States to make endeavours to reduce the consumption of alcohol, in order to keep the health and social order, the State regulates the manufacturing, sale and consumption of alcohol. Similarly, the law may direct the States to prohibit the proliferation of pornography industry and not recognise it as a constitutional right to trade and business. However, it may yet regulate it in the interest of general public and the players with a view to prevent the unwarranted implications of non-recognition of pornography contracts.

Lastly, it is submitted that gradual development of sexual mores has greatly altered perception and acceptance of the commerciality of sexual conduct. The rise of the pornography contract suggests that the time for sexual reconsideration in our legal system may have arrived.

UNITED STATES ACTS AND ORDINANCES

THE MINNEAPOLIS ORDINANCE, 1983

An Ordinance of the City of Minneapolis

Amending Title 7, Chapter 139 of the Minneapolis Code of Ordinances relating to Civil Rights: In General.

The City Council of the City of Minneapolis do ordain as follows:—

Section 1. That section 139.10 of the above-entitled ordinance be amended to read as follows:—

139.10 Findings, declaration of policy and purpose

(a) Findings.—The council finds that discrimination in employment, labor union membership, housing accommodations, property rights, education, public accommodations and public services based on race, color, creed, religion, ancestry, national origin, sex, including sexual harassment AND PORNOGRAPHY, affectional preference, disability, age, marital status, or status with regard to public assistance or in housing accommodations based on familial status adversely affects the health, welfare, peace and safety of the community. Such discriminatory practices degrade individuals, foster intolerance and hate, and create and intensify unemployment, sub-standard housing, under-education, ill health, lawlessness and poverty, thereby injuring the public welfare.

(1) **Special Findings on Pornography:** The council finds that pornography is central in creating and maintaining the civil inequality of the sexes. Pornography is a systematic practice of exploitation and subordination based on sex which differentially harms women. The bigotry and contempt it promotes, with the acts of aggression it fosters, harm women's opportunities for equality of rights in employment, education, property rights, public accommodations and public services; create public harassment and private denigration; promote injury and degradation such as rape, battery and prostitution and inhibit just enforcement of laws against these acts; contribute significantly to restricting women from full exercise of citizenship and participation in public life, including in neighborhoods; damage relations between the sexes; and undermine women's equal exercise of rights to speech and action guaranteed to all citizens under the constitutions and laws of the united states and the state of minnesota.

(b) Declaration of policy and purpose.—It is the public policy of the City of Minneapolis and the purpose of this title:

(1) To recognize and declare that the opportunity to obtain employment, labor union membership, housing accommodations, property rights, education, public accommodations and public services without discrimination based on race, color, creed, religion, ancestry, national origin, sex, including sexual harassment AND PORNOGRAPHY, affectional preference, disability, age, marital status, or status with regard to public assistance or to obtain housing accommodations without discrimination based on familial status is a civil right;

(2) To prevent and prohibit all discriminatory practices based on race, color, creed, religion, ancestry, national origin, sex, including sexual harassment AND PORNOGRAPHY, affectional preference, disability, age, marital status, or status with regard to public assistance with respect to employment, labor union membership, housing accommodations, property rights, education, public accommodations or public services;

(3) To prevent and prohibit all discriminatory practices based on familial status with respect to housing accommodations;

(4) To prevent and prohibit all discriminatory practices of sexual subordination or inequality through pornography;

(5) To protect all persons from unfounded charges of discriminatory practices;

(6) To eliminate existing and the development of any ghettos in the community; and

(7) To effectuate the foregoing policy by means of public information and education, mediation and conciliation, and enforcement.

Section 3. That Section 139.20 of the above-entitled ordinance be amended by adding thereto a new sub-section (gg) to read as follows:—

(gg) Pornography.—Pornography is a form of discrimination on the basis of sex.

(1) Pornography is the sexually explicit subordination of women, graphically depicted, whether in pictures or in words, that also includes one or more of the following:—

(i) women are presented dehumanized as sexual objects, things or commodities; or

(ii) women are presented as sexual objects who enjoy pain or humiliation; or

(iii) women are presented as sexual objects who experience sexual pleasure in being raped; or

(iv) women are presented as sexual objects tied up or cut up or mutilated or bruised or physically hurt; or

(v) women are presented in postures of sexual submission; or

(vi) women's body parts - including but not limited to vaginas, breasts, and buttocks - are exhibited, such that women are reduced to those parts; or

(vii) women are presented as whores by nature; or

(viii) women are presented being penetrated by objects or animals; or

(ix) women are presented in scenarios of degradation, injury, abasement, torture, shown as filthy or inferior, bleeding, bruised, or hurt in a context that makes these conditions sexual.

(2) The use of men, children, or transsexuals in the place of women in (1) (i-ix) above is pornography for purposes of sub-sections (l) - (p) of this statute.

Section 4. That section 139.40 of the above-mentioned ordinance be amended by adding thereto new sub-sections (l), (m), (n), (o), (p), (q), (r) and (s) to read as follows:—

(1) **Discrimination by trafficking in pornography.**—The production, sale, exhibition, or distribution of pornography is discrimination against women by means of trafficking in pornography:—

(1) City, state, and federally funded public libraries or private and public university and college libraries in which pornography is available for study, including on open shelves, shall not be construed to be trafficking in pornography but

special display presentations of pornography in said places is sex discrimination.

(2) The formation of private clubs or associations for purposes of trafficking in pornography is illegal and shall be considered a conspiracy to violate the civil rights of women.

(3) Any woman has a cause of action hereunder as a woman acting against the subordination of women. Any man or transsexual who alleges injury by pornography in the way women are injured by it shall also have a cause of action.

(m) Coercion into pornographic performances.—Any person, including transsexual, who is coerced, intimidated, or fraudulently induced (hereafter "coerced") into performing for pornography shall have a cause of action against the maker(s), seller(s), exhibitor(s) or distributor(s) of said pornography for damages and for the elimination of the products of the performance(s) from the public view.

(1) **Limitation of action.**—This claim shall not expire before five years have elapsed from the date of the coerced performance(s) or from the last appearance or sale of any product of the performance(s), whichever date is later;

(2) Proof of one or more of the following facts or conditions shall not, without more, negate a finding of coercion;

(i) that the person is a woman; or

(ii) that the person is or has been a prostitute; or

(iii) that the person has attained the age of majority; or

(iv) that the person is connected by blood or marriage to anyone involved in or related to the making of the pornography; or

(v) that the person has previously had, or been thought to have had, sexual relations with anyone, including anyone involved in or related to the making of the pornography; or

(vi) that the person has previously posed for sexually explicit pictures for or with anyone, including anyone involved in or related to the making of the pornography at issue; or

(vii) that anyone else, including a spouse or other relative, has given permission on the person's behalf; or

(viii) that the person actually consented to a use of the performance that is changed into pornography; or

(ix) that the person knew that the purpose of the acts or events in question was to make pornography; or

(x) that the person showed no resistance or appeared to cooperate actively in the photographic sessions or in the sexual events that produced the pornography; or

(xi) that the person signed a contract, or made statements affirming a willingness to cooperate in the production of pornography; or

(xii) that no physical force, threats, or weapons were used in the making of the pornography; or

(xiii) that the person was paid or otherwise compensated.

(n) Forcing pornography on a person.—Any woman, man, child, or transsexual who has pornography forced on him/her in any place of employment, in education, in a home, or in any public place has a cause of action against the perpetrator and/or institution.

(o) Assault or physical attack due to pornography.—Any woman, man, child, or transsexual who is assaulted, physically attacked or injured in a way that is directly caused by specific pornography has a claim for damages against the perpetrator, the maker(s), distributor(s), seller(s), and/or exhibitor(s), and for an injunction against the specific pornography's further exhibition, distribution, or sale. No damages shall be assessed (A) against maker(s) for pornography made, (B) against distributor(s) for pornography distributed, (C) against seller(s) for pornography sold, or (D) against exhibitors for pornography exhibited prior to the enforcement date of this act.

(p) Defenses.—Where the materials which are the subject matter of a cause of action under sub-sections (l), (m), (n), or (o) of this section are pornography, it shall not be a defense that the defendants did not know or intend that the materials were pornography or sex discrimination.

(q) Severability.—Should any part(s) of this ordinance be found legally invalid, the remaining part(s) remain valid.

(r) Sub-sections (l), (m), (n), and (o) of this section are exceptions to the second clause of section 141.90 of this title.

(s) Effective date.—Enforcement of this ordinance of December 30, 1983, shall be suspended until July 1, 1984 ("enforcement date") to facilitate training, education, voluntary compliance, and implementation taking into consideration the opinions of the City Attorney and the Civil Rights Commission. No liability shall attach under (l) or as specifically provided in the second sentence of (o) until the enforcement date. Liability under all other sections of this act shall attach as of December 30, 1983.

Amending Title 7, Chapter 141 of the Minneapolis Code of Ordinances relating to Civil Rights: Administration and Enforcement.

The City Council of the City of Minneapolis do ordain as follows:—

Section 1. That section 141.50 (l) of the above-entitled ordinance be amended by adding thereto a new sub-section (3) to read as follows:

(3) Pornography: The hearing committee or court may order relief, including the removal of violative material, permanent injunction against the sale, exhibition or distribution of violative material, or any other relief deemed just and equitable, including reasonable attorney's fees.

Section 2. That Section 141.60 of the above-entitled ordinance be amended as follows:

141.60 Civil action, judicial review and enforcement.

(a) **Civil actions.**

(1) An individual alleging a violation of this ordinance may bring a civil action directly in court.

(2) A complainant may bring a civil action at the following times:

(i) Within forty-five (45) days after the director, a review committee or a hearing committee has dismissed a complaint for reasons other than conciliation agreement to which the complainant is a signator; or

(ii) After forty-five (45) days from the filing of a verified complaint if a hearing has not been held pursuant to section 141.50 or the department has not entered into a conciliation agreement to which the complainant is a signator. The complainant shall notify the department of his/her intention to bring a civil action, which shall be commenced within ninety (90) days of giving the notice. A complainant bringing a civil action shall mail, by registered or certified mail, a copy of the summons and complaint to the department and upon receipt of same, the director shall terminate all proceedings before the department relating to the complaint and shall dismiss the complaint.

No complaint shall be filed or reinstituted with the department after a civil action relating to the same unfair discriminatory practice has been brought unless the civil action has been dismissed without prejudice.

GOVT OPS - Your Committee, to whom was referred ordinances amending Title 7 of the Minneapolis Code of Ordinances, to add pornography as discrimination against women and provide just and equitable relief upon finding of discrimination by hearing committee of the Civil Rights Commission, and having held public hearings thereon, recommends that the following ordinances be given their second readings for amendment and passage:

a. Ordinance amending Chap 139 relating to Civil Rights: In General;

b. Ordinance amending Chap 141 relating to Civil Rights: Administration and Enforcement.

CODE OF ALABAMA

Title 13A: Criminal Code – Section 13A-12-200.2 – Distribution, possession with intent to distribute, production, etc., of obscene material prohibited; penalties; distribution of fines

Section 13A-12-200.2 - Distribution, possession with intent to distribute, production, etc., of obscene material prohibited; penalties; distribution of fines.

(a)(1) It shall be unlawful for any person to knowingly distribute, possess with intent to distribute, or offer or agree to distribute any obscene material or any device designed or marketed as useful primarily for the stimulation of human genital organs for any thing of pecuniary value. Material not otherwise obscene may be obscene under this section if the distribution of the material, the offer to do so, or the possession with the intent to do so is a commercial exploitation of erotica solely for the sake of prurient appeal. Any person who violates this sub-section shall be guilty of a misdemeanor and, upon conviction, shall be punished by a fine of not more than ten thousand dollars ($10,000) and may also be imprisoned in the county jail or sentenced to hard labor for the county for not more than one year. A second or subsequent violation of this subdivision is a Class C felony if the second or subsequent violation occurs after a conviction has been obtained for a previous violation. Upon a second violation, a corporation or business entity shall be fined not less than ten thousand dollars ($10,000) nor more than fifty thousand dollars ($50,000).

(2) It shall be unlawful for any person, being a wholesaler, to knowingly distribute, possess with intent to distribute, or offer or agree to distribute, for the purpose of resale or commercial distribution at retail, any obscene material or any device designed or marketed as useful primarily for the stimulation of human genital organs for any thing of pecuniary value. Material not otherwise obscene may be obscene under this section if the distribution of the material, the offer to do so, or the possession with the intent to do so is a commercial exploitation of erotica solely for the sake of their prurient appeal. Any person who violates this sub-section shall be guilty of a misdemeanor and, upon conviction, shall be punished by a fine of not more than twenty thousand dollars ($20,000) and may also be imprisoned in the county jail or sentenced to hard labor for the county for not more than one year. A second or subsequent violation of this sub-division is a Class C felony if the second or subsequent violation occurs after a conviction has been obtained for a previous violation. Upon a second violation, a corporation or business entity shall be fined not less than ten thousand dollars ($10,000) nor more than fifty thousand dollars ($50,000).

(3) It shall be unlawful for any person to knowingly produce, or offer or agree to produce, any obscene material or any device designed or marketed as useful primarily for the stimulation of human genital organs for any thing of pecuniary value. Material not otherwise obscene may be obscene under this section if the distribution of the material, the offer to do so, or the possession with the intent to do so is a commercial exploitation of erotica solely for the sake of prurient appeal. Any person who violates this sub-section shall be guilty of a Class C felony.

(4) If a person is held under this section in the county jail, one-half of any fines collected and due to be deposited to the State General Fund for violations of this section shall be paid by the Comptroller to the general fund of the county where the person is held for the operation of the county jail.

UNITED KINGDOM

OBSCENE PUBLICATIONS ACT, 1959

CHAPTER 66

An Act to amend the law relating to the publication of obscene matter; to provide for the protection of literature; and to strengthen the law concerning pornography.

[*29th July, 1959*]

Be it enacted by the Queen's most Excellent Majesty, by and with the advice and consent of the Lords Spiritual and Temporal, and Commons, in this present Parliament assembled, and by the authority of the same, as follows:—

1. Test of obscenity.—(l) For the purposes of this Act an article shall be deemed to be obscene if its effect or (where the article comprises two or more distinct items) the effect of any one of its items is, if taken as a whole, such as to tend to deprave and corrupt persons who are likely, having regard to all relevant circumstances, to read, see or hear the matter contained or embodied in it.

(2) In this Act "article" means any description of article containing or embodying matter to be read or looked at or both, any sound record, and any film or other record of a picture or pictures.

(3) For the purposes of this Act a person publishes an article who—

(a) distributes, circulates, sells, lets on hire, gives, or lends it, or who offers it for sale or for letting on hire; or

(b) in the case of an article containing or embodying matter to be looked at or a record, shows, plays or projects it

or, where the matter is data stored electronically, transmits that data:

(4) For the purposes of this Act a person also publishes an article to the extent that any matter recorded on it is included by him in a programme included in a programme service.

(5) Where the inclusion of any matter in a programme so included would, if that were recorded matter, constitute the publication of an obscene article for the purposes of this Act by virtue of sub-section (4) above, this Act shall have effect in relation to the inclusion of that matter in that programme as if it were recorded matter.

(6) In this section "programme" and "programme service" have the same meaning as in the Broadcasting Act, 1990.

2. Prohibition of publication of obscene matter.—(1) Subject as hereinafter provided, any person who, whether for gain or not, publishes an obscene article shall be liable—

(a) on summary conviction to a fine not exceeding one hundred pounds or to imprisonment for a term not exceeding six months;

(b) on conviction on indictment to a fine or to imprisonment for a term not exceeding three years or both.

(2) [***]

(3) A prosecution for an offence against this section shall not be commenced more than two years after the commission of the offence.

(3A) Proceedings for an offence under this section shall not be instituted except by or with the consent of the Director of Public Prosecutions in any case where the article in question is a moving picture film of a width of not less than sixteen millimeters and the relevant publication or the only other publication which followed or could reasonably have been expected to follow from the relevant publication took place or (as the case may be) was to take place in the course of a film exhibition;

and in this sub-section "the relevant publication" means—

(a) in the case of any proceedings under this section for publishing an obscene article, the publication in respect of which the defendant would be charged if the proceedings were brought; and

(b) in the case of any proceedings under this section for having an obscene article for publication for gain, the publication which, if the proceedings were brought, the defendant would be alleged to have had in contemplation.

(4) A person publishing an article shall not be proceeded against for an offence at common law consisting of the publication of any matter contained or embodied in the article where it is of the essence of the offence that the matter is obscene.

(4A) Without prejudice to sub-section (4) above, a person shall not be proceeded against for an offence at common law—

(a) in respect of a film exhibition or anything said or done in the course of a film exhibition, where it is of the essence of the common law offence that the exhibition or, as the case may be, what was said or done was obscene, indecent, offensive, disgusting or injurious to morality; or

(b) in respect of an agreement to give a film exhibition or to cause anything to be said or done in the course of such an exhibition where the common law offence consists of conspiring to corrupt public morals or to do any act contrary to public morals or decency.

(5) A person shall not be convicted of an offence against this section if he proves that he had not examined the article in respect of which he is charged and had no reasonable cause to suspect that it was such that his publication of it would make him liable to be convicted of an offence against this section.

(6) In any proceedings against a person under this section the question whether an article is obscene shall be determined without regard to any publication by another person unless it could reasonably have been expected that the publication by the other person would follow from publication by the person charged.

(7) In this section "film exhibition" has the same meanings as in the Cinemas Act, 1985.

3. Powers of search and seizure.—(1) If a justice of the peace is satisfied by information on oath that there is reasonable ground for suspecting that, in any premises in.the petty sessions area for which he acts, or on any stall or vehicle in that area, being premises or a stall or vehicle specified in the information, obscene articles are, or are from time to time, kept for publication for gain, the justice may issue a warrant under his hand empowering any constable to enter (if need be by force) and search the premises, or to search the stall or vehicle, within fourteen days from the date of the warrant, and to seize and remove any articles found therein or thereon which the constable has reason to believe to be obscene articles and to be kept for publication for gain.

(2) A warrant under the foregoing sub-section shall, if any obscene articles are seized under the warrant, also empower the seizure and removal of any documents found in the premises or, as the case may be, on the stall or vehicle which relate to a trade or business carried on at the premises or from the stall or vehicle.

(3) Subject to sub-section (3A) of this section any articles seized under sub-section (1) of this section shall be brought before a justice of the peace acting for the same petty sessions area as the justice who issued the warrant, and the justice before whom the articles are brought may thereupon issue a summons to the occupier of the premises or, as the case may be, the user of the stall or vehicle to appear on a day specified in the summons before a magistrates' court for that petty sessions area to show cause why the articles or any of them should not be forfeited; and if the court is satisfied, as respects any of the articles, that at the time when they were seized they were obscene articles kept for publication for gain, the court shall order those articles to be forfeited:

Provided that if the person summoned does not appear, the court shall not make an order unless service of the summons is proved:

Provided also that this sub-section does not apply in relation to any article seized under sub-section (1) of this section which is returned to the occupier of the premises or, as the case may be, to the user of the stall or vehicle in or on which it was found.

(3A) Without prejudice to the duty of a court to make an order for the forfeiture of an article where section 1(4) of the Obscene Publications Act, 1964 applies (orders made on conviction), in a case where by virtue of sub-section (3A) of section 2 of this Act proceedings under the said section 2 for having an article for publication for gain could not be instituted except by or with the consent of the Director of Public Prosecutions, no order for the forfeiture of the article shall be made under this section unless the warrant under which the article was seized was issued on an information laid by or on behalf of the Director of Public Prosecutions.

(4) In addition to the person summoned, any other person being the owner, author or maker of any of the articles brought before the court, or any other person through whose hands they had passed before being seized, shall be entitled to appear before the court on the day specified in the summons to show cause why they should not be forfeited.

(5) Where an order is made under this section for the forfeiture of any articles, any person who appeared, or was entitled to appear, to show cause against the making of the order may appeal to the Crown Court; and no such order shall take effect until the expiration of the period within which notice of appeal to the Crown Court may be given against the order, or, if before the expiration thereof notice of appeal is duly given or application is made for the statement of a case for the opinion of the High Court, until the final determination or abandonment of the proceedings on the appeal or case.

(6) If as respects any articles brought before it the court does not order forfeiture, the court may if it thinks fit order the person on whose information the warrant for the seizure of the articles was issued to pay such costs as the court thinks reasonable to any person who has appeared before the court to show cause why those articles should not be forfeited; and costs ordered to be paid under this sub-section shall be enforceable as a civil debt.

(7) For the purposes of this section the question whether an article is obscene shall be determined on the assumption that copies of it would be published in any manner likely having regard to the circumstances in which it was found, but in no other manner.

(8) The Obscene Publications Act, 1857, is hereby repealed, without prejudice, however, to the execution of any warrant issued thereunder before the commencement of this Act or to the taking of any proceedings in pursuance of a warrant so issued.

4. Defence of public good.—(1) Subject to sub-section (1A) of this section a person shall not be convicted of an offence against section two of this Act, and an order for forfeiture shall not be made under the foregoing section, if it is proved that publication of the article in question is justified as being for the public good on the ground that it is in the interests of science, literature, art or learning, or of other objects of general concern.

(1A) Sub-section (1) of this section shall not apply where the article in question is a moving picture film or soundtrack, but—

(a) a person shall not be convicted of an offence against section 2 of this Act in relation to any such film or soundtrack, and

(b) an order for forfeiture of any such film or soundtrack shall not be made under section 3 of this Act, if it is proved that publication of the film or soundtrack is justified as being for the public good on the ground that it is in the interests of drama, opera, ballet or any other art, or of literature or learning.

(2) It is hereby declared that the opinion of experts as to the literary, artistic, scientific or other merits of an article may be admitted in any proceedings under this Act either to establish or to negative the said ground.

(3) In this section "moving picture soundtrack" means any sound record designed for playing with a moving picture film, whether incorporated with the film or not.

5. Citation, commencement and extent.—(1) This Act may be cited as the Obscene Publications Act, 1959.

(2) This Act shall come into operation on the expiration of one month beginning with the date of the passing thereof.

(3) This Act shall not extend to Scotland or to Northern Ireland.

OBSCENE PUBLICATIONS ACT, 1964

CHAPTER 74

An Act to strengthen the law for preventing the publication for gain of obscene matter and the publication of things intended for the production of obscene matter.

[*31st July 1964*]

1. Obscene articles intended for publication for gain

(1) In section 2(1) of the Obscene Publications Act, 1959 (under which it is an offence punishable on summary conviction or an indictment to publish an obscene article, whether for gain or not) after the words "any person who, whether for gain or not, publishes an obscene article" there shall be inserted the words "or who has an obscene article for publication for gain (whether gain to himself or another)".

(2) For the purpose of any proceedings for an offence against the said section 2 a person shall be deemed to have an article for publication for gain if with a view to such publication he has the article in his ownership, possession or control.

(3) In proceedings brought against a person under the said section 2 for having an obscene article for publication for gain the following provisions shall apply in place of sub-sections (5) and (6) of that section, that is to say,—

(a) he shall not be convicted of that offence if he proves that he had not examined the article and had no reasonable cause to suspect that it was such that his having it would make him liable to be convicted of an offence against that section; and

(b) the question whether the article is obscene shall be determined by reference to such publication for gain of the article as in the circumstances it may reasonably be inferred he had in contemplation and to any further publication that could reasonably be expected to follow from it, but not to any other publication.

(4) Where articles are seized under section 3 of the Obscene Publications Act, 1959 (which provides for the seizure and forfeiture of obscene articles kept for publication for gain), and a person is convicted under section 2 of that Act of having them for publication for gain, the court on his conviction shall order the forfeiture of those articles:

Provided that an order made by virtue of this sub-section (including an order so made on appeal) shall not take effect until the expiration of the ordinary time within which an appeal in the matter of the proceedings in which the order was made may be instituted or, where such an appeal is duly instituted, until the appeal is finally decided or abandoned; and for this purpose—

(a) an application for a case to be stated or for leave to appeal shall be treated as the institution of an appeal; and

(b) where a decision on appeal is subject to a further appeal, the appeal shall not be deemed to be finally decided until the expiration of the ordinary time within which a further appeal may be instituted or, where a further appeal is duly instituted, until the further appeal is finally decided or abandoned.

(5) References in section 3 of the Obscene Publications Act, 1959 and this section to publication for gain shall apply to any publication with a view to gain, whether the gain is to accrue by way of consideration for the publication or in any other way.

2. Negatives, etc. for production of obscene articles

(1) The Obscene Publications Act, 1959 (as amended by this Act) shall apply in relation to anything which is intended to be used, either alone or as one of a set, for the reproduction or manufacture there from of articles containing or embodying matter to be read, looked at or listened to, as if it were an article containing or embodying that matter so far as that matter is to be derived from it or from the set.

(2) For the purposes of the Obscene Publications Act, 1959 (as so amended) an article shall be deemed to be had or kept for publication if it is had or kept for the reproduction or manufacture there from of articles for publication; and the question whether an article so had or kept is obscene shall—

(a) for purposes of section 2 of the Act be determined in accordance with section 1(3)(b) above as if any reference there to publication of the article were a reference to publication of articles reproduced or manufactured from it; and

(b) for purposes of section 3 of the Act be determined on the assumption that articles reproduced or manufactured from it would be published in any manner likely having regard to the circumstances in which it was found, but in no other manner.

3. Citation, commencement and extent

(1) This Act may be cited as the Obscene Publications Act, 1964, and this Act and the Obscene Publications Act, 1959 may be cited together as the Obscene Publications Acts 1959 and 1964.

(2) This Act shall come into operation on the expiration of one month beginning with the date of the passing thereof.

(3) This Act shall not extend to Scotland or to Northern Ireland.

CHILDREN AND YOUNG PERSONS (HARMFUL PUBLICATIONS) ACT, 1955

An Act to prevent the dissemination of certain pictorial publications harmful to children and young persons.

[*6th May, 1955*]

1. Works to which this Act applies.

This Act applies to any book, magazine or other like work which is of a kind likely to fall into the hands of children or young persons and consists wholly or mainly of stories told in pictures (with or without the addition of written matter), being stories portraying—

(a) the commission of crimes; or

(b) acts of violence or cruelty; or

(c) incidents of a repulsive or horrible nature;

in such a way that the work as a whole would tend to corrupt a child or young person into whose hands it might fall.

2. Penalty for printing, publishing, selling, & c., works to which this Act applies.

(1) A person who prints, publishes, sells or lets on hire a work to which this Act applies, or has any such work in his possession for the purpose of selling it or letting it on hire, shall be guilty of an offence and liable, on summary conviction, to imprisonment for a term not exceeding four months or to a fine not exceeding level 3 on the standard scale]or to both:

Provided that, in any proceedings taken under this sub-section against a person in respect of selling or letting on hire a work or of having it in his possession for the purpose of selling it or letting it on hire, it shall be a defence for him to prove that he had not examined the contents of the work and had no reasonable cause to suspect that it was one to which this Act applies.

(2) A prosecution for an offence under this section shall not, in England or Wales, be instituted except by, or with the consent of, the Attorney General.

3. Power to search for, and dispose of, works to which this Act applies and articles for printing them.

(1) Where, upon an information being laid before a justice of the peace that a person has, or is suspected of having, committed an offence under the last foregoing section with respect to a work (hereafter in this sub-section referred to as "the relevant work"), the justice issues a summons directed to that person requiring him to answer to the information or issues a warrant to arrest that person, that or any other justice, if satisfied by written information substantiated on oath that there is reasonable ground for suspecting that the said person has in his possession or under his control—

(a) any copies of the relevant work or any other work to which this Act applies; or

(b) any plate prepared for the purpose of printing copies of the relevant work or any other work to which this Act applies or any photographic film prepared for that purpose;

may grant a search warrant authorising any constable named therein to enter (if necessary by force) any premises specified in the warrant and any vehicle or stall used by the said person for the purposes of trade or business and to search the premises, vehicle or stall and seize any of the following things which the constable finds therein or thereon, that is to say:

(i) any copies of the relevant work and any copies of any other work which the constable has reasonable cause to believe to be one to which this Act applies; and

(ii) any plate which the constable has reasonable cause to believe to have been prepared for the purpose of printing copies of any such work as is mentioned in paragraph (i) of this sub-section and any photographic film which he has reasonable cause to believe to have been prepared for that purpose.

(2) The court by or before which a person is convicted of an offence under the last foregoing section with respect to a work may order any copies of that work and any plate prepared for the purpose of printing copies of that work or photographic film prepared for that purpose, being copies which have, or a plate or film which has, been found in his possession or under his control, to be forfeited:

Provided that an order made under this sub-section by a magistrate's court or, on appeal from a magistrate's court, by the Crown Court shall not take effect until the expiration of the ordinary time within which an appeal in the matter of the proceedings in which the order was made may be lodged (whether by giving notice of appeal or applying for a case to be stated for the opinion of the High Court) or, where such an appeal is duly lodged, until the appeal is finally decided or abandoned.

(3) In the application of this section to Scotland there shall be substituted in sub-section (1) for the words from the beginning of the sub-section to "any other justice" the words "Where proceedings have been instituted against a person in respect of an offence under the last foregoing section with respect to a work (hereafter in this sub-section referred to as "the relevant work'), the sheriff"; and for the proviso to sub-section (2) there shall be substituted the following proviso:

"Provided that an order made under this sub-section shall not take effect until the expiration of the time within which an appeal under section 442 of the Criminal Procedure (Scotland) Act, 1975, may be taken in respect of the proceedings in which the order was made or, where such an appeal is taken, until the appeal is finally disposed of or abandoned."

4. Prohibition of importation of works to which this Act applies and articles for printing them.

The importation of—

(a) any work to which this Act applies; and

(b) any plate prepared for the purpose of printing copies of any such work and any photographic film prepared for that purpose; is hereby prohibited.

5. Short title, interpretation, extent, commencement and duration.

(1) This Act may be cited as the Children and Young Persons (Harmful Publications) Act, 1955.

(2) In this Act the expressions "child" and "young person" have the meanings assigned to them respectively by section one hundred and seven of the Children and Young Persons Act, 1933, or, in Scotland, by section one hundred and ten of the Children and Young Persons (Scotland) Act, 1937, the expression "plate"(except where it occurs in the expression "photographic plate") includes block, mould, matrix and stencil and the expression "photographic film" includes photographic plate.

(3) No provision of this Act, other than the provisions of the last foregoing section, shall extend to Northern Ireland.

(4) This Act shall come into operation at the expiration of one month beginning with the date of its passing.

SEXUAL OFFENCES ACT, 2003

(Relevant Provisions)

Section 45: Indecent photographs of persons aged 16 or 17

This clause redefines a "child" for the purposes of the Protection of Children Act, 1978 ("the 1978 Act") as a person under 18 years, rather than under 16 years, of age. This change means the offences under that Act of taking, making, permitting to take, distributing, showing, possessing with intent to distribute, and advertising indecent photographs or pseudo-photographs of children will now also be applicable where the photographs concerned are of children of 16 or 17 years of age. The same change applies to the offence of possessing an indecent photograph or pseudo-photograph of a child at section 160 of the Criminal Justice Act, 1988 [section 160(4) applies the 1978 Act definition of "child"].

However, the clause also creates a number of conditions which if satisfied will mean that the defendant is not guilty of an offence under section 1(1) (a), (b) or (c) of the 1978 Act (provided that the offence charged relates to a photograph and not a pseudo-photograph).

The conditions in relation to an offence under section 1(1)(a) of the 1978 Act (taking or making indecent photographs) are as follows:

Firstly, the defendant must prove that the photograph in question was of the child aged 16 or over and that at the time of the taking or making of the photograph he and the child were married or living together as partners in an enduring family relationship [section 1A(1)].

Secondly, the defendant must show that there is enough evidence to raise an issue as to whether the child consented to the photograph being taken or made, or as to whether the defendant reasonably believed that the child consented [section 1A(4)].

Thirdly, the photograph must not be one that shows a person other than the child and the defendant [section 1A (3)].

If any of these conditions is not satisfied, the prosecution need only prove the offence as set out in section 1(1)(a) of the 1978 Act. But if the three conditions are satisfied, the defendant is not guilty of the offence unless the prosecution also prove that the child did not consent and that the defendant did not reasonably believe that the child consented [section 1A(4)].

The conditions in relation to an offence under section 1(1)(b) of the 1978 Act (distributing or showing indecent photographs) are as follows;

Firstly, the defendant must prove that the photograph in question was of the child aged 16 or over, and that either at the time of distributing or showing it, or at the time of obtaining it, he and the child were married or living together as partners in an enduring family relationship [section 1A(1) and (2)].

Secondly, the photograph must not be one that shows a person other than the child and the defendant [section 1A(3)].

If either of these conditions is not satisfied, the prosecution need only prove the offence as set out in section 1(1)(b) of the 1978 Act. But if both the conditions are satisfied, the defendant is not guilty of the offence unless the prosecution prove that the showing or distribution was to a person other than the child [section 1A(5)].

The conditions in relation to an offence under section 1(1)(c) of the 1978 Act (being in possession of indecent photographs with a view to their being distributed or shown) is as follows:

Firstly, the defendant must prove that the photograph in question was of the child aged 16 or over and that either at the time of his possession of it with a view to distributing or showing it, or at the time when he obtained it, he and the child were married or living together as partners in an enduring family relationship [section 1A(1) and (2)].

Secondly, the defendant must show that there is enough evidence to raise an issue as to whether the child consented (or the defendant reasonably believed that the child consented) to the photograph's being in the defendant's possession, and also as to whether the defendant had the photograph in his possession with a view to distributing or showing it to a person other than the child [section 1A(6)].

Thirdly, the photograph must not be one that shows a person other than the child and the defendant [section 1A(3)].

If any of these conditions is not satisfied, the prosecution need only prove the offence as set out in section 1(1)(c) of the 1978 Act. But if the three conditions are satisfied, the defendant is not guilty of the offence unless the prosecution also prove either that the child did not so consent and that the defendant did not reasonably believe that the child so consented, or that the defendant had the photograph in his possession with a view to its being distributed to a person other than the child.

Similar provision is made in relation to an offence under section 160 of the Criminal Justice Act, 1988 (possession of indecent photograph of a child). The conditions are as follows:

Firstly, the defendant must prove that the photograph in question was of the child aged 16 or over and that at the time when he possessed the photograph, or at the time when he obtained it, he and the child were married or living together as partners in an enduring family relationship [section 160A(1) and (2)].

Secondly, the defendant must show that there is enough evidence to raise an issue as to whether the child consented to the photograph being in his possession or as to whether the defendant reasonably believed that the child so consented [section 160A(4)].

Thirdly, the photograph must not be one that shows a person other than the child and the defendant [section 160A(3)].

If any of these conditions is not satisfied, the prosecution need only prove the offence as set out in section 160 of the Criminal Justice Act, 1988. But if the three conditions are satisfied, the defendant is not guilty of the offence unless the prosecution prove that the child did not consent and that the defendant did not reasonably believe that the child consented [section 160A(4)].

Section 48: Causing or inciting child prostitution or pornography

Section 48 makes it an offence for a person (A) intentionally to cause or incite a child under 18(B) into prostitution or involvement in pornography anywhere in the world. The offence is aimed at persons who recruit into prostitution or pornography (whether on a one-off basis or longer term) those who are not involved or not currently involved in it. This could be where A makes a living from the prostitution of others and encourages new recruits to work for him or another (whether those recruits do actually then engage in prostitution or not). It could also cover the situation where A and B live together and A compels B to become involved in pornography, for example in order to pay their rent, or for any other reason. Unlike the prostitution offence at section 53, there is no requirement that the causing or inciting of a child prostitute must be done for gain. The prostitution or pornography can take place, or be intended to take place, in any part of the world. Where B is 13 or over, the offence will not be committed where A reasonably believes that B is 18 or over. (It will be for the prosecution to prove that A does not reasonably believe that B is 18 or over). However, where B is under 13, A will commit the offence regardless of any reasonable belief he may have about B's age. The terms "pornography" and "prostitute" are defined in section 51.

Section 49: Controlling a child prostitute or a child involved in pornography

Section 49 makes it an offence for a person (A) intentionally to control any of the activities of a child (B) that relate to the child's prostitution or involvement in pornography in any part of the world. The offence is committed even if B's activities in relation to prostitution or pornography are controlled for part of the time by another person. An example of the behaviour that might be caught by this offence is where A requires or directs B to charge a certain price or to use a particular hotel for her sexual services or to pose for a certain photographer and B complies with this request or direction. The prostitution or pornography can take place in any part of the world. Where B is 13 or over, the offence will not be committed where A reasonably believes that B is 18 or over. (It will be for the prosecution to prove that A does not reasonably believe that B is 18 or over). However, where B is under 13, A will commit the offence regardless of any belief he may have about B's age. The terms "pornography" and "prostitution" are defined in section 51.

Section 50: Arranging or facilitating child prostitution or pornography

Section 50 makes it an offence for a person (A) to arrange or facilitate the involvement of a child (B) in prostitution or pornography in any part of the world. This offence would cover for example, delivering B to a place where he will be used to make pornography or making arrangements for B's prostitution to take place in a particular room. Where B is 13 or over, the offence will not be committed where A reasonably believes that B is 18 or over. (It will be for the prosecution to prove that A does not reasonably believe that B is 18 or over). However, where B is under 13, A will commit the offence regardless of any reasonable belief he may have about B's age. The terms "pornography" and "prostitution" are defined in section 51

CRIMINAL JUSTICE AND IMMIGRATION ACT, 2008

(Relevant Provisions)

PART 5

63. Possession of extreme pornographic images

(1) It is an offence for a person to be in possession of an extreme pornographic image.

(2) An "extreme pornographic image" is an image which is both—

(a) pornographic, and

(b) an extreme image.

(3) An image is "pornographic" if it is of such a nature that it must reasonably be assumed to have been produced solely or principally for the purpose of sexual arousal.

(4) Where (as found in the person's possession) an image forms part of a series of images, the question whether the image is of such a nature as is mentioned in sub-section (3) is to be determined by reference to—

(a) the image itself, and

(b) (if the series of images is such as to be capable of providing a context for the image) the context in which it occurs in the series of images.

(5) So, for example, where—

(a) an image forms an integral part of a narrative constituted by a series of images, and

(b) having regard to those images as a whole, they are not of such a nature that they must reasonably be assumed to have been produced solely or principally for the purpose of sexual arousal,

the image may, by virtue of being part of that narrative, be found not to be pornographic, even though it might have been found to be pornographic if taken by itself.

(6) An "extreme image" is an image which—

(a) falls within sub-section (7), and

(b) is grossly offensive, disgusting or otherwise of an obscene character.

(7) An image falls within this sub-section if it portrays, in an explicit and realistic way, any of the following—

(a) an act which threatens a person's life,

(b) an act which results, or is likely to result, in serious injury to a person's anus, breasts or genitals,

(c) an act which involves sexual interference with a human corpse, or

(d) a person performing an act of intercourse or oral sex with an animal (whether dead or alive),

and a reasonable person looking at the image would think that any such person or animal was real.

(8) In this section "image" means—

(a) a moving or still image (produced by any means); or

(b) data (stored by any means) which is capable of conversion into an image within paragraph (a).

(9) In this section references to a part of the body include references to a part surgically constructed (in particular through gender reassignment surgery).

(10) Proceedings for an offence under this section may not be instituted—

(a) in England and Wales, except by or with the consent of the Director of Public Prosecutions; or

(b) in Northern Ireland, except by or with the consent of the Director of Public Prosecutions for Northern Ireland.

64. Exclusion of classified films etc.

(1) Section 63 does not apply to excluded images.

(2) An "excluded image" is an image which forms part of a series of images contained in a recording of the whole or part of a classified work.

(3) But such an image is not an "excluded image" if—

(a) it is contained in a recording of an extract from a classified work, and

(b) it is of such a nature that it must reasonably be assumed to have been extracted (whether with or without other images) solely or principally for the purpose of sexual arousal.

(4) Where an extracted image is one of a series of images contained in the recording, the question whether the image is of such a nature as is mentioned in sub-section (3)(b) is to be determined by reference to—

(a) the image itself, and

(b) (if the series of images is such as to be capable of providing a context for the image) the context in which it occurs in the series of images;

and section 63(5) applies in connection with determining that question as it applies in connection with determining whether an image is pornographic.

(5) In determining for the purposes of this section whether a recording is a recording of the whole or part of a classified work, any alteration attributable to—

(a) a defect caused for technical reasons or by inadvertence on the part of any person, or

(b) the inclusion in the recording of any extraneous material (such as advertisements), is to be disregarded.

(6) Nothing in this section is to be taken as affecting any duty of a designated authority to have regard to section 63 (along with other enactments creating criminal offences) in determining whether a video work is suitable for a classification certificate to be issued in respect of it.

(7) In this section—

- "classified work" means (subject to sub-section (8)) a video work in respect of which a classification certificate has been issued by a designated authority (whether before or after the commencement of this section);
- "classification certificate" and "video work" have the same meanings as in the Video Recordings Act, 1984 (c. 39);
- "designated authority" means an authority which has been designated by the Secretary of State under section 4 of that Act;

- "extract" includes an extract consisting of a single image;
- "image" and "pornographic" have the same meanings as in section 63;
- "recording" means any disc, tape or other device capable of storing data electronically and from which images may be produced (by any means).

(8) Section 22(3) of the Video Recordings Act, 1984 (effect of alterations) applies for the purposes of this section as it applies for the purposes of that Act.

65. Defences: general

(1) Where a person is charged with an offence under section 63, it is a defence for the person to prove any of the matters mentioned in sub-section (2).

(2) The matters are—

(a) that the person had a legitimate reason for being in possession of the image concerned;

(b) that the person had not seen the image concerned and did not know, nor had any cause to suspect, it to be an extreme pornographic image;

(c) that the person—

(i) was sent the image concerned without any prior request having been made by or on behalf of the person, and

(ii) did not keep it for an unreasonable time.

(3) In this section "extreme pornographic image" and "image" have the same meanings as in section 63.

66. Defence: participation in consensual acts

(1) This section applies where—

(a) a person ("D") is charged with an offence under section 63, and

(b) the offence relates to an image that portrays an act or acts within paragraphs (a) to (c) (but none within paragraph (d)) of sub-section (7) of that section.

(2) It is a defence for D to prove—

(a) that D directly participated in the act or any of the acts portrayed, and

(b) that the act or acts did not involve the infliction of any non-consensual harm on any person, and

(c) if the image portrays an act within section 63(7)(c), that what is portrayed as a human corpse was not in fact a corpse.

(3) For the purposes of this section harm inflicted on a person is "non-consensual" harm if—

(a) the harm is of such a nature that the person cannot, in law, consent to it being inflicted on himself or herself; or

(b) where the person can, in law, consent to it being so inflicted, the person does not in fact consent to it being so inflicted.

67. Penalties etc. for possession of extreme pornographic images

(1) This section has effect where a person is guilty of an offence under section 63.

(2) Except where sub-section (3) applies to the offence, the offender is liable—

(a) on summary conviction, to imprisonment for a term not exceeding the relevant period or a fine not exceeding the statutory maximum or both;

(b) on conviction on indictment, to imprisonment for a term not exceeding 3 years or a fine or both.

(3) If the offence relates to an image that does not portray any act within section 63(7)(a) or (b), the offender is liable—

(a) on summary conviction, to imprisonment for a term not exceeding the relevant period or a fine not exceeding the statutory maximum or both;

(b) on conviction on indictment, to imprisonment for a term not exceeding 2 years or a fine or both.

(4) In sub-section (2)(a) or (3)(a) "the relevant period" means—

(a) in relation to England and Wales, 12 months;

(b) in relation to Northern Ireland, 6 months.

68. Special rules relating to providers of information society services

Schedule 14 makes special provision in connection with the operation of section 63 in relation to persons providing information society services within the meaning of that Schedule.

69. Indecent photographs of children: England and Wales

(1) The Protection of Children Act, 1978 (c. 37) is amended as follows.

(2) In section 1B(1)(b) (exception for members of the Security Service)—

(a) after "Security Service" insert "or the Secret Intelligence Service";

(b) for "the Service" substitute "that Service".

(3) After section 7(4) (meaning of photograph), insert—

"(4A) References to a photograph also include—

(a) a tracing or other image, whether made by electronic or other means (of whatever nature)—

(i) which is not itself a photograph or pseudo-photograph, but

(ii) which is derived from the whole or part of a photograph or pseudo-photograph (or a combination of either or both); and

(b) data stored on a computer disc or by other electronic means which is capable of conversion into an image within paragraph (a);

and sub-section (8) applies in relation to such an image as it applies in relation to a pseudo-photograph."

(4) In section 7(9)(b) (meaning of indecent pseudo-photograph), for "a pseudo-photograph" substitute "an indecent pseudo-photograph".

70. Indecent photographs of children: Northern Ireland

(1) The Protection of Children (Northern Ireland) Order, 1978 (S.I. 1978/1047 (N.I. 17)) is amended as follows.

(2) In Article 2(2) (interpretation) in paragraph (b) of the definition of "indecent pseudo-photograph", for "a pseudo-photograph" substitute "an indecent pseudo-photograph".

(3) After Article 2(2) insert—

"(2A) In this Order, references to a photograph also include—

(a) a tracing or other image, whether made by electronic or other means (of whatever nature)—

(i) which is not itself a photograph or pseudo-photograph, but

(ii) which is derived from the whole or part of a photograph or pseudo-photograph (or a combination of either or both); and

(b) data stored on a computer disc or by other electronic means which is capable of conversion into an image within paragraph (a);

and paragraph (3)(c) applies in relation to such an image as it applies in relation to a pseudo-photograph."

(4) In article 3A(1)(b) (exception for members of the Security Service)—

(a) after "Security Service" insert "or the Secret Intelligence Service";

(b) for "the Service" substitute "that Service".

71. Maximum penalty for publication etc. of obscene articles

In section 2(1)(b) of the Obscene Publications Act, 1959 (c. 66) (maximum penalty on indictment for publication etc. of obscene articles) for "three years" substitute "five years".

INDIAN STATUTES

THE YOUNG PERSONS (HARMFUL PUBLICATIONS) ACT, 1956

(93 of 1956)

[*28th December, 1956*]

An Act to prevent the dissemination of certain publications harmful to young persons.

BE it enacted by Parliament in the Seventh Year of the Republic of India as follows:—

1. Short title, extent and commencement.—(1) This Act may be called the Young Persons (Harmful Publications) Act, 1956.

(2) It extends to the whole of India except the State of Jammu and Kashmir.

(3) It shall come into force on such date as the Central Government may, by notification in the Official Gazette, appoint.

2. Definitions.—In this Act,—

(a) "harmful publication" means any book, magazine, pamphlet, leaflet, newspaper or other like publication which consists of stories told with the aid of pictures or without the aid of pictures or wholly in pictures, being stories portraying wholly or mainly—

(i) the commission of offences; or

(ii) acts of violence or cruelty; or

(iii) incidents of a repulsive or horrible nature;

in such a way that the publication as a whole would tend to corrupt a young person into whose hands it might fall, whether by inciting or encouraging him to commit offences or acts of violence or cruelty or in any other manner whatsoever;

(b) "State Government" in relation to a Union territory, means the administrator thereof;

(c) "young person" means a person under the age of twenty years.

3. Penalty for sale, etc., of harmful publications.—(1) If a person—

(a) sells, lets to hire, distributes, publicly exhibits or in any manner puts into circulation, any harmful publication, or

(b) for purposes of sale, hire, distribution, public exhibition or circulation, prints, makes or produces or has in his possession any harmful publication, or

(c) advertises or makes known by any means whatsoever that any harmful publication can be procured from or through any person,

he shall be punishable with imprisonment which may extend to six months, or with fine, or with both.

(2) On a conviction under this section, the court may order the destruction of all the copies of the harmful publication in respect of which the conviction was had and which are in the custody of court or remain in the possession or power of the person convicted.

4. Power of Government to declare harmful publications forfeited.—(1) The State Government may, if it is of opinion after consultation with the principal law officer of the State, whether called the Advocate-General or by any other name, that any publication is a harmful publication, declare, by order notified in the Official Gazette, that every copy of such publication shall be forfeited to the Government and every such notification shall state the ground for the order.

(2) Without prejudice to the provisions contained in sub-section (1) of section 6, where there is an order of forfeiture under sub-section (1) in respect of any publication it shall be lawful for any police officer to seize the same wherever found in the territories to which this Act extends.

5. Appeal to High Court against order of forfeiture.—Any person aggrieved by an order of forfeiture passed by the State Government under section 4 may, within sixty days of the date of such order, apply to the High Court to set aside such order, and upon such application the High Court may pass such order as it deems fit.

6. Power to seize and destroy harmful publications.—(1) Any police officer or any other officer empowered in this behalf by the State Government may seize any harmful publication.

(2) Any magistrate of the first class may, by warrant, authorise any police officer not below the rank of sub-inspector to enter and search any place where any stock of harmful publications may be or may be resonably suspected to be, and such police officer may seize any publication found in such place if in his opinion it is a harmful publication.

(3) Any publication seized under sub-section (1) shall be produced, as soon as may be, before a magistrate of the first class, and any publication seized under sub-section (2) shall be produced, as soon as may be, before the court which issued the warrant.

(4) If in the opinion of the magistrate or court such publication is a harmful publication, the magistrate or court may cause it to be destroyed, but if, in the opinion of the magistrate or court, such publication is not a harmful publication, the magistrate or court shall dispose of it in the manner provided in sections 523, 524 and 525 of the Code of Criminal Procedure, 1898 (5 of 1898).

7. Offences under this Act to be cognizable.—Notwithstanding anything contained in the Code of Criminal Procedure, 1898 (5 of 1898), any offence punishable under this Act shall be cognizable.

THE INDECENT REPRESENTATION OF WOMEN (PROHIBITION) ACT, 1986[1]

(60 of 1986)

[*23rd December, 1986*]

An Act to prohibit indecent representation of women through advertisements or in publications, writings, paintings, figures or in any other manner and for matters connected therewith or incidental thereto

BE it enacted by Parliament in the Thirty-seventh Year of the Republic of India as follows:—

1. Short title, extent and commencement.—(1) This Act may be called the Indecent Representation of Women (Prohibition) Act, 1986.

(2) It extends to the whole of India, except the State of Jammu and Kashmir.

(3) It shall come into force on such date[2] as the Central Government may, by notification in the Official Gazette, appoint.

2. Definitions.—In this Act, unless the context otherwise requires,—

(a) "advertisement" includes any notice, circular, label, wrapper or other document and also includes any visible representation made by means of any light, sound, smoke or gas;

(b) "distribution" includes distribution by way of samples whether free or otherwise;

(c) "indecent representation of women" means the depiction in any manner of the figure of a woman, her form or body or any part thereof in such a way as to have the effect of being indecent, or derogatory to, or denigrating, women, or is likely to deprave, corrupt or injure the public morality or morals;

(d) "label" means any written, marked, stamped, printed or graphic matter, affixed to, or appearing upon, any package;

(e) "package" includes a box, carton, tin or other container;

(f) "prescribed" means prescribed by rules made under this Act.

3. Prohibition of advertisements containing indecent representation of women.—No person shall publish, or cause to be published, or arrange or take part in the publication or exhibition of, any advertisement which contains indecent representation of women in any form.

4. Prohibition of publication or sending by post of books, pamphlets, *etc.*, containing indecent representation of women.—No person shall produce or cause to be produced, sell, let to hire, distribute, circulate or send by post any book, pamphlet, paper, slide, film, writing, drawing, painting, photograph, representation or figure which contains indecent representation of women in any form:

Provided that nothing in this section shall apply to—

---

1. Published in the Gazette of India, Extra., Pt. II, Sec. 1, dated 23rd December, 1986.
2. 2-10-1987 *vide* Notification No. G.S.R. 821(E), dated 25th September, 1987, *see* Gazette of India, Extra., 1987, Pt. II, Sec. 3(i).

(a) any book, pamphlet, paper, slide, film, writing, drawing, painting, photograph, representation or figure—

(i) the publication of which is proved to be justified as being for the public good on the ground that such book, pamphlet, paper, slide, film, writing, drawing, painting, photograph, representation or figure is in the interest of science, literature, art, or learning or other objects of general concern; or

(ii) which is kept or used *bona fide* for religious purposes;

(b) any representation sculptured, engraved, painted or otherwise represented on or in—

(i) any ancient monument within the meaning of the Ancient Monument and Archaeological Sites and Remains Act, 1958 (24 of 1958); or

(ii) any temple, or on any car used for the conveyance of idols, or kept or used for any religious purpose.

(c) any film in respect of which the provisions of Part II of the Cinematograph Act, 1952 (37 of 1952), will be applicable.

5. Powers to enter and search.—(1) Subject to such rules as may be prescribed, any Gazetted Officer authorised by the State Government may, within the local limits of the area for which he is so authorised,—

(a) enter and search at all reasonable times, with such assistance, if any, as he considers necessary, any place in which he has reason to believe that an offence under this Act has been or is being committed;

(b) seize any advertisement or any book, pamphlet, paper, slide, film, writing, drawing, painting, photograph, representation or figure which he has reason to believe contravenes any of the provisions of this Act;

(c) examine any record, register, document or any other material object found in any place mentioned in clause (a) and seize the same if he has reason to believe that it may furnish evidence of the commission of an offence punishable under this Act:

Provided that no entry under this sub-section shall be made into a private dwelling house without a warrant:

Provided further that the power of seizure under this sub-section may be exercised in respect of any document, article or thing which contains any such advertisement, including the contents, if any, of such document, article or thing if the advertisement cannot be separated by reason of its being embossed or otherwise from such document, article or thing without affecting the integrity, utility or saleable value thereof.

(2) The provisions of the Code of Criminal Procedure, 1973 (2 of 1974), shall, so far as may be, apply to any search or seizure under this Act as they apply to any search or seizure made under the authority of a warrant issued under section 94 of the said Code.

(3) Where any person seizes anything under clause (b) or clause (c) of sub-section (1), he shall, as soon as may be, inform the nearest Magistrate and take his orders as to the custody thereof.

6. Penalty.—Any person who contravenes the provisions of section 3 or section 4 shall be punishable on first conviction with imprisonment of either description for a term which may extend to two years, and with fine which may extend to two thousand rupees, and in the event of a second or subsequent conviction with imprisonment for a term of not less than six months but which may extend to five years and also with a fine not less than ten thousand rupees but which may extend to one lakh rupees.

7. Offences by companies.—(1) Where an offence under this Act has been committed by a company, every person, who, at the time the offence was committed, was in charge of, and was responsible to, the company for the conduct of the business of the company, as well as the company, shall be deemed to be guilty of the offence and shall be liable to be proceeded against and punished accordingly:

Provided that nothing contained in this sub-section shall render any such person liable to any punishment, if he proves that the offence was committed without his knowledge or that he had exercised all due diligence to prevent the commission of such offence.

(2) Notwithstanding anything contained in sub-section (1), where any offence under this Act has been committed by a company and it is proved that the offence has been committed with the consent or connivance of, or is attributable to any neglect on the part of, any director, manager, secretary or other officer of the company, such director, manager, secretary or other officer shall be proceeded against and punished accordingly.

Explanation.—For the purposes of this section,—

(a) "company" means any body corporate and includes a firm or other association of individuals; and

(b) "director", in relation to a firm, means a partner in the firm.

8. Offences to be cognizable and bailable.—(1) Notwithstanding anything contained in the Code of Criminal Procedure, 1973 (2 of 1974), an offence punishable under this Act shall be bailable.

(2) An offence punishable under this Act shall be cognizable.

9. Protection of action taken in good faith.—No suit, prosecution or other legal proceeding shall lie against the Central Government or any State Government or any officer of the Central Government or any State Government for anything which is in good faith done or intended to be done under this Act.

10. Power to make rules.—(1) The Central Government may, by notification in the Official Gazette, make rules to carry out the provisions of this Act.

(2) In particular and without prejudice to the generality of the foregoing power, such rules may provide for all or any of the following matters, namely:—

(a) the manner in which the seizure of advertisements or other articles shall be made, and the manner in which the seizure list shall be prepared and delivered to the person from whose custody any advertisement or other article has been seized;

(b) any other matter which is required to be, or may be, prescribed.

(3) Every rule made under this Act, shall be laid, as soon as may be after it is made, before each House of Parliament, while it is in session for a total period of thirty days, which may be comprised in one session or in two or more successive sessions, and if, before the expiry of the session immediately following the session or the successive sessions aforesaid, both Houses agree in making any modification in the rule or both Houses agree that the rule should not be made, the rule shall thereafter have effect only in such modified form or be of no effect, as the case may be; so, however, that any such modification or annulment shall be without prejudice to the validity of anything previously done under that rule.

THE INFORMATION TECHNOLOGY ACT, 2000

(Relevant Provisions)

2. Definitions.—(1) In this Act, unless the context otherwise requires,—

(a) "access", with its grammatical variations and cognate expressions, means gaining entry into, instructing or communicating with the logical, arithmetical or memory function resources of a computer, computer system or computer network;

(b) "addressee" means a person who is intended by the originator to receive the electronic record but does not include any intermediary;

(c) "adjudicating officer" means an adjudicating officer appointed under sub-section (1) of section 46;

(d) "affixing electronic signature", with its grammatical variations and cognate expressions means adoption of any methodology or procedure by a person for the purpose of authenticating an electronic record by means of electronic signature;

(e) "appropriate Government" means as respects any matter,—

(i) enumerated in List II of the Seventh Schedule to the Constitution;

(ii) relating to any State law enacted under List III of the Seventh Schedule to the Constitution,

the State Government and in any other case, the Central Government;

(f) "asymmetric crypto system" means a system of a secure key pair consisting of a private key for creating a digital signature and a public key to verify the digital signature;

(g) "Certifying Authority" means a person who has been granted a licence to issue a electronic signature Certificate under section 24;

(h) "certification practice statement" means a statement issued by a Certifying Authority to specify the practices that the Certifying Authority employs in issuing Electronic Signature Certificates;

(ha) "communication device" means cell phones, personal digital assistance or combination of both or any other device used to communicate, send or transmit any text, video, audio or image;

(i) "computer" means any electronic, magnetic, optical or other high-speed data processing device or system which performs logical, arithmetic and memory functions by manipulations of electronic, magnetic or optical impulses, and includes all input, output, processing, storage, computer software or communication facilities which are connected or related to the computer in a computer system or computer network;

(j) "computer network" means the inter-connection of one or more computers or computer systems or communication device through—

(i) the use of satellite, microwave, terrestrial line, wire, wireless or other communication media; and

(ii) terminals or a complex consisting of two or more inter-connected computers or communication device whether or not the inter-connection is continuously maintained;

(k) "computer resource" means computer, computer system, computer network, data, computer data base or software;

(l) "computer system" means a device or collection of devices, including input and output support devices and excluding calculators which are not programmable and capable of being used in conjunction with external files which contain computer programmes, electronic instructions, input data and output data that performs logic, arithmetic, data storage and retrieval, communication control and other functions;

(m) "Controller" means the Controller of Certifying Authorities appointed under sub-section (l) of section 17;

(n) "Cyber Appellate Tribunal" means the Cyber Appellate Tribunal established under sub-section (1) of section 48;

(na) "cyber cafe" means any facility from where access to the internet is offered by any person in the ordinary course of business to the members of the public;

(nb) "cyber security" means protecting information, equipment, devices computer, computer resource, communication device and information stored therein from unauthorised access, use, disclosure, disruption, modification or destruction;

(o) "data" means a representation of information, knowledge, facts, concepts or instructions which are being prepared or have been prepared in a formalised manner, and is intended to be processed, is being processed or has been processed in a computer system or computer network, and may be in any form (including computer printouts magnetic or optical storage media, punched cards, punched tapes) or stored internally in the memory of the computer;

(p) "digital signature" means authentication of any electronic record by a subscriber by means of an electronic method or procedure in accordance with the provisions of section 3;

(q) "Digital Signature Certificate" means a Digital Signature Certificate issued under sub-section (4) of section 35;

(r) "electronic form", with reference to information, means any information generated, sent, received or stored in media, magnetic, optical, computer memory, micro film, computer generated micro fiche or similar device;

(s) "Electronic Gazette" means the Official Gazette published in the electronic form;

(t) "electronic record" means data, record or data generated, image or sound stored, received or sent in an electronic form or micro film or computer generated micro fiche;

(ta) "electronic signature" means authentication of any electronic record by a subscriber by means of the electronic technique specified in the Second Schedule and includes digital signature;

(tb) "Electronic Signature Certificate" means an Electronic Signature Certificate issued under section 35 and includes Digital Signature Certificate;

(u) "function", in relation to a computer, includes logic, control, arithmetical process, deletion, storage and retrieval and communication or telecommunication from or within a computer;

(ua) "Indian Computer Emergency Response Team" means an agency established under sub-section (1) of section 70B;

(v) "information" includes data, message, text, images, sound, voice, codes, computer programmes, software and data bases or micro film or computer generated micro fiche;

(w) "intermediary", with respect to any particular electronic records, means any person who on behalf of another person receives, stores or transmits that record or provides any service with respect to that record and includes telecom service providers, network service providers, internet service providers, web-hosting service providers, search engines, online payment sites, online-auction sites, online-market places and cyber cafes;

(x) "key pair", in an asymmetric crypto system, means a private key and its mathematically related public key, which are so related that the public key can verify a digital signature created by the private key;

(y) "law" includes any Act of Parliament or of a State Legislature, Ordinances promulgated by the President or a Governor, as the case may be, Regulations made by the President under article 240, Bills enacted as President's Act under sub-clause (a) of clause (1) of article 357 of the Constitution and includes rules, regulations, bye-laws and orders issued or made thereunder;

(z) "licence" means a licence granted to a Certifying Authority under section 24;

(za) "originator" means a person who sends, generates, stores or transmits any electronic message; or causes any electronic message to be sent, generated, stored or transmitted to any other person but does not include an intermediary;

(zb) "prescribed" means prescribed by rules made under this Act;

(zc) "private key" means the key of a key pair used to create a digital signature;

(zd) "public key" means the key of a key pair used to verify a digital signature and listed in the Digital Signature Certificate;

(ze) "secure system" means computer hardware, software, and procedure that—

(a) are reasonably secure from unauthorised access and misuse;

(b) provide a reasonable level of reliability and correct operation;

(c) are reasonably suited to performing the intended functions; and

(d) adhere to generally accepted security procedures;

(zf) "security procedure" means the security procedure prescribed under section 16 by the Central Government;

(zg) "subscriber" means a person in whose name the Electronic Signature Certificate is issued;

(zh) "verify", in relation to a digital signature, electronic record or public key, with its grammatical variations and cognate expressions, means to determine whether—

(a) the initial electronic record was affixed with the digital signature by the use of private key corresponding to the public key of the subscriber;

(b) the initial electronic record is retained intact or has been altered since such electronic record was so affixed with the digital signature.

(2) Any reference in this Act to any enactment or any provision thereof shall, in relation to an area in which such enactment or such provision is not in force, be construed as a reference to the corresponding law or the relevant provision of the corresponding law, if any, in force in that area.

66. Computer related offences.—If any person, dishonestly or fraudulently, does any act referred to in section 43, he shall be punishable with imprisonment for a term which may extend to three years or with fine which may extend to five lakh rupees or with both.

Explanation.—For the purposes of this section,—

(a) the word "dishonestly" shall have the meaning assigned to it in section 24 of the Indian Penal Code (45 of 1860);

(b) the word "fraudulently" shall have the meaning assigned to it in section 25 of the Indian Penal Code (45 of 1860).

66A. Punishment for sending offensive messages through communication service, etc.—Any person who sends, by means of a computer resource or a communication device,—

(a) any information that is grossly offensive or has menacing character; or

(b) any information which he knows to be false, but for the purpose of causing annoyance, inconvenience, danger, obstruction, insult, injury, criminal intimidation, enmity, hatred or ill will, persistently by making use of such computer resource or a communication device; or

(c) any electronic mail or electronic mail message for the purpose of causing annoyance or inconvenience or to deceive or to mislead the addressee or recipient about the origin of such messages,

shall be punishable with imprisonment for a term which may extend to three years and with fine.

Explanation.—For the purpose of this section, terms "electronic mail" and "electronic mail message" means a message or information created or transmitted or received on a computer, computer system, computer resource or communication device including attachments in text, image, audio, video and any other electronic record, which may be transmitted with the message.

66C. Punishment for identity theft.—Whoever, fraudulently or dishonestly make use of the electronic signature, password or any other unique identification feature of any other person, shall be punished with imprisonment of either description for a term which may extend to three years and shall also be liable to fine with may extend to rupees one lakh.

66D. Punishment for cheating by personation by using computer resource.—Whoever, by means for any communication device or computer resource cheats by personating, shall be punished with imprisonment of either description for a term which may extend to three years and shall also be liable to fine which may extend to one lakh rupees.

66E. Punishment for violation of privacy.—Whoever, intentionally or knowingly captures, publishes or transmits the image of a private area of any person without his or her consent, under circumstances violating the privacy of that person, shall be punished with imprisonment which may extend to three years or with fine not exceeding two lakh rupees, or with both.

Explanation.—For the purposes of this section—

(a) "transmit" means to electronically send a visual image with the intent that it be viewed by a person or persons;

(b) "capture", with respect to an image, means to videotape, photograph, film or record by any means;

(c) "private area" means the naked or undergarment clad genitals, pubic area, buttocks or female breast;

(d) "publishes" means reproduction in the printed or electronic form and making it available for public;

(e) "under circumstances violating privacy" means circumstances in which a person can have a reasonable expectation that;—

(i) he or she could disrobe in privacy, without being concerned that an image of his private area was being captured; or

(ii) any part of his or her private area would not be visible to the public, regardless of whether that person is in a public or private place.

67. Punishment for publishing or transmitting obscene material in electronic form.—Whoever publishes or transmits or causes to be published or transmitted in the electronic form, any material which is lascivious or appeals to the prurient interest or if its effect is such as to tend to deprave and corrupt persons who are likely, having regard to all relevant circumstances, to read, see or hear the matter contained or embodied in it, shall be punished on first conviction with imprisonment of either description for a term which may extend to three years and with fine which may extend to five lakh rupees and in the event of second or subsequent conviction with imprisonment of either description for a term which may extend to five years and also with fine which may extend to ten lakh rupees.

67A. Punishment for publishing or transmitting of material containing sexually explicit act, etc., in electronic form.—Whoever publishes or transmits or causes to be published or transmitted in the electronic form any material which contains sexually explicit act or conduct shall be punished on first conviction with imprisonment of either description for a term which may extend to five years and with fine which may extend to ten lakh rupees and in the event of second or subsequent conviction with imprisonment of either description for a term which may extend to seven years and also with fine which may extend to ten lakh rupees.

67B. Punishment for publishing or transmitting of material depicting children in sexually explicit act, etc., in electronic form.—Whoever—

(a) publishes or transmits or causes to be published or transmitted material in any electronic form which depicts children engaged in sexually explicit act or conduct; or

(b) creates text or digital images, collects, seeks, browses, downloads, advertises, promotes, exchanges or distributes material in any electronic form depicting children in obscene or indecent or sexually explicit manner; or

(c) cultivates, entices or induces children to online relationship with one or more children for and on sexually explicit act or in a manner that may offend a reasonable adult on the computer resource; or

(d) facilitates abusing children online, or

(e) records in any electronic form own abuse or that of others pertaining to sexually explicit act with children,

shall be punished on first conviction with imprisonment of either description for a term which may extend to five years and with fine which may extend to ten lakh rupees and in the event of second or subsequent conviction with imprisonment of either discription for a term which may extend to seven years and also with fine which may extend to ten lakh rupees:

Provided that provisions of section 67, section 67A and this section does not extend to any book, pamphlet, paper, writing, drawing, painting representation or figure in electronic form—

(i) the publication of which is proved to be justified as being for the public good on the ground that such book, pamphlet, paper, writing drawing, painting representation or figure is in the interest of science, literature, art or learning or other objects of general concern; or

(ii) which is kept or used for *bona fide* heritage or religious purposes.

Explanation.—For the purposes of this section "children" means a person who has not completed the age of 18 years.

71. Penalty for misrepresentation.—Whoever makes any misrepresentation to, or suppresses any material fact from the Controller or the Certifying Authority for obtaining any licence or Electronic Signature Certificate, as the case may be, shall be punished with imprisonment for a term which may extend to two years, or with fine which may extend to one lakh rupees, or with both.

72. Penalty for breach of confidentiality and privacy.—Save as otherwise provided in this Act or any other law for the time being in force, if any person who, in pursuance of any of the powers conferred under this Act, rules or regulations made thereunder, has secured access to any electronic record, book, register, correspondence, information, document or other material without the consent of the person concerned discloses such electronic record, book, register, correspondence, information, document or other material to any other person shall be punished with imprisonment for a term which may extend to two years, or with fine which may extend to one lakh rupees, or with both.

75. Act to apply for offence or contravention committed outside India.—(1) Subject to the provisions of sub-section (2), the provisions of this Act shall apply also to any offence or contravention committed outside India by any person irrespective of his nationality.

(2) For the purposes of sub-section (1), this Act shall apply to an offence or contravention committed outside India by any person if the act or conduct constituting the offence or contravention involves a computer, computer system or computer network located in India.

79. Exemption from liability of intermediary in certain cases.—(1) Notwithstanding anything contained in any law for the time being in force but subject to the provisions of sub-sections (2) and (3), an intermediary shall not be liable for any third party information, data, or communication link made available or hosted by him.

(2) The provisions of sub-section (1) shall apply if—

(a) the function of the intermediary is limited to providing access to a communication system over which information made available by third parties is transmitted or temporarily stored or hosted; or

(b) the intermediary does not—

(i) initiate the transmission,

(ii) select the receiver of the transmission, and

(iii) select or modify the information contained in the transmission;

(c) the intermediary observes due diligence while discharging his duties under this Act and also observes such other guidelines as the Central Government may prescribe in this behalf.

(3) The provisions of sub-section (1) shall not apply if—

(a) the intermediary has conspired or abetted or aided or induced, whether by threats or promise or othorise in the commission of the unlawful act;

(b) upon receiving actual knowledge, or on being notified by the appropriate Government or its agency that any information, data or communication link residing in or connected to a computer resource, controlled by the intermediary is being used to commit the unlawful act, the intermediary fails to expeditiously remove or disable access to that material on that resource without vitiating the evidence in any manner.

Explanation.—For the purpose of this section, the expression "third party information" means any information dealt with by an intermediary in his capacity as an intermediary.

80. Power of police officer and other officers to enter, search, etc.—(1) Notwithstanding anything contained in the Code of Criminal Procedure, 1973 (2 of 1974), any police officer, not below the rank of a Inspector, or any other officer of the Central Government or a State Government authorised by the Central Government in this behalf may enter any public place and search and arrest without warrant any person found therein who is reasonably suspected of having committed or of committing or of being about to commit any offence under this Act.

Explanation.—For the purposes of this sub-section, the expression "public place" includes any public conveyance, any hotel, any shop or any other place intended for use by, or accessible to the public.

(2) Where any person is arrested under sub-section (1) by an officer other than a police officer, such officer shall, without unnecessary delay, take or send the person arrested before a magistrate having jurisdiction in the case or before the officer-in-charge of a police station.

(3) The provisions of the Code of Criminal Procedure, 1973 (2 of 1974), shall, subject to the provisions of this section, apply, so far as may be, in relation to any entry, search or arrest, made under this section.

THE CABLE TELEVISION NETWORKS (REGULATION) ACT, 1995

(Relevant Provisions)

19. Power to prohibit transmission of certain programmes in public interest.—Where any authorised officer thinks it necessary or expedient so to do in the public interest, he may, by order, prohibit any cable operator from transmitting or re-transmitting any programme or channel if, it is not in conformity with the prescribed programme code referred to in section 5 and advertisement code referred to in section 6 or if it is likely to promote, on grounds of religion, race, language, caste or community or any other ground whatsoever, disharmony or feelings of enmity, hatred or ill-will between different religious, racial, linguistic or regional groups or castes or communities or which is likely to disturb the public tranquillity.

20. Power to prohibit operation of cable television network in public interest.—(1) Where the Central Government thinks it necessary or expedient so to do in public interest, it may prohibit the operation of any cable television network in such areas as it may, by notification in the Official Gazette, specify in this behalf.

(2) Where the Central Government thinks it necessary or expedient so to do in the interest of the—

(i) sovereignty or integrity of India; or

(ii) security of India; or

(iii) friendly relations of India with any foreign State; or

(iv) public order, decency or morality,

it may, by order, regulate or prohibit the transmission or re-transmission of any channel or programme.

(3) Where the Central Government considers that any programme of any channel is not in conformity with the prescribed programme code referred to in section 5 or the prescribed advertisement code referred to in section 6, it may by order, regulate or prohibit the transmission or re-transmission of such programme.

THE CABLE TELEVISION NETWORKS RULES, 1994

(Relevant Provisions)

6. Programme Code.—(1) No programme should be carried in the cable service which—

(a) offends against good taste or decency;

(d) contains anything obscene, defamatory, deliberate, false and suggestive innuendos and half truths;

(k) denigrates women through the depiction in any manner of the figure of a woman, her form or body or any part thereof in such a way as to have the effect of being indecent, or derogatory to women, or is likely to deprave, corrupt or injure the public morality or morals;

(l) denigrates children;

(n) contravenes the provisions of the Cinematograph Act, 1952 (37 of 1952);

(n)contravenes the provisions of the Cinematograph Act, 1952 (37 of 1952);

(o) is not suitable for unrestricted public exhibition.

(2) The cable operator should strive to carry programmes in his cable service which project women in a positive, leadership role of sobriety, moral and character building qualities.

(4) Care should be taken to ensure that programmes meant for children do not contain any bad language or explicit scenes of violence.

(5) Programmes unsuitable for children must not be carried in the cable service at times when the largest numbers of children are viewing.

THE CINEMATOGRAPH ACT, 1952

(Relevant Provisions)

5A. Certification of films.—(1) If, after examining a film or having it examined in the prescribed manner, the Board considers that—

(a) the film is suitable for unrestricted public exhibition, or, as the case may be, for unrestricted public exhibition with an endorsement of the nature mentioned in the proviso to clause (i) of sub-section (1) of section 4, it shall grant to the person applying for a certificate in respect of the film a "U" certificate or, as the case may be, a "UA" certificate; or

(b) the film is not suitable for unrestricted public exhibition, but is suitable for public exhibition restricted to adults or, as the case may be, is suitable for public exhibition restricted to members of any profession or any class of persons, it shall grant to the person applying for a certificate in respect of the film an "A" certificate or, as the case may be, a "S" certificate,

and cause the film to be so marked in the prescribed manner:

Provided that the applicant for the certificate, any distributor or exhibitor or any other person to whom the rights in the film have passed shall not be liable for punishment under any law relating to obscenity in respect of any matter contained in the film for which certificate has been granted under clause (a) or clause (b).

(2) A certificate granted or an order refusing to grant a certificate in respect of any film shall be published in the Gazette of India.

(3) Subject to the other provisions contained in this Act, a certificate granted by the Board under this section shall be valid throughout India for a period of ten years.

5B. Principles for guidance in certifying films.—(1) A film shall not be certified for public exhibition if, in the opinion of the authority competent to grant the certificate, the film or any part of it is against the interests of the sovereignty and integrity of India the security of the State, friendly relations with foreign States, public order, decency or morality, or involves defamation or contempt of court or is likely to incite the commission of any offence.

(2) Subject to the provisions contained in sub-section (1), the Central Government may issue such directions as it may think fit setting out the principles which shall guide the authority competent to grant certificates under this Act in sanctioning films for public exhibition.

5C. Appeals.—(1) Any person applying for a certificate in respect of a film who is aggrieved by any order of the Board—

(a) refusing to grant a certificate; or

(b) granting only an "A" certificate; or

(c) granting only a "S" certificate; or

(d) granting only a "UA" certificate; or

(e) directing the applicant to carry out any excisions or modifications,

may, within thirty days from the date of such order, prefer an appeal to the Tribunal:

Provided that the Tribunal may, if it is satisfied that the appellant was prevented by sufficient cause from filing the appeal within the aforesaid period of thirty days, allow such appeal to be admitted within a further period of thirty days.

(2) Every appeal under this section shall be made by a petition in writing and shall be accompanied by a brief statement of the reasons for the order appealed against where

such statement has been furnished to the appellant and by such fees, not exceeding rupees one thousand, as may be prescribed.

16. Power to make rules.—(1) The Central Government may, by notification in the Official Gazette, make rules—

(a) prescribing the terms, conditions and restrictions, if any, subject to which licences may be granted under this Part;

(b) providing for the regulation of cinematograph exhibitions for securing the public safety;

(c) prescribing the time within which and the conditions subject to which an appeal under sub-section (3) of section 12 may be preferred.

(2) Every rule made by the Central Government under this Part shall be laid, as soon as may be after it is made, before each House of Parliament, while it is in session, for a total period of thirty days which may be comprised in one session or in two or more successive sessions, and if, before the expiry of the session immediately following the session or the successive sessions aforesaid, both Houses agree in making any modification in the rule or both Houses agree that the rule should not be made, the rule shall thereafter have effect only in such modified form or be of no effect, as the case may be; so, however, that any such modification or annulment shall be without prejudice to the validity of anything previously done under that rule.

THE INDIAN PENAL CODE

(Relevant Provisions)

292. Sale, etc., of obscene books, etc.—(1) For the purposes of sub-section (2), a book, pamphlet, paper, writing, drawing, painting, representation, figure or any other object, shall be deemed to be obscene if it is lascivious or appeals to the prurient interest or if its effect, or (where it comprises two or more distinct items) the effect of any one of its items, is, if taken as a whole, such as to tend to deprave and corrupt person, who are likely, having regard to all relevant circumstances, to read, see or hear the matter contained or embodied in it.

(2) Whoever—

(a) sells, lets to hire, distributes, publicly exhibits or in any manner puts into circulation, or for purposes of sale, hire, distribution, public exhibition or circulation, makes, produces or has in his possession any obscene book, pamphlet, paper, drawing, painting, representation or figure or any other obscene object whatsoever, or

(b) imports, exports or conveys any obscene object for any of the purposes aforesaid, or knowing or having reason to believe that such object will be sold, let to hire, distributed or publicly exhibited or in any manner put into circulation, or

(c) takes part in or receives profits from any business in the course of which he knows or has reason to believe that any such obscene objects are for any of the purposes aforesaid, made, produced, purchased, kept, imported, exported, conveyed, publicly exhibited or in any manner put into circulation, or

(d) advertises or makes known by any means whatsoever that any person is engaged or is ready to engage in any act which is an offence under this section, or that any such obscene object can be procured from or through any person, or

(e) offers or attempts to do any act which is an offence under this section,

shall be punished on first conviction with imprisonment of either description for a term which may extend to two years, and with fine which may extend to two thousand rupees, and, in the event of a second or subsequent conviction, with imprisonment of either description for a term which may extend to five years, and also with fine which may extend to five thousand rupees.

Exception.—This section does not extend to—

(a) any book, pamphlet, paper, writing, drawing, painting, representation or figure—

(i) the publication of which is proved to be justified as being for the public good on the ground that such book, pamphlet, paper, writing, drawing, painting, representation or figure is in the interest of science, literature, art or learning or other objects of general concern, or

(ii) which is kept or used *bona fide* for religious purposes;

(b) any representation sculptured, engraved, painted or otherwise represented on or in--

(i) any ancient monument within the meaning of the Ancient Monuments and Archaeological Sites and Remains Act, 1958 (24 of 1958), or

(ii) any temple, or on any car used for the conveyance of idols, or kept or used for any religious purpose.

CLASSIFICATION OF OFFENCE

Punishment—On first conviction, with imprisonment for 2 years, and with fine of 2,000 rupees, and, in the event of second or subsequent conviction, with imprisonment for five years and with fine of 5,000 rupees—Cognizable—Bailable—Triable by any Magistrate—Non-compoundable.

293. Sale, etc., of obscene objects to young person.—Whoever sells, lets to hire, distributes, exhibits or circulates to any person under the age of twenty years any such obscene object as is referred to in the last preceding section, or offers or attempts so to do, shall be punished on first conviction with imprisonment of either description for a term which may extend to three years, and with fine which may extend to two thousand rupees, and, in the event of a second or subsequent conviction, with imprisonment of either description for a term which may extend to seven years, and also with fine which may extend to five thousand rupees.

CLASSIFICATION OF OFFENCE

Punishment—On first conviction, with imprisonment for 3 years, and with fine of 2,000 rupees, and, in the event of second or subsequent conviction, with imprisonment for 7 years, and with fine of 5,000 rupees—Cognizable—Bailable—Triable by any Magistrate—Non-compoundable.

294. Obscene acts and songs.—Whoever, to the annoyance of others—

(a) does any obscene act in any public place, or

(b) sings, recites or utters any obscene song, ballad or words, in or near any public place,

shall be punished with imprisonment of either description for a term which may extend to three months, or with fine, or with both.

CLASSIFICATION OF OFFENCE

Punishment—Imprisonment for 3 months, or fine, or both—Cognizable—Bailable—Triable by any Magistrate—Non-compoundable.

THE DRUGS AND MAGIC REMEDIES (OBJECTIONABLE ADVERTISEMENTS) ACT, 1954[1]

(21 of 1954)

[*30th April, 1954*]

An Act to control the advertisement of drugs in certain cases, to prohibit the advertisement for certain purposes of remedies alleged to possess magic qualities and to provide for matters connected therewith.

Be it enacted by Parliament as follows:—

1. Short title, extent and commencement.—(1) This Act may be called the Drugs and Magic Remedies (Objectionable Advertisements) Act, 1954.

(2) It extends to the whole of India except the State of Jammu and Kashmir, and applies also to persons domiciled in the territories to which this Act extends who are outside the said territories.

(3) It shall come into force on such date[2] as the Central Government may, by notification in the Official Gazette, appoint.

2 Definitions.—In this Act, unless the context otherwise requires,—

(a) 'advertisement' includes any notice, circular, label, wrapper, or other document, and any announcement made orally or by any means of producing or transmitting light, sound or smoke;

(b) 'drug' includes—

(i) a medicine for the internal or external use of human beings or animals;

(ii) any substance intended to be used for or in the diagnosis, cure, mitigation, treatment or prevention of disease in human beings or animals;

(iii) any article, other than food, intended to affect or influence in any way the structure or any organic function of the body of human beings or animals;

(iv) any article intended for use as a component of any medicine, substance or article, referred to in sub-clauses (i), (ii) and (iii);

(c) 'magic remedy' includes a *talisman, mantra, kavacha,* and any other charm of any kind which is alleged to possess miraculous powers for or in the diagnosis, cure, mitigation, treatment or prevention of any disease in human beings or animals or for affecting or influencing in any way the structure or any organic function of the body of human beings or animals;

[3][(cc) 'registered medical practitioner' means any person,—

(i) who holds a qualification granted by an authority specified in, or notified under, section 3 of the Indian Medical Degrees Act, 1916 (7 of 1916) or specified in the Schedules to the Indian Medical Council Act, 1956 (102 of 1956); or

---

1. Extended to Dadra and Nagar Haveli by Reg. 6 of 1963 (w.e.f. 1-7-1965) and to Pondicherry by Reg. 7 of 1963 (w.e.f. 1-10-1963), Goa, Daman and Diu by Reg. 11 of 1963 (w.e.f. 1-7-1965) and to Sikkim with modifications w.e.f. 1-11-1989, *vide* S.O. 852(E), dated 26th October, 1989.
2. Came into force on 1-4-1955, *vide* S.R.O. 511, dated 26th February, 1955, published in Gazette of India, 1955, Pt. II, Sec. 3, p. 449.
3. Ins. by Act 42 of 1963, sec. 2 (w.e.f. 7-12-1963).

(ii) who is entitled to be registered as a medical practitioner under any law for the time being in force in any State to which this Act extends relating to the registration of medical practitioners;]

(d) 'taking any part in the publication of any advertisement' includes—

(i) the printing of the advertisement;

(ii) the publication of any advertisement outside the territories to which this Act extends by or at the instance of a person residing within the said territories.

[1][***]

3. Prohibition of advertisement of certain drugs for treatment of certain diseases and disorders.—Subject to the provisions of this Act, no person shall take any part in the publication of any advertisement referring to any drug in terms which suggest or are calculated to lead to the use of that drug for—

(a) the procurement of miscarriage in women or prevention of conception in women; or

(b) the maintenance or improvement of the capacity of human beings for sexual pleasure; or

(c) the correction of menstrual disorder in women; or

[2][(d) the diagnosis, cure, mitigation, treatment or prevention of any disease, disorder or condition specified in the Schedule, or any other disease, disorder or condition (by whatsoever name called) which may be specified in the rules made under this Act:

Provided that no such rule shall be made except—

(i) in respect of any disease, disorder or condition which requires timely treatment in consultation with a registered medical practitioner or for which there are normally no accepted remedies, and

(ii) after consultation with the Drugs Technical Advisory Board constituted under the Drugs and Cosmetics Act, 1940 (23 of 1940) and, if the Central Government considers necessary, with such other persons having special knowledge or practical experience in respect of Ayurvedic or Unani systems of medicines as that Government deems fit.]

4. Prohibition of misleading advertisements relating to drugs.—Subject to the provisions of this Act, no person shall take any part in the publication of any advertisement relating to a drug if the advertisement contains any matter which—

(a) directly or indirectly gives a false impression regarding the true character of the drug; or

(b) makes a false claim for the drug; or

(c) is otherwise false or misleading in any material particular.

5. Prohibition of advertisement of magic remedies for treatment of certain diseases and disorders.—No person carrying on or purporting to carry on the profession of administering magic remedies shall take any part in the publication of any advertisement referring to any magic remedy which directly or indirectly claims to be efficacious for any of the purposes specified in section 3.

6. Prohibition of import into, and export from, India of certain advertise-ments.— No person shall import into, or export from, the territories to which this Act extends any document containing an advertisement of the nature referred to in section 3, or section 4, or section 5, and any documents containing any such advertisement shall be deemed

1. Clause (e) omitted by Act 42 of 1963, sec. 2 (w.e.r. 7-12-1963).
2. Subs. by Act 42 of 1963, sec. 3, for clause (d) (w.e.f. 7-12-1963).

to be goods of which the import or export has been prohibited under section 19 of the Sea Customs Act, 1878 (8 of 1878) and all the provisions of that Act shall have effect accordingly, except that section 183 thereof shall have effect as if for the word 'shall' therein the word 'may' were substituted.

7. Penalty.—Whoever contravenes any of the provisions of this Act [1][or the rules made thereunder] shall, on conviction, be punishable—

(a) in the case of a first conviction, with imprisonment which may extend to six months, or with fine, or with both;

(b) in the case of a subsequent conviction, with imprisonment which may extend to one year, or with fine, or with both.

[2][**8. Powers of entry, search, etc.**—(1) Subject to the provisions of any rules made in this behalf, any Gazetted Officer authorised by the State Government may, within the local limits of the area for which he is so authorised,—

(a) enter and search at all reasonable times, with such assistants, if any, as he considers necessary, any place in which he has reason to believe that an offence under this Act has been or is being committed;

(b) seize any advertisement which he has reason to believe contravenes any of the provisions of this Act:

Provided that the power of seizure under this clause may be exercised in respect of any document, article or thing which contains any such advertisement, including the contents, if any, of such document, article or thing, if the advertisement cannot be separated by reason of its being embossed or otherwise, from such document, article or thing without affecting the integrity, utility or saleable value thereof;

(c) examine any record, register, document or any other material object found in any place mentioned in clause (a) and seize the same if he has reason to believe that it may furnish evidence of the commission of an offence punishable under this Act.

(2) The provisions of the Code of Criminal Procedure, 1898 (5 of 1898) shall, so far as may be, apply to any search or seizure under this Act as they apply to any search or seizure made under the authority of a warrant issued under section 98 of the said Code.

(3) Where any person seizes anything under clause (b) or clause (c) of sub-section (1), he shall, as soon as may be, inform a Magistrate and take his orders as to the custody thereof.]

9. Offences by companies.—(1) If the person contravening any of the provisions of this Act is a company, every person who, at the time the offence was committed, was in charge of, and was responsible to, the company for the conduct of the business of the company as well as the company shall be deemed to be guilty of the contravention and shall be liable to be proceeded against and punished accordingly:

Provided that nothing contained in this sub-section shall render any such person liable to any punishment provided in this Act if he proves that the offence was committed without his knowledge or that he exercised all due diligence to prevent the commission of such offence.

(2) Notwithstanding anything contained in sub-section (1) where an offence under this Act has been committed by a company and it is proved that the offence was committed with the consent or connivance of, or is attributable to any neglect on the part of, any director or manager, secretary or the officer of the company, such director,

---

1. Ins. by Act 42 of 1963, sec. 4 (w.e.f. 7-12-1963).
2. Subs. by Act 42 of 1963, sec. 5, for section 8 (w.e.f. 7-12-1963).

manager, secretary or other officer of the company shall also be deemed to be guilty of that offence and shall be liable to be proceeded against and punished accordingly.

Explanation.—For the purposes of this section,—

(a) 'company' means any body corporate and includes a firm or other association of individuals, and

(b) 'director' in relation to a firm means a partner in the firm.

[1][**9A. Offences to be cognizable.**—Notwithstanding anything contained in the Code of Criminal Procedure, 1898 (5 of 1898), an offence punishable under this Act shall be cognizable.]

10. Jurisdiction to try offences.—No court inferior to that of a Presidency Magistrate or a Magistrate of the first class shall try any offence punishable under this Act.

[2][**10A. Forfeiture.**—Where a person has been convicted by any court for contravening any provision of this Act or any rule made thereunder, the court may direct that any document (including all copies thereof), article or thing, in respect of which the contravention is made, including the contents thereof where such contents are seized under clause (b) of sub-section (1) of section 8, shall be forfeited to the Government.]

11. Officers to be deemed to be public servants.—Every person authorised under section 8 shall be deemed to be a public servant within the meaning of section 21 of the Indian Penal Code (45 of 1860).

Illustration

A Municipal Commissioner is a public servant.

Explanation 1.—Persons falling under any of the above descriptions are public servants, whether appointed by the Government or not.

Explanation 2.—Wherever the words "public servant" occur, they shall be understood of every person who is in actual possession of the situation of a public servant, whatever legal defect there may be in his right to hold that situation.

Explanation 3.—The word "election" denotes an election for the purpose of selecting members of any legislative, municipal or other public authority, of whatever character, the method of selection to which is by, or under any law prescribed as by election.

12. Indemnity.—No suit, prosecution or other legal proceeding shall lie against any person for anything which is in good faith done or intended to be done under this Act.

13. Other laws not affected.—The provisions of this Act are in addition to, and not in derogation of the provisions of any other law for the time being in force.

[3][**14. Savings.**—Nothing in this Act shall apply to—

(a) any signboard or notice displayed by a registered medical practitioner on his premises indicating that treatment for any disease, disorder or condition specified in section 3, the Schedule or the rules made under this Act is undertaken in those premises; or

(b) any treatise or book dealing with any of the matters specified in section 3 from a *bona fide* scientific or social standpoint; or

(c) any advertisement relating to any drug sent confidentially in the manner prescribed under section 16 only to a registered medical practitioner; or

(d) any advertisement relating to a drug printed or published by the Government; or

(e) any advertisement relating to a drug printed or published by any person with the previous sanction of the Government granted prior to the

1. Ins. by Act 42 of 1963, sec. 6 (w.e.f. 7-12-1963).
2. Ins. by Act 42 of 1963, sec. 7 (w.e.f. 7-12-1963).
3. Subs. by Act 42 of 1963, sec. 8, for section 14 (w.e.f. 7-12-1963).

commencement of the Drugs and Magic Remedies (Objectionable Advertisements) Amendment Act, 1963 (42 of 1963):

Provided that the Government may, for reasons to be recorded in writing, withdraw the sanction after giving the person an opportunity of showing cause against such withdrawal.]

15. Power to exempt from application of Act.—If in the opinion of the Central Government public interest requires that the advertisement of any specified drug or class of drugs [1][or any specified class of advertisements relating to drugs] should be permitted, it may, by notification in the Official Gazette, direct that the provisions of sections 3, 4, 5 and 6 or any one of such provisions shall not apply or shall apply subject to such conditions as may be specified in the notification to or in relation to the advertisement of any such drug or class of drugs [1][or any such class of advertisements relating to drugs].

16. Power to make rules.—(1) The Central Government may, by notification in the Official Gazette, make rules for carrying out the purposes of this Act.

(2) In particular and without prejudice to the generality of the foregoing power, such rules may—

(a) specify any [2][disease, disorder or condition] to which the provisions of section 3 shall apply;

(b) prescribe the manner in which advertisements of articles or things referred to in clause (c) of [3][***] section 14 may be sent confidentially.

[4][(3) Every rule made under this Act shall be laid, as soon as may be after it is made, before each of House of Parliament while it is in session for a total period of thirty days which may be comprised in one session or in two or more successive sessions and if before the expiry of the session in which it is so laid or the successive sessions aforesaid, both Houses agree in making any modification in the rule or both Houses agree that the rule should not be made, the rule shall thereafter have effect only in such modified form or be of no effect, as the case may be; so however, that any such modification or annulment shall be without prejudice to the validity of anything previously done under that rule.]

[5][*THE SCHEDULE*

[*See* sections 3(d) and 14]

S.No.	*Name of the disease, disorder or condition*	*S.No.*	*Name of the disease, disorder or condition*
1.	Appendicitis	9.	Diabetes
2.	Arteriosclerosis	10.	Diseases and disorders of the brain
3.	Blindness	11.	Diseases and disorders of the optical system
4.	Blood poisoning	12.	Diseases and disorders of the uterus
5.	Bright's disease	13.	Disorders of menstrual flow
6.	Cancer	14.	Disorders of the nervous system
7.	Cataract	15.	Disorders of the prostatic gland
8.	Deafness		

1. Ins. by Act 42 of 1963, sec. 9 (w.e.f. 7-12-1963).
2. Subs. by Act 42 of 1963, sec. 10, for "disease or condition" (w.e.f. 7-12-1963).
3. The words "sub-section (1) of" omitted by Act 42 of 1963, sec. 10 (w.e.f. 7-12-1963).
4. Ins. by Act 42 of 1963, sec. 10 (w.e.f. 7-12-1963).
5. Added by Act 42 of 1963, sec. 11 (w.e.f. 7-12-1963).

S.No.	Name of the disease, disorder or condition	S.No.	Name of the disease, disorder or condition
16.	Dropsy	36.	Lupus
17.	Epilepsy	37.	Nervous debility
18.	Female diseases (in general)	38.	Obesity
19.	Fevers (in general)	39.	Paralysis
20.	Fits	40.	Plague
21.	Form and structure of the female bust	41.	Pleurisy
22.	Gall stones, kidney stones and bladder stones	42.	Pneumonia
23.	Gangrene	43.	Rheumatism
24.	Glaucoma	44.	Ruptures
25.	Goitre	45.	Sexual impotence
26.	Heart diseases	46.	Smallpox
27.	High or low blood pressure	47.	Stature of persons
28.	Hydrocele	48.	Sterility in women
29.	Hysteria	49.	Trachoma
30.	Infantile paralysis	50.	Tuberculosis
31.	Insanity	51.	Tumours
32.	Leprosy	52.	Typhoid fever
33.	Leucoderma	53.	Ulcers of the gastro-intestinal tract
34.	Lockjaw	54.	Venereal diseases, including syphilis, gonorrhoea, soft chancre, venereal granuloma and lympho granuloma.]
35.	Locomotor ataxia		

THE CONSTITUTION OF INDIA

(Relevant Provisions)

19. Protection of certain rights regarding freedom of speech, etc.—(1) All citizens shall have the right—

(a) to freedom of speech and expression;

(b) to assemble peaceably and without arms;

(c) to form associations or unions;

(d) to move freely throughout the territory of India;

(e) to reside and settle in any part of the territory of India; and

(g) to practise any profession, or to carry on any occupation, trade or business.

(2) Nothing in sub-clause (a) of clause (1) shall affect the operation of any existing law, or prevent the State from making any law, in so far as such law imposes reasonable restrictions on the exercise of the right conferred by the said sub-clause in the interests of the sovereignty and integrity of India, the security of the State, friendly relations with Foreign States, public order, decency or morality or in relation to contempt of court, defamation or incitement to an offence.

THE CUSTOMS ACT, 1962
(Relevant Provisions)

CHAPTER IV

PROHIBITIONS ON IMPORTATION AND EXPORTATION OF GOODS

11. Power to prohibit importation or exportation of goods.—(1) If the Central Government is satisfied that it is necessary so to do for any of the purposes specified in sub-section (2), it may, by notification in the Official Gazette, prohibit either absolutely or subject to such conditions (to be fulfilled before or after clearance) as may be specified in the notification, the import or export of goods of any specified description.

(2) The purposes referred to in sub-section (1) are the following:—

(a) the maintenance of the security of India;

(b) the maintenance of public order and standards of decency or morality;

(c) the prevention of smuggling;

(d) the prevention of shortage of goods of any description;

(e) the conservation of foreign exchange and the safeguarding or balance of payments;

(f) the prevention of injury to the economy of the country by the uncontrolled import or export of gold or silver;

(g) the prevention of surplus of any agricultural product or the product of fisheries;

(h) the maintenance of standards for the classification, grading or marketing of goods in international trade;

(i) the establishment of any industry;

(j) the prevention of serious injury to domestic production of goods of any description;

(k) the protection of human, animal or plant life or health;

(l) the protection of national treasures of artistic, historic or archaeological value;

(m) the conservation of exhaustible natural resources;

(n) the protection of patents, trade marks and copyrights;

(o) the prevention of deceptive practices;

(p) the carrying on of foreign trade in any goods by the State, or by a Corporation owned or controlled by the State to the exclusion, complete or partial, or citizens of India;

(q) the fulfilment of obligations under the Charter of the United Nations for the maintenance of international peace and security;

(r) the implementation of any treaty, agreements or convention with any country;

(s) the compliance of imported goods with any laws which are applicable to similar goods produced or manufactured in India;

(t) the prevention of dissemination of documents containing any matter which is likely to prejudicially affect friendly relations with any foreign State or is derogatory to national prestige;

(u) the prevention of the contravention of any law for the time being in force; and

(v) any other purpose conducive to the interests of the general public.

THE INDIAN POST OFFICE ACT, 1898

(Relevant Provisions)

20. Transmission by post of anything indecent, etc., prohibited.—No person shall send by post—

(a) any indecent or obscene printing, painting, photograph, lithograph, engraving, book or card, or any other indecent or obscene article, or

(b) any postal article having thereon, or on the cover thereof, any words, marks or designs of an indecent, obscene, seditious, scurrilous, threatening or grossly offensive character.

23. Power to deal with postal articles posted in contravention of Act.—(1) Any postal article sent by post in contravention of any of the provisions of this Act may be detained and either returned to the sender or forwarded to destination, in each case charged with such additional postage (if any), as the Central Government may, by rule, direct.

(2) Any officer in charge of a post office or authorized by the Post Master General in this behalf may open or unfasten any newspaper or any book, pattern or sample packet, in course of transmission by post, which he suspects to have been sent by post in contravention of section 20, clause (a), or of section 21 or of any of the provisions of this Act relating to postage.

(3) Notwithstanding anything in sub-section (1)—

(a) any postal article sent by post in contravention of the provisions of section 19 or section 19A may, under the authority of the Post Master General, if necessary, be opened and destroyed; and

(b) any postal article sent by post in contravention of the provisions of section 20 may be disposed of in such manner as the Central Government may, by rule, direct.

THE PRESS COUNCIL ACT, 1978

(Relevant Provisions)

13. Objects and functions of the Council.—(1) The objects of the Council shall be to preserve the freedom of the Press and to maintain and improve the standards of newspapers and news agencies in India.

(2) The Council may, in furtherance of its objects, perform the following functions, namely:—

(a) to help newspapers and news agencies to maintain their independence;

(b) to build up a code of conduct for newspapers, news agencies and journalists in accordance with high professional standards;

(c) to ensure on the part of newspapers, news agencies and journalists, the maintenance of high standards of public taste and foster a due sense of both the rights and responsibilities of citizenship;

(d) to encourage the growth of a sense of responsibility and public service among all those engaged in the profession of journalism;

(e) to keep under review any development likely to restrict the supply and dissemination of news of public interest and importance;

(f) to keep under review cases of assistance received by any newspaper or news agency in India from any foreign source including such cases as are referred to it by the Central Government or are brought to its notice by any individual, association of persons or any other organisation:

Provided that nothing in this clause shall preclude the Central Government from dealing with any case of assistance received by a newspaper or news agency in India from any foreign source in any other manner it thinks fit;

(g) to undertake studies of foreign newspapers, including those brought out by any embassy or other representative in India of a foreign State, their circulation and impact.

Explanation.—For the purposes of this clause, the expression "foreign State" has the meaning assigned to it in section 87A of the Code of Civil Procedure, 1908 (5 of 1908);

(h) to promote a proper functional relationship among all classes of persons engaged in the production or publication of newspapers or in news agencies:

Provided that nothing in this clause shall be deemed to confer on the Council any functions in regard to disputes to which the Industrial Disputes Act, 1947 (14 of 1947), applies;

(i) to concern itself with developments such as concentration of or other aspects of ownership of newspapers and news agencies which may affect the independence of the Press;

(j) to undertake such studies as may be entrusted to the Council and to express its opinion in regard to any matter referred to it by the Central Government;

(k) to do such other acts as may be incidental or conducive to the discharge of the above functions.

14. Power to censure.—(1) Where, on receipt of a complaint made to it or otherwise, the Council has reason to believe that a newspaper or news agency has offended against the standards of journalistic ethics or public taste or that an editor or a working journalist has committed any professional misconduct, the Council may, after giving the newspaper, or news agency, the editor or journalist concerned an opportunity of being heard, hold an inquiry in such manner as may be provided by regulations made under this Act and, if it is satisfied that it is necessary so to do, it may, for reasons to be recorded in writing, warn, admonish or censure the newspaper, the news agency, the editor or the journalist or disapprove the conduct of the editor or the journalist, as the case may be:

Provided that the Council may not take cognizance of a complaint if in the opinion of the Chairman, there is no sufficient ground for holding an inquiry.

(2) If the Council is of the opinion that it is necessary or expedient in the public interest so to do, it may require any newspaper to publish therein in such manner as the Council thinks fit, any particulars relating to any inquiry under this section against a newspaper or news agency, an editor or a journalist working therein, including the name of such newspaper, news agency, editor or journalist.

(3) Nothing in sub-section (1) shall be deemed to empower the Council to hold an inquiry into any matter in respect of which any proceeding is pending in a court of law.

(4) The decision of the Council under sub-section (1), or sub-section (2), as the case may be, shall be final and shall not be questioned in any court of law.

THE DRAMATIC PERFORMANCES ACT, 1876

(Relevant Provisions)

12. Exclusion of performances at religious festivals.—Nothing in this Act applies to any jatras or performances of a like kind at religious festivals.

ONE HUNDRED AND NINTH REPORT

LAW COMMISSION OF INDIA

OBSCENE AND INDECENT ADVERTISEMENTS AND DISPLAYS: SECTIONS 292-293, INDIAN PENAL CODE

CHAPTER 1

INTRODUCTORY

1.1. Scope and significance.—The question dealt with in this Report is this. Is there any need for reforming the law relating to indecent advertisements and displays in India ? An examination of the question has been taken up by the Law Commission of its own, in view of the feeling occasionally expressed that indecent advertisements of various types find display in the streets or are published in newspapers, periodicals and other media, and that these could harm the morals of society, apart from their being derogatory to the honour and dignity of the fair sex.

1.2. Utility of a study of the law on the subject.—There does exist, in the Indian statute book, a variety of provisions intended to check the evil referred to above. Some of the provisions are of a general character, while a few are of a specialised nature.[1] Whether or not these provisions, taken in their totality, are adequate for checking indecent advertisements, will be a matter of opinion. But an examination of these provisions could at least help in clarifying one's thoughts on the subject and in enabling a serious student of the problems to acquire a better familiarity with the terrain covered by the present law.

1.3. Methodology.—Accordingly, we propose to deal, in brief, with the present law, and then to examine if any improvements are needed therein. The subject of indecency has received some attention in England very recently, where an Act[2] has been passed on the subject of indecent displays. It will be useful to have a look at the recent developments in England also—though it must be pointed out that the focus in the recent English Act is not on the whole gamut of indecent advertisements, but rather on certain outrageously explicit displays that might, by reason of their taking place at public places (particularly, the market- place), "shock and disgust" the people.[3]

1.4. Working Paper.—It may be mentioned that in order to elicit opinion on the subject, we had prepared a Working Paper and circulated it to interested persons and bodies, inviting their comments. A few comments have been received on the Working Paper, which will be discussed in a later chapter.[4]

---

1. *See* Chapter 2, *infra*.
2. Indecent Displays (Control) Act, 1981, (Ch. 42) (Eng.).
3. *See* paras. 3.7 to 3.12, *infra*.
4. Chapter 6, *infra*.

CHAPTER 2

THE PRESENT LAW IN INDIA AS TO OFFENSIVE ADVERTISEMENTS

2.1. General and special provisions as to offensive advertisements.—The punishment of offensive advertisements is, under the present law in India, permissible under a number of statutory provisions. These can be broadly classified into—

(1) General provisions; and

(ii) Special provisions.

By "general"' provisions, we have in mind the provision in the Indian Penal Code relating to obscenity (section 292).[1] This section applies to a variety of matters and is comprehensive enough to cover all obscene publications. In contrast, special provisions are confined to special types of writings or other obscene matter.

2.2. General provision (section 292, I.P.C.).—The general provision on the subject is, as stated above, contained in section 292 of the Indian Penal Code. It reads as under:—

> "292. *Sale, etc. of obscene books etc.*—(1) For the purposes of sub-section (2), a book, pamphlet, paper, writing, drawing, painting, representation, figure or any other object, shall be deemed to be obscene if it is lascivious or appeals to the prurient interest or if its effect, or (where it comprises two or more distinct items) the effect of any one of its items is, if taken as a whole, such as to tend to deprave and corrupt persons who are likely, having regard to all relevant circumstances, to read, see or hear the matter contained or embodied in it.
>
> (2) Whoever—
>
> (a) sells, lets to hire, distributes, publicly exhibits or in any manner puts into circulation, or for purposes of sale, hire, distribution, public exhibition or circulation, makes, produces or has in his possession any obscene book, pamphlet, paper, drawing, painting, representation or figure or any other obscene object whatsoever, or
>
> (b) imports, exports or conveys any obscene object for any of the purposes aforesaid, or knowing or having reason to believe that such object will be sold, let to hire, distributed or publicly exhibited or in any manner put into circulation, or
>
> (c) takes part in or receives profits from any business in the course of which he knows or has reason to believe that any such obscene objects are, for any of the purposes aforesaid, made, produced, purchased, kept, imported, exported, conveyed, publicly exhibited or in any manner put into circulation, or
>
> (d) advertises or makes known by any means whatsoever that any person is engaged or is ready to engage in any act which is an offence under this section, or that any such obscene object can be procured from or through any person, or
>
> (e) offers or attempts to do any act which is an offence under this section, shall be punished on first conviction with imprisonment of either description for a term which may extend to two years, and with fine which may extend to two thousand rupees, and, in the event of a second or subsequent conviction, with imprisonment of either description for a term which may extend to five years, and also with fine which may extend to five thousand rupees.
>
> *Exception*—This section does not extend to—
>
> (a) any book, pamphlet, paper, writing, drawing, painting, representation or figure—

1. Para. 2.2, *infra*.

(i) the publication of which is proved to be justified as being for the public good on the ground that such book, pamphlet, paper, writing, drawing, painting, representation or figure is in the interest of science, literature, art or learning or other objects of general concern, or

(ii) which is kept or used bona fide for religious purposes;

(b) any representation sculptured, engraved, painted or otherwise represented on or in—

(i) any ancient monument within the meaning of the Ancient Monuments and Archaeological Sites and Remains Act, 1958, or

(ii) any temple, or on any car used for the conveyance of idols or kept or used for any religious purposes."

2.3. Section 293—Sale, etc., of obscene objects to young person.—Section 293, Indian Penal Code, reads as under:—

"293. Whoever sells, lets to hire, distributes, exhibits or circulates to any person under the age of twenty years any such obscene object as is referred to in the last preceding section, or offers or attempts so to do, shall be punished on first conviction with imprisonment of either description for a term which may extend to three years, and with fine which may extend to two thousand rupees, and in the event of a second or subsequent conviction, with imprisonment of either description for a term which may extend to seven years, and also with fine which may extend to five thousand rupees".

2.4. Section 294—obscene acts and songs.—Section 294 of the same Code reads:—

"294. Whoever, to the annoyance of others—

(a) does any obscene act in any public place, or

(b) sings, recites or utters any obscene song, ballad or words, in or near any public place, shall be punished with imprisonment of either description for a term which may extend to three months, or with fine, or with both."

2.5. Provision in special laws.—The special provisions relating to indecency or obscenity are to be found in—

(a) the Drugs Magic Remedies (Objectionable Advertisements) Act, 1954;

(b) the Young Persons (Harmful Publications) Act, 1955;

(c) Section 20, Indian Post Office Act, 1898;

(d) Section 11, Customs Act, 1962.

The Act mentioned at (a) above, while it does cover some indecent advertisements, is confined to advertisements of drugs and remedies connected with sexual disorders. Its target is not indecency or obscenity, as such.

2.6. Importance of section 292, I.P.C.—The special statutory provisions mentioned in the preceding paragraph are rarely invoked in practice,[1] in the context of obscenity. For all practical purposes, the provision of a comprehensive character with an all-India operation which can be pressed into service for punishing obscene publications and exhibitions is section 292 of the Indian Penal Code.[2] A later chapter will, therefore, concentrate on that section and examine how far the section needs expansion, so as to make it an effective instrument for checking offensive advertisements.[3]

Before doing so, we proceed to examine the English Law on the subject.

---

1. This also applies to stray local enactments relating to indecent advertisements.
2. Para. 2.2, *supra*.
3. Chapter 4, *infra*.

CHAPTER 3

THE LAW IN ENGLAND

3.1. The common Law.—At common law,[1] it is an indictable offence, punishable by fine and imprisonment at the discretion of the court, to say or do or exhibit anything in public which outrages public decency, whether or not it tends to deprave or corrupt those who see it. There are, however, restrictions on prosecutions for this common law offence.

3.2. Indecent Advertisements Act, 1989.—Under the Indecent Advertisements Act, 1889, (as supplemented by later enactments), a person,[2] affixing or inscribing on any building walls, post, tree etc. anything whatsoever so as to be visible to a person in any street or footpath or affixing on a public urinal or delivering to any person in street or footpath or exhibiting to public view in the window of a house or shop any picture or printed or written matter which is of an indecent or obscene nature is liable, on summary conviction, to a penalty not exceeding £ 20 or to imprisonment for any term not exceeding one month, any person who gives or delivers to any other person any such pictures or printed or written matter with the intent that it should be so affixed, inscribed, delivered or exhibited is liable, on summary conviction, to penalty not exceeding £ 50 or to imprisonment for a term not exceeding 3 months.

A constable or other peace officer may arrest without warrant any person found committing an offence[3] against the Indecent Advertisements Act, 1889, wilfully exposing any obscene print, picture etc. in any public place is punishable under the Vagrancy Act, 1824;[4] now the Indecent Displays (Control) Act, 1981.

3.3. Venereal disease.—There are also restrictions on advertisements relating to the treatment of venereal disease.[5]

3.4. Publication of obscene article.—The general law of obscenity in England is contained in the Obscene Publications Act, 1959. A person who—

(i) publishes an obscene article, whether for gain or not; or

(ii) "has" an obscene article for gain (whether gain to himself or gain to another),[6]

is punishable.

The meaning of the expression "publishes" is defined, *inter alia*, as covering anyone who distributes or circulates an obscene article.[7] An elaborate test[8] of obscenity is also laid down.

3.5. Sanction for prosecution.—A prosecution for obscenity in England requires consent of the Director of Public Prosecutions where the article is a moving picture film not less than 16 mm. wide and its publication takes place, or is expected to take place only in the course of a cinematograph exhibition.[9]

---

1. *Halsbury's*, 4th Edn., Vol. 11 (Criminal Law), p. 587, paras. 10-26.
2. Section 3, Indecent Advertisements Act, 1889, as amended and supplemented by section 1(2), Criminal Law Act, 1948, and section 92(1), Criminal Justice Act, 1967.
3. Section 6, Indecent Advertisements Act, 1889, as amended by section 2, Indecent Advertisements (Amendment) Act, 1970.
4. *Halsbury's*, 4th Edn., Vol. 11 (Criminal Law), paras. 118-119.
5. Section 2, Venereal Disease Act, 1917; *Halsbury's*, 4th Edn., (Vol. on Medicine).
6. Section 2(1), Obscene Publications Act, 1959.
7. Section 1(3), Obscene Publications Act, 1959.
8. Section 2(6), Obscene Publications Act, 1959.
9. Section 2(3), Obscene Publications Act, 1959.

3.6. Sending unsolicited matter.—Sending unsolicited matter describing human sexual techniques or unsolicited advertisements of such matter is an offence.[1]

3.7. The Act of 1981.—Recently, there has been enacted in England (in 1981) an Act to make "fresh provision" with respect to the public display of indecent matter. Its main target is the "public nuisance" aspect of indecent displays *e.g.*, (i) cinema club posters; (ii) bookshop window displays that people cannot avoid, seeing as they walk along the pavement or go into a shop to buy (say) cigarettes or chocolates; (iii) sex show window displays.[2]

The Act[3] makes it an offence to "make", "cause" or "permit" the public display of any indecent matter. The old statutory offences are repealed.

3.8. Section 1(1), Indecent Displays etc. Act, 1981.—The principal provision [section 1(1)] of the Act of 1981 reads as under:—

> "1(1) If any indecent matter is publicly displayed, the person making the display and any person causing or permitting the display to be made shall be guilty of an offence."

The section does not apply to television broadcasts by the BBC or ITA, to art galleries or museums, performance of plays, and cinematograph exhibitions in licensed places.

3.9. Indecent matter.—The expression "matter" includes anything capable of being displayed, but does not include an actual human body or part thereof [section 1(5)].

The expression "indecent" is riot defined in the Act of 1981. Rulings on analogous laws hold that the word should be given its ordinary meaning.[4]

3.10. The punishment under the English Act of 1981 is—

(a) fine not exceeding the statutory maximum, on summary conviction;

(b) imprisonment upto two years or fine or both, on conviction on indictment (section 4).

3.11. Arrest under the 1981 Act.—The offender against the Act of 1981 cannot be arrested without warrant unless he gives a false name and address, but a constable may seize any article which he has reasonable grounds for believing to be or to contain indecent matter and to have been used in the commission of an offence under the Act.

---

1. Section 4, Unsolicited Goods and Services Act, 1971. See *D.P.P.* v. *Beate Uhso (UK) Ltd.*, (1974) 1 All ER 753.
2. Mr. T. Sainsbury, H.C. Debates, Vol. 997, Col. 1167.
3. Indecent Displays (Control) Act, 1971 (Ch. 42) (Eng.). *See* R.T.H. Stone *Out of Sight, out of Mind* (January 1982) 45 Modern Law Review.
4. *R.* v. *Stamford*, (1972) 2 WLR 1055.

CHAPTER 4

CHANGE NEEDED IN SECTION 292, INDIAN PENAL CODE

4.1. Whether reform needed.—Having set out the position under the present statutory framework in India, and having noted certain other developments, we have now to examine the question whether any changes are needed to deter a tendency to publish obscene or indecent advertisements. *Prima facie,* it would appear that the general provision in the Indian Penal Code, section 292, punishing[1] obscene publications, is intended to check and (on one view)[2] can be pressed into service for checking obscene advertisements without much difficulty. The definition of obscenity, as enacted in section 292(1), seems to take in all publications that can be reasonably objected to on the score of possible evil effects on the morals of listeners or readers of obscene matter.

4.2. Scheme of section 292, I.P.C.—However, as will be indicated presently, there is scope for improvement in certain respects in the law as contained in section 292. We first address ourselves to a lacuna in existing section 292(2). For understanding this lacuna, it is desirable first to analyse section 292. Leaving aside the Exception to the section,[3] the scheme of the section is as follows. The section does not begin with the *substantive* penal provision, but with a definition of "obscene" [contained in sub-section (1)]. The penal provision creating and punishing the offence appears in sub-section (2). Here also, one can concentrate on clause (a), the remaining clauses not being material for the present purpose.

4.3. Section 292(1) and section 292(2) compared.—Now, if one goes through the text of sub-sections (1) and (2) of section 292 carefully, one finds that in one respect, there is a hiatus between the two, though it may perhaps be regarded as only a verbal hiatus. The relevant portions of the two sub-sections can be put in two parallel columns as under:—

Section 292(1), Indian Penal Code	*Section 292(2)(a), Indian Penal Code*
"For the purposes of sub-section (2), a book, pamphlet, paper, writing, drawing, painting, representation, figure or any other object, shall be deemed to be obscene.................."	"Whoever sells, lets to hire, distributes publicly exhibits or in any manner puts into circulation........any obscene book, pamphlet, paper, drawing, painting, representation or figure or any other obscene object whatsoever........".

It will be noticed that the word "writing" is specifically mentioned in section 292(1), but that word does not appear in section 292(2)(a). The latter does not get the full advantage of the definition contained in the former.

Since section 292(2)(a) is the substantive penal provision, it is desirable that it gets the full advantage of section 292(1), which is the defining provision.

4.4. Possible amendment of section 292(2)(a), I.P.C.—Of course, it can be argued that the disharmony between section 292(1) and section 292(2)(a), Indian Penal Code, as revealed by the above analysis,[4] can, in practice, be tided over by recourse to the residuary words "any other obscene object whatsoever", which occur in section 292(2)(a). However, in order to avoid controversy, it appears desirable that section 292(2)(a) of the Indian Penal Code should be amended by inserting, after the word "paper", the word "writing". After this amendment, the section would cover obscene advertisements in writing, particularly those in periodicals and posters.

---

1. Para. 2.2, *supra.*
2. *See* para. 4.4, *infra.*
3. Para. 2.2, *supra.*
4. Para. 4.3, *supra.*

CHAPTER 5

INDECENCY AND OBSCENITY: NEED TO INSERT SECTION 293A

5.1. Indecent matter.—It is also necessary to examine in detail another question concerning the scope of the law. The public exhibition of obscene matter is a subject falling within section 292, Indian Penal Code. But the section is silent about matter which is merely *indecent,* without being obscene. Should the scope of the penal law be extended to cover such matter ? That is the precise question to be considered.

5.2. Questions considered.—*Prima facie,* it would appear that the law should cover such acts. The Constitution in Article 19(2), permits such legislation and it would seem that, on the merits, there is a case for punishing public display of indecent matter. No doubt, a pretty large number of writings, pictures and gestures which are indecent on the score of their sexually explicit character would also be obscene, in the sense of, the likelihood of depraving and corrupting the minds of the audience or the readers. But, at least in theory, one can conceive of indecent matter that is not obscene. Although the amount of harm caused by its display or publication may be negligible and its frequency may not be alarming, the matter requires consideration. It may be mentioned that section 292 of the Indian Penal Code[1] does not punish the publication of indecent matter as such.

5.3. Question to be considered.—Before formulating any concrete proposal on the subject of indecency, two points require consideration, namely—

(a) the scope of the expression "indecent", *in general;* and

(b) one *special* question, namely, whether the concept of "indecent" is, in its content, confined to matters dealing with sex, or whether it can take within its sweep other matters also.

5.4. Legislative usage.—As to the first question, legislative precedents do not appear to furnish much guidance. The expression "indecent" does not carry any legislative definition. The expression occurs occasionally in legislative usage, sometimes singly, at other times in conjunction with words like "obscene" or "lewd". But its exact ambit remains undefined.

The fact that the word "indecent" has not been defined and different people have different standards, was accepted[2] in the debate on the English Act of 1980. The Williams Committee in England thought that the word "indecent" was surrounded with vagueness[3] and confusion, as to be useless. In fact, when the Bill leading to the Protection of Children Act, 1978 was debated in England, the vagueness of "indecent" was used as a justification for requiring the consent of the Director of Public Prosecutions for prosecutions under the Act.[4]

5.5. Suggestion of the Williams Committee.—The William Committee[5] in England, while noting the vagueness of the expression "indecent", seems to have, taken the view that if the expression *had* to be defined, then some such formula as "offensive to reasonable people" might be considered.

5.6. An American ruling.—It may also be of relevance to refer, at this stage, to a decision of the Supreme Court of the United States, where the Court had to consider the question of "indecent" speech in the context of regulation of broadcast matter.[6] In that case, the authority of the Federal Communications Commission to effect qualitative

1. Chapter 2, *supra.*
2. T. Benyon, H.C. Debates, Vol. 997, Col. 1196.
3. Committee on Obscenity & Film Censorship (1979), Cmd. 7772, para. 9.21.
4. *R.* v. *Khuller,* 1973 AC 435 (HL).
5. Committee on Obscenity and Film Censorship Report (1979), Cmd. 7772, para. 9.21.
6. *F.C.C.* v. *Pacifica Foundation,* (1978), 98 S Ct 3026.

content control through the regulation of radio broadcast which that Commission finds "indecent but not obscene", was challenged. The case concerned a recorded monologue, broadcast on the New York radio station in the early afternoon, as part of a discussion of contemporary attitudes towards language. The title of the monologue was "Filthy Words" and the broadcast was prefaced by an advice that the record contained "sensitive language which might be regarded as offensive to some". Five weeks later, the Federal Communications Commission received a complaint about the programme from a listener who had heard the broadcast while driving with his fifteen year old son. The Commission granted the complaint, though it declined to impose formal sanctions on the Radio Station. The Commission's conclusion was, that the seven words which had been broadcast and objected to, depicted "sexual and excretory activities and organs in a manner patently offensive by contemporary community standards for the broadcast medium". The words in question were therefore "indecent" and prohibited by 18 United States Code, section 1464, which forbids the use of "any obscene, indecent, or profane language by means of a radio communication". Expressly stating that the "indecent" speech which it sought to control was not subsumed by the concept of obscenity, the Commission justified using the broader category by reference to the "unique qualities" of the broadcast media.

5.7. The action of the Federal Communications Commission was reversed by a divided panel of the U.S. Court of Appeal for the District of Columbia Circuit. On appeal, the Supreme Court of the United States (by a majority of five against four) reversed the judgment of the Court of Appeal. Mr. Justice Stevens rejected the contention that "indecent" means no more than obscene in 18 U.S. Code, section 1464. He determined that "prurient appeal is an element of the obscene, but the normal definition of "indecent" merely refers to non-conformance with "accepted standards of morality". He conceded that the Supreme Court had previously construed the expression "indecent" (as occurring in similar statutes) to mean "obscene". But he reasoned that the history of section 1464, and the type of media to which it was addressed (broadcast as opposed to print), warranted a different construction in its case.

5.8. The constitutional question.—This determined the question whether the statute in issue authorised the Commission to regulate the speech at issue. The constitutional question still remained, namely, would the interpretation placed by the Supreme Court forbid constitutionally accepted speech? Mr. Justice Stevens isolated two characteristics of the broadcast media to justify lesser constitutional protection for the airing of indecent material: (1) the broadcast media are a uniquely pervasive presence, intruding into the protected enclave of the home; and (2) broadcasts are uniquely accessible to unsupervised children.

A learned commentor, commenting on the above case,[1] expressed the view that while the privacy argument, put forth by Justice Stevens, had some weakness, the argument of protection of the young children might be stronger. The comment further states that the case must not be read as "permissive", in the sense of defining the inner core of the Federal Communications Commission's power to regulate indecent speech, but must be read rather as "restrictive" and as marking the outer limit of that power. The comment further points out that the case authorises "time zoning" of broadcast, only when the broadcast—(1) uses language offensive to most people in depicting sexual or excretory activities, (2) uses that language not incidentally, but repetitively, (3) is at the time of the day when children are likely to be in the audience, and (4) is likely to influence children.[2]

5.9. Possible approach towards defining obscenity.—This ruling of the American Supreme Court, it must be pointed out, does not seek to define "indecency". It upholds

1. Supreme Court 1977 Term, (1978) 92 Harvard Law Review 57, 162.
2. F.C.C. v. *Pacifica Foundation*, (1978), 98 S Ct 3026 (3035, 3040, 3041), notes 29 and 3052.

the action of Federal Communications Commission in restraining an indecent programme, in the context of the time at which, and the manner in which, the matter was, broadcast. Infact, the ruling indirectly draws attention to the constitutional aspect, and reminds us that a restraint on speech and expression—including a restraint on indecent speech—must still pass the constitutional test.

It is possible that the ambiguity residing in the expression "indecent" could, to some extent, be reduced if the magnitude of the vice is defined by some qualifying words, which would introduce a modicum of precision. We shall make a concrete suggestion later.[1]

5.10. Sexual content of 'indecency'.—Another question pertains to sexual content. According to one view[2] indecency is not confined to sexual indecency and includes anything which an ordinary decent man or woman would find to be shocking, disgusting and revolting. This view was referred to in the debates on the Bill which led to the English Act of 1981, but most speakers in the debate regarded "indecency" as confined to indecency with a sexual content.

5.11. "Indecent" and "obscene" in Post Office Act.—In England, the sending by post of "indecent or obscene" writings etc. or indecent or obscene article is punishable by statute. It has been held that in section 11 of the Post Office Act, 1953, the words "indecent or obscene" convey one idea, namely, "offending against the recognised standards of propriety, indecent being at the lower end of the scale and obscene at the upper end of the scale .... an indecent article is not necessarily obscene whereas an obscene article must almost certainly be indecent."[3] It is possible that the expression "indecent" (in the Post Office Act) is not confined to sexual indecency, and extends to other improper matter.[4]

5.12. Sexual indecency whether necessary.—On some consideration, it seems that while most matters of an "indecent" character would be offensive because of their sexual implications, there could possibly be other matters which offend decency by non-sexual descriptions or depictions. It may not therefore, be necessary to confine any proposal in this regard to sexual indecency.

5.13. Indecent displays.—The problem of indecency is mainly to be tackled in regard to public outrage of indecency constituted by public displays and advertisements. Legislative proposals on the subject will, of course, have to take note of the issues discussed in the preceding paragraphs, and take particular care of the need to confine themselves to matter that offends reasonable persons—they need not cover everything that may offend a hyper-sensitive person.

5.14. Indecent advertisements and displays: possible amendment.—Taking all the above aspects into consideration, one possible course would be to insert in the Indian Penal Code a specific section to cover indecency. The following is a possible amendment by way of adding a new section:—

Section 293A, to be inserted in the Indian Penal Code

"(1) The provisions of sections 292 and 293 shall apply to a person who publicly displays any indecent matter, as they apply to a person who commits any offence under those sections in relation to obscene matter falling within those sections.

(2) For the purposes of this section, matter is indecent if it is offensive to reasonable persons from the point of view of decency."

---

1. Para. 5.14, *infra*.
2. *R.* v. *Khuller*, 1973 AC 435 (HL) (per Lord Reid).
3. *R.* v. *Stanley*, (1965) 1 All ER 1035.
4. Smith & Hogan *Criminal Law*, (1978), pp. 796, 797.

CHAPTER 6

COMMENTS RECEIVED ON THE WORKING PAPER

6.1. Working paper.—In the Working Paper which the Commission had circulated on the subject, the points made in the preceding Chapters were incorporated,[1] in order to present the issues in a concrete form and to facilitate a consideration of the important aspects. Comments of interested persons and bodies were invited as to the need for—

(1) amendment of section 292(2)(a) of the Indian Penal Code, on the lines indicated in the Working Paper, which were the same as those mentioned in this Report,[2] and

(2) also the insertion of a new section 293A in that Code, as proposed in the Working Paper—the proposal being the same as has been mentioned in this Report.[3]

6.2. Comments received on the Working Paper.—Comments have been received on the Working Paper[4] from—

(a) two State Government;[5]

(b) one High Court;[6]

(c) a social organisation[7] based at Delhi, and certain gentlemen associated with that organisation[8]; and

(d) one individual.[9]

6.3. Comments favouring the amendment.—(a) The comments received on the Working Paper from the State Governments, and from one High Court whose comments has been received,[10] favour both the amendments that were put forth in the Working Paper.[11]

(b) The comments received from the social organisation mentioned above and certain gentlemen associated with it, while favouring, in substance, the amendments put forth[12] by the Commission; have made certain additional suggestions. We shall, later in this Chapter,[13] deal with such of the additional points as are of importance.

(c) Finally, one gentlemen[9] has drawn attention to the need for using the mass media by stressing the ill-effects of (indecent) advertisements.

6.4. Some points considered: whether definition of 'obscene' to be revised.—To come, now, to the additional points made in some of the comments, there is, in the first place, the suggestion that the definition of "obscene" should be re-framed, so as to provide that matter which is capable of arousing lustful thought, action or sensation should be

1. Law Commission Working Paper, dated 15th September, 1984.
2. Para. 4.4, *supra*.
3. Para. 5.14, *supra*.
4. All comments received upto 10th November, 1984 have been taken into account.
5. Law Commission File No. F.2(12)84-L.C., letters dated 17th and 29th October, 1984.
6. Law Commission File No. F.2(12)84-L.C., letter of 25th October, 1984.
7. The Neeti Manch, Delhi.
8. Law Commission File No. F.2(12)84-L.C., S. No. 3 to S. No. 5.
9. Law Commission File No. F.2(12)84-L.C., S. No. 6.
10. Law Commission File No. F.2(12)84-L.C., letters of 17th, 25th and 29th October, 1984.
11. Para. 6.1, *supra*.
12. Law Commission File No. F.2(12)84-L.C., S. Nos. 3, 4, 5.
13. Para. 6.4, *infra*.

regarded as obscene. There is also a suggestion that the matter should be treated as obscene which one cannot see in the presence of one's grown up children.

We do not, however, think that the present concept of obscenity as provided in the Penal Code[1] needs any substantial change, from the angle mentioned above. No serious problem of substance has arisen from the present concept of obscenity, a concept which has evolved as a result of judicial decisions and takes due note of constitutional requirements. At least, no defect in the direction of the definition being too liberal has been noticed. No doubt, various components of the concept may have to be applied by the judiciary. And the interpretation placed by one judge may differ from another. But this is unavoidable.

6.5. Other suggestions.—There has been made a suggestion that the jury system should be introduced in the trial of charges for obscenity. The suggestion seems to be based on the assumption that judges are, at present, taking too liberal a view of the law. Reported decisions on section 292, however, do not appear to bear out this assumption. Similarly, the suggestion that the punishment for obscenity should be more severe has not appealed to us. In fact, we find from some of the views forwarded to us that there are several persons—particularly, women—who realise the limitations of the law in dealing with obscenity and who have sought to emphasise the role of society in creating a better moral climate in this field.

We have very carefully, gone through all the comments and have come to the conclusion that so far as the points made therein are concerned, they do not call for any other reforms in section 292 of the Indian Penal Code.

6.6. The question of pre-censorship.—It is sometimes suggested—though faintly—that there should be a system of censorship of advertisements. We are strongly opposed to any such course of action. Apart from anything else, the constitutionality of such a legal provision (in regard to advertisements) would be extremely difficult to sustain,[2] in the context of the heads of "decency" or and "morality", specified in Article 19(2) of the Constitution.

---

1. Section 292, I.P.C.
2. Cf. *Usha Uthup* v. *State of West Bengal*, AIR 1984 Cal 268 (275) (September).

CHAPTER 7

RECOMMENDATIONS

7.1. Recommendations.—In the light of the discussion in the preceding chapters, we make the following recommendations for amending the Indian Penal Code:—

(1) Section 292(2)(a) of the Code should be amended on the lines already indicated.[1] What we recommend is that section 292(2)(a) of the Indian Penal Code should be amended by inserting after the word "paper" the word "writing".

(2) The following section should be inserted in the Code :—

Section 293A (as recommended)

"(1) The provisions of sections 292 and 293 shall apply to a person who publicly displays any indecent matter, as they apply to a person who commits any offence under these sections in relation to obscene matter falling within those sections.

(2) For the purpose of this section, matter is indecent if it is offensive to reasonable person from the point of view of decency."

K.K. Mathew	*Chairman.*
J.P. Chaturvedi Dr. M.B. Rao	*Members.*
P.M. Bakshi Vepa P. Sarathi	*Part-time Members.*
A.K. Srinivasamurthy	*Member-Secretary.*

Dated: 8th January, 1985.

---

1. Para. 4.4, *supra*.

SUBJECT INDEX

•••